—ADJECTIVES.

The syntax of the English Adjective is fully embraced in the following brief rule, together with the exceptions, observations, and notes, which are, in due order, subjoined.

RULE IX.—ADJECTIVES.

Adjectives relate to nouns or pronouns: as, "*Miserable* comforters are ye *all*"—*Job*, xvi, 2. "*No worldly* enjoyments are *adequate* to the *high* desires and powers of an *immortal* spirit."—*Blair*.

> "Whatever faction's *partial* notions are,
> *No* hand is wholly *innocent* in war."
> —*Rowe's Lucan*, B. vii, l. 191.

EXCEPTION FIRST.

An adjective sometimes relates to a *phrase* or *sentence* which is made the subject of an intervening verb; as, "*To insult the afflicted, is impious*"—*Dillwyn*. "*That he should refuse, is not strange*"—"*To err is human*." *Murray* says, "*Human* belongs to its substantive 'nature' understood."—*Gram.*, p. 233. From this I dissent.

EXCEPTIONSECOND.

In combined arithmetical numbers, one adjective often relates *to an other,* and the whole phrase, to a subsequent noun; as, *"One thousand four hundred and fifty-six* men."—"Six dollars and *eighty-seven and a half* cents for *every five* days' service."—"In the *one hundred and twenty-second* year."—*"One seven* times more than it was wont to be heated."—*Daniel,* iii, 19.

EXCEPTIONTHIRD.

With an infinitive or a participle denoting being or action in the abstract, an adjective is sometimes also taken *abstractly*; (that is, without reference to any particular noun, pronoun, or other subject;) as, "To be *sincere,* is to be *wise, innocent,* and *safe."—Hawkesworth. "Capacity* marks the abstract quality of being *able* to receive or hold."—*Crabb's Synonymes.* "Indeed, the main secret of being *sublime,* is to say great things in few and plain words."—*Hiley's Gram.,* p. 215. "Concerning being *free* from sin in heaven, there is no question."—*Barclay's Works,* iii, 437. Better: "Concerning *freedom* from sin," &c.

EXCEPTIONFOUR TH.

Adjectives are sometimes substituted for their corresponding abstract nouns; (perhaps, in most instances, *elliptically,* like Greek neuters;) as, "The sensations of *sublime* and *beautiful* are not always distinguished by very distant boundaries."—*Blair's Rhet.,* p. 47. That is, "of *sublimity* and *beauty."* "The faults opposite to *the sublime* are chiefly two: *the frigid,* and *the bombast"—Ib.,* p. 44. Better: "The faults opposite to *sublimity,* are chiefly two; *frigidity* and *bombast."* "Yet the ruling character of the nation was that of *barbarous* and *cruel."—Brown's Estimate,* ii, 26. That is, "of *barbarity* and *cruelty."* "In a word, *agreeable* and *disagreeable* are qualities

Advanced English Grammar:

Adjectives, Pronouns, and Verbs

Goold Brown

of the objects we perceive," &c.—*Kames, El. of Crit.*, i, 99. "*Polished*, or *refined*, was the idea which the author had in view."—*Blair's Rhet.*, p. 219.

OBSERVATIONSONRULEIX.

OBS. 1.—Adjectives often relate to nouns or pronouns *understood*; as, "A new sorrow recalls *all* the *former*" [sorrows].—*Art of Thinking*, p. 31. [The place] "*Farthest* from him is best."—*Milton, P. L.* "To whom they all gave heed, from the *least* [person] to the *greatest*" [person].—*Acts*, viii, 10. "The Lord your God is God of gods, and Lord of lords, a great God, a *mighty* [God], and a *terrible*" [God].—*Deut.*, x, 17. "Every one can distinguish an *angry* from a *placid*, a *cheerful* from a *melancholy*, a *thoughtful* from a *thoughtless*, and a *dull* from a penetrating, countenance."—*Beattie's Moral Science*, p. 192. Here the word *countenance* is understood seven times; for eight different countenances are spoken of. "He came unto his *own* [possessions], and his *own* [men] received him not."—*John*, i, 11. The *Rev. J. G. Cooper*, has it: "He came unto his own (*creatures*,) and his own (*creatures*) received him not."—*Pl. and Pract. Gram.*, p. 44. This ambitious editor of Virgil, abridger of Murray, expounder of the Bible, and author of several "new and improved" grammars, (of different languages,) should have understood this text, notwithstanding the obscurity of our version. " [Greek: Eis ta idia ælthe. kai oi idioi auton ou parelabon]."—"In *propria* venit, et *proprii* eum non receperunt."—*Montanus.* "Ad *sua* venit, et sui eum non exceperunt."—*Beza.* "Il est venu *chez soi*; et *les siens* ne l'ont point reçu."—*French Bible.* Sometimes the construction of the adjective involves an ellipsis of *several words*, and those perhaps the principal parts of the clause; as, "The sea appeared to be agitated more than [in that degree *which* is] *usual*."—*Murray's Key*, 8vo, p. 217. "During the course of the sentence, the scene should be changed as little as [in the least] *possible*" [degree].—*Blair's Rhet.*, p. 107; *Murray's Gram.*, 8vo, p. 312.

"Presumptuous man! the reason wouldst thou find,
Why [*thou art*] form'd so *weak*, so *little*, and so *blind*"
 —*Pope.*

OBS. 2.—Because *qualities* belong only to *things*, most grammarians teach, that, "*Adjectives* are capable of being added *to nouns only*."— *Buchanan's Syntax*, p. 26. Or, as Murray expresses the doctrine: "Every adjective, and every adjective pronoun, *belongs to a substantive*, expressed or understood."—*Octavo Gram.*, p. 161. "The adjective *always* relates to a *substantive*."—*Ib.*, p. 169. This teaching, which is alike repugnant to the true *definition* of an adjective, to the true *rule* for its construction, and to *all the exceptions* to this rule, is but a sample of that hasty sort of induction, which is ever jumping to false conclusions for want of a fair comprehension of the facts in point. The position would not be tenable, even if all our *pronouns* were admitted to be *nouns*, or "*substantives*;" and, if these two parts of speech are to be distinguished, the consequence must be, that Murray supposes a countless number of unnecessary and absurd *ellipses*. It is sufficiently evident, that in the construction of sentences, adjectives often relate immediately to *pronouns*, and only through them to the nouns which they represent. Examples: "I should like to know who has been carried off, except *poor dear me*."—*Byron*. "To *poor us* there is not much hope remaining."—*Murray's Key*, 8vo, p 204. "It is the final pause *which alone*, on many occasions, marks the difference between prose and verse."— *Murray's Gram.*, p. 260. "And sometimes after *them both*."—*Ib.*, p. 196. "All men hail'd *me happy*."—*Milton*. "To receive *unhappy me*."—*Dryden*. "Superior to *them all*."—*Blair's Rhet.*, p. 419. "*They* returned to their own country, *full* of the discoveries which they had made."—*Ib.*, p. 350. "*All ye* are brethren."—*Matt.*, xxiii, 8. "And *him only* shalt thou serve."—*Matt.*, iv, 10.

"Go *wiser thou,* and in thy scale of sense
Weigh thy opinion against Providence."—*Pope.*

OBS. 3.—When an adjective follows a finite verb, and is not followed by a noun, it generally relates to the subject of the verb; as, "*I* am *glad* that the *door* is made *wide.*"—"An unbounded *prospect* doth not long continue *agreeable.*"—*Kames, El. of Crit.,* i, 244. "Every thing which is *false, vicious,* or *unworthy,* is *despicable* to him, though all the world should approve it."—*Spectator,* No. 520. Here *false, vicious,* and *unworthy,* relate to *which*; and *despicable* relates to *thing.* The practice of Murray and his followers, of supplying a "substantive" in all such cases, is absurd. "When the Adjective forms the *Attribute* of a Proposition, it belongs to the noun [or pronoun] which serves as the *Subject* of the Proposition, and cannot be joined to any other noun, since it is of the Subject that we affirm the quality expressed by this Adjective."—*De Sacy, on General Gram.,* p. 37. In some peculiar phrases, however, such as, *to fall short of, to make bold with, to set light by,* the adjective has such a connexion with the verb, that it may seem questionable how it ought to be explained in parsing. Examples: (1.) "This latter mode of expression falls *short* of the force and vehemence of the former."—*L. Murray's Gram.,* p. 353. Some will suppose the word *short* to be here used *adverbially,* or to qualify *falls* only; but perhaps it may as well be parsed as an adjective, forming a predicate with "*falls,*" and relating to "*mode,*" the nominative. (2.) "And that I have made so *bold* with thy glorious Majesty."—*Jenks's Prayers,* p. 156. This expression is perhaps elliptical: it may mean, "that I have made *myself* so bold," &c. (3.) "Cursed be he that *setteth light* by his father or his mother: and all the people shall say, Amen."—*Deut.,* xxvii, 16. This may mean, "that setteth light *esteem* or *estimation,*" &c.

OBS. 4.—When an adjective follows an infinitive or a participle, the noun or pronoun to which it relates, is sometimes before it, and sometimes after it, and often considerably remote; as, "A real gentleman cannot but practice those virtues *which*, by an intimate knowledge of mankind, he has found to be *useful* to them."—"He [a melancholy enthusiast] thinks *himself* obliged in duty to be *sad* and *disconsolate*."—*Addison*. "He is scandalized at *youth* for being *lively*, and at *childhood* for being *playful*."—*Id*. "But growing *weary* of one who almost walked him out of breath, *he* left him for Horace and Anacreon."—*Steele*.

OBS. 5.—Adjectives preceded by the definite article, are often used, by *ellipsis*, as *nouns*; as, *the learned*, for *learned men*. Such phrases usually designate those classes of persons or things, which are characterized by the qualities they express; and this, the reader must observe, is a use quite different from that *substitution* of adjectives for nouns, which is noticed in the fourth exception above. In *our* language, the several senses in which adjectives may thus be taken, are not distinguished with that clearness which the inflections of other tongues secure. Thus, *the noble, the vile, the excellent,* or *the beautiful,* may be put for three extra constructions: first, for *noble persons, vile persons,* &c.; secondly, for *the noble man, the vile man,* &c.; thirdly, for the abstract qualities, *nobility, vileness, excellence, beauty.* The last-named usage forms an exception to the rule; in the other two the noun is understood, and should be supplied by the parser. Such terms, if elliptical, are most commonly of the plural number, and refer to the word *persons* or *things* understood; as, "*The careless* and *the imprudent, the giddy* and *the fickle, the ungrateful* and *the interested,* everywhere meet us."—*Blair*. Here the noun *persons* is to be six times supplied. "Wherever there is taste, *the witty* and *the humorous* make themselves perceived."—*Campbell's Rhet.,* p. 21. Here the author meant, simply, the qualities *wit* and *humour,* and he ought to have used these words, because the others are equivocal, and are more naturally conceived to refer to persons. In the following couplet, the noun *places* or *things* is understood after "*open,*" and again after "*covert,*" which last word is sometimes misprinted "*coverts:*"

"Together let us beat this ample field,
Try what *the open*, what *the covert*, yield."—*Pope, on Man.*

OBS. 6.—The adjective, in English, is generally placed immediately *before its noun*; as, "*Vain* man! is grandeur given to *gay* attire?"—*Beattie.* Those adjectives which relate to *pronouns*, most commonly follow them; as, "They left *me weary* on a grassy turf."—*Milton.* But to both these general rules there are many exceptions; for the position of an adjective may be varied by a variety of circumstances, not excepting the mere convenience of emphasis: as, "And Jehu said, Unto *which* of *all us*?"—*2 Kings*, ix, 5. In the following instances the adjective is placed *after the word* to which it relates:

1. When other words depend on the adjective, or stand before it to qualify it; as, "A mind *conscious of right*,"—"A wall *three feet thick*,"—"A body of troops *fifty thousand strong*."

2. When the quality results from an action, or receives its application through a verb or participle; as, "Virtue renders *life happy*."—"He was in Tirzah, drinking *himself drunk* in the house of Arza."—*1 Kings*, xvi, 9. "All men agree to call *vinegar sour, honey sweet*, and *aloes bitter*."—*Burke, on Taste*, p. 38. "God made *thee perfect*, not *immutable*."—*Milton.*

3. When the quality excites admiration, and the adjective would thus be more clearly distinctive; as, "Goodness *infinite*,"—"Wisdom *unsearchable*."—*Murray.*

4. When a verb comes between the adjective and the noun; as, "Truth stands *independent* of all external things."—*Burgh.* "Honour is not *seemly* for a fool."—*Solomon.*

5. When the adjective is formed by means of the prefix *a*; as, *afraid, alert, alike, alive, alone, asleep, awake, aware, averse, ashamed, askew*. To these may be added a few other words; as, *else, enough, extant, extinct, fraught, pursuant.*

6. When the adjective has the nature, but not the form, of a participle; as, "A queen *regnant*,"—"The prince *regent*,"—"The heir *apparent*,"—"A lion, not *rampant*, but *couchant* or *dormant*"—"For the time then *present*."

OBS. 7.—In some instances, the adjective may *either precede or follow* its noun; and the writer may take his choice, in respect to its position: as, 1. In *poetry*—provided the sense be obvious; as,

———————————"Wilt thou to the *isles*
Atlantic*, to the *rich Hesperian clime,*
Fly in the train of Autumn?"
    —*Akenside, P. of I.*, Book i, p. 27.

————————————————-"Wilt thou fly
With laughing Autumn to *the Atlantic isles*,
And range with him th' *Hesperian field*?"
    —*Id. Bucke's Gram.*, p. 120.

2. When technical usage favours one order, and common usage an other; as, "A notary *public*," or, "A *public* notary;"—"The heir *presumptive*," or, "The *presumptive* heir."—See *Johnson's Dict.*, and *Webster's.*

3. When an adverb precedes the adjective; as, "A Being *infinitely* wise," or, "An *infinitely wise* Being." Murray, Comly, and others, here approve only the former order; but the latter is certainly not ungrammatical.

4. When several adjectives belong to the same noun; as, "A woman, *modest, sensible,* and *virtuous,*" or, "A *modest, sensible,* and *virtuous* woman." Here again, Murray, Comly, and others, approve only the former order; but I judge the latter to be quite as good.

5. When the adjective is emphatic, it may be *foremost* in the sentence, though the natural order of the words would bring it last; as, "*Weighty* is the anger of the righteous."—*Bible.* "*Blessed* are the pure in heart."—*Ib.* "*Great* is the earth, *high* is the heaven, *swift* is the sun in his course."—*1 Esdras*, iv, 34. "*The more laborious* the life is, *the less populous* is the country."—*Goldsmith's Essays*, p. 151.

6. When the adjective and its noun both follow a verb as parts of the predicate, either may possibly come before the other, yet the arrangement is *fixed by the sense intended*: thus there is a great difference between the assertions, "We call the *boy good*," and, "We call the *good boy*"

OBS. 8.—By an ellipsis of the noun, an adjective with a preposition before it, is sometimes equivalent to an adverb; as, *"In particular;"* that is, *"In a particular manner;"* equivalent to *particularly.* So *"in general"* is equivalent to *generally.* It has already been suggested, that, in parsing, the scholar should here supply the ellipsis. See Obs. 3d, under Rule vii.

OBS. 9.—Though English adjectives are, for the most part, incapable of any *agreement,* yet such of them as denote unity or plurality, ought in general to have nouns of the same number: as, *this man, one man, two men, many men.*[372] In phrases of this form, the rule is well observed; but in some peculiar ways of numbering things, it is commonly disregarded; for certain nouns are taken in a plural sense without assuming the plural termination. Thus people talk of many *stone* of cheese,—many *sail* of vessels,—many *stand* of arms,—many *head* of cattle,—many *dozen* of eggs,—many *brace* of partridges,—many *pair* of shoes. So we read in the

Bible of "two hundred *pennyworth* of bread," and "twelve *manner* of fruits." In all such phraseology, there is, in regard to the *form* of the latter word, an evident disagreement of the adjective with its immediate noun; but sometimes, (where the preposition *of* does not occur,) expressions that seem somewhat like these, may be elliptical: as when historians tell of *many thousand foot* (soldiers), or *many hundred horse* (troops). To denote a collective number, a singular adjective may precede a plural one; as, "*One* hundred men,"—"*Every* six weeks." And to denote plurality, the adjective many may, in like manner, precede *an* or *a* with a singular noun; as, "The Odyssey entertains us with *many a wonderful adventure*, and *many a landscape* of nature."—*Blair's Rhet.*, p. 436." There *starts up many* a writer."—*Kames, El. of Crit.*, i, 306.

"Full *many a flower is born* to blush unseen,
And waste its sweetness on the desert air."—*Gray*.

OBS. 10.—Though *this* and *that* cannot relate to plurals, many writers do not hesitate to place them before singulars taken conjointly, which are equivalent to plurals; as, "*This power and will* do necessarily produce that which man is empowered to do."—*Sale's Koran*, i, 229. "*That sobriety and self-denial* which are essential to the support of virtue."—*Murray's Key*, 8vo, p. 218. "*This modesty and decency* were looked upon by them as a law of nature."—*Rollin's Hist.*, ii, 45. Here the plural forms, *these* and *those*, cannot be substituted; but the singular may be repeated, if the repetition be thought necessary. Yet, when these same pronominal adjectives are placed *after* the nouns to suggest the things again, they must be made plural; as, "*Modesty and decency* were thus carefully guarded, for *these* were looked upon as being enjoined by the law of nature."

OBS. 11.—In prose, the use of adjectives for adverbs is improper; but, in poetry, an adjective relating to the noun or pronoun, is sometimes elegantly used in stead of an adverb qualifying the verb or participle; as; "*Gradual* sinks the breeze Into a perfect calm."—*Thomson's Seasons*, p. 34. "To Thee I bend the knee; to Thee my thoughts *Continual* climb."—*Ib.*, p. 48. "As on he walks *Graceful*, and crows defiance."—*Ib.*, p. 56. "As through the falling glooms *Pensive* I stray."—*Ib.*, p. 80. "They, *sportive*, wheel; or, sailing down the stream, Are snatch'd *immediate* by the quick-eyed trout."—*Ib.*, p. 82. "*Incessant* still you flow."—*Ib.*, p. 91. "The shatter'd clouds *Tumultuous* rove, the interminable sky *Sublimer* swells."—*Ib.*, p. 116. In order to determine, in difficult cases, whether an adjective or an adverb is required, the learner should carefully attend to the definitions of these parts of speech, and consider whether, in the case in question, *quality* is to be expressed, or *manner*: if the former, an adjective is always proper; if the latter, an adverb. That is, in this case, the adverb, though not always required in poetry, is specially requisite in prose. The following examples will illustrate this point: "She looks *cold*;"—"She looks *coldly* on him."—"I sat *silent*;"—"I sat *silently* musing."—"Stand *firm*; maintain your cause *firmly*." See *Etymology*, Chap, viii, Obs. 4th, 5th, 6th, and 7th, on the Modifications of Adverbs.

OBS. 12.—In English, an adjective and its noun are often taken as a sort of compound term, to which other adjectives may be added; as, "An *old man*; a *good* old man; a very *learned, judicious*, good old man."—*L. Murray's Gram.*, p. 169; *Brit. Gram.*, 195; *Buchanan's*, 79. "Of an *other determinate positive new* birth, subsequent to baptism, we know nothing."—*West's Letters*, p. 183. When adjectives are thus accumulated, the subsequent ones should convey such ideas as the former may consistently qualify, otherwise the expression will be objectionable. Thus the ordinal adjectives, *first, second, third, next*, and *last*, may qualify the cardinal numbers, but they cannot very properly be qualified by them. When, therefore, we specify any part of a series, the cardinal adjective ought, by good right, to follow the ordinal, and not, as in the following phrase, be placed before it: "In reading the *nine last chapters* of John."—*Fuller*. Properly speaking, there is but one last chapter in any book. Say, therefore, "the *last nine* chapters;" for, out of the twenty-one chapters in John, a man may select several different nines. (See *Etymology,* Chap, iv, Obs. 7th, on the Degrees of Comparison.) When one of the adjectives merely qualifies the other, they should be joined together by a hyphen; as, "A *red-hot* iron."—"A *dead-ripe* melon." And when both or all refer equally and solely to the noun, they ought either to be connected by a conjunction, or to be separated by a comma. The following example is therefore faulty: "It is the business of an epic poet, to form a *probable interesting* tale."—*Blair's Rhet.*, p. 427. Say, "probable *and* interesting;" or else insert a comma in lieu of the conjunction.

> "Around him wide a sable army stand,
> A *low-born, cell-bred, selfish, servile band.*"
> —*Dunciad*, B. ii, l. 355.

OBS. 13.—Dr. Priestley has observed: "There is a remarkable ambiguity in the use of the negative adjective *no*; and I do not see," says he, "how it can be remedied in any language. If I say, '*No laws are better than the English,*' it is only my known sentiments that can inform a person whether I mean to praise, or dispraise *them.*"—*Priestley's Gram.*, p. 136. It may not be possible to remove the ambiguity from the phraseology here cited, but it is easy enough to avoid the form, and say in stead of it, "*The English laws are worse than none,*" or, "*The English laws are as good as any*;" and, in neither of these expressions, is there any ambiguity, though the other may doubtless be taken in either of these senses. Such an ambiguity is sometimes used on purpose: as when one man says of an other, "He is no small knave;" or, "He is no small fool."

"There liv'd in primo Georgii (they record)

A worthy member, *no small fool, a lord*."—*Pope*, p. 409.

NOTEST ORULEIX.

NOTE I.—Adjectives that imply unity or plurality, must agree with their nouns in number: as, "*That sort, those sorts*;"—"*This hand, these hands*." [373]

NOTE II.—When the adjective is necessarily plural, or necessarily singular, the noun should be made so too: as, "*Twenty pounds*" not, "Twenty *pound*;"—"*Four feet* long," not, "*Four foot* long;"—"*One session*" not, "One *sessions*."

NOTE III.—The reciprocal expression, *one an other*, should not be applied to two objects, nor *each other*, or *one the other*, to more than two; as, "Verse and prose, on some occasions, run into *one another*, like light and shade."—*Blair's Rhet.*, p. 377; *Jamieson's*, 298. Say, "into *each other*" "For mankind have always been butchering *each other*"—*Webster's Essays*, p. 151. Say, "*one an other*" See *Etymology*, Chap, iv, Obs. 15th, 16th, 17th, and 18th, on the Classes of Adjectives.

NOTE IV.—When the comparative degree is employed with *than*, the latter term of comparison should *never include* the former; nor the former the latter: as, "*Iron is more useful* than *all the metals*"—"*All the metals are less useful* than *iron*." In either case, it should be, "all the other metals,"

NOTE V.—When the superlative degree is employed, the latter term of comparison, which is introduced by *of*, should *never exclude* the former; as, "A fondness for show, is, of all *other* follies, the most vain." Here the word *other* should be expunged; for this latter term must *include* the former: that is, the fondness for show must be one of the follies of which it is the vainest.

NOTE VI.—When equality is denied, or inequality affirmed, neither term of the comparison should *ever include* the other; because every thing must needs be equal to itself, and it is absurd to suggest that a part surpasses the whole: as, "*No writings whatever* abound *so much* with the bold and animated figures, *as the sacred books.*"—*Blair's Rhet.*, p. 414. Say, "No *other* writings whatever;" because the sacred books are "*writings*" See *Etymology*, Chap, iv, Obs. 6th, on Regular Comparison.

NOTE VII.—Comparative terminations, and adverbs of degree, should not be applied to adjectives that are not susceptible of comparison; and all double comparatives and double superlatives should be avoided: as, "*So universal* a complaint:" say rather, "*So general.*"—"Some *less nobler* plunder:" say, "*less noble*"—"The *most straitest* sect:" expunge *most*. See *Etymology*, Chap, iv, from Obs. 5th to Obs. 13th, on Irregular Comparison. [374]

NOTE VIII.—When adjectives are connected by *and, or,* or *nor,* the shortest and simplest should in general be placed first; as, "He is *older* and *more respectable* than his brother." To say, "*more respectable* and *older*" would be obviously inelegant, as possibly involving the inaccuracy of "*more older.*"

NOTE IX.—When one adjective is superadded to an other without a conjunction expressed or understood, the most distinguishing quality must be expressed next to the noun, and the latter must be such as the former may consistently qualify; as, "An *agreeable young* man," not, "A *young agreeable* man."—"The art of speaking, like *all other practical* arts, may be facilitated by rules,"—*Enfield's Speaker*, p. 10. Example of error: "The Anglo-Saxon language possessed, for the *two first* persons, a *Dual* number."—*Fowler's E. Gram.*, 1850, p. 59. Say, "the *first two* persons;" for the *second* of three can hardly be one of the *first*; and "*two first*" with the *second* and *third* added, will clearly make *more* than three. See Obs. 12th, above.

NOTE X.—In prose, the use of adjectives for adverbs, is a vulgar error; the adverb alone being proper, when *manner* or *degree* is to be expressed, and not *quality*; as, "He writes *elegant*;" say, "*elegantly*."—"It is a *remarkable* good likeness;" say, "*remarkably good*."

NOTE XI.—The pronoun *them* should never be used as an adjective, in lieu of *those*: say, "I bought *those* books;" not, "*them* books." This also is a vulgar error, and chiefly confined to the conversation of the unlearned.[375]

NOTE XII.—When the pronominal adjectives, *this* and *that*, or *these* and *those*, are contrasted; *this* or *these* should represent the latter of the antecedent terms, and *that* or *those* the former: as,

"And, reason raise o'er instinct as you can,
In *this* 'tis God directs, in *that* 'tis man."—*Pope.*

"Farewell my friends! farewell my foes!
My peace with *these*, my love with *those*!"—*Burns.*

NOTE XIII.—The pronominal adjectives *either* and *neither*, in strict propriety of syntax, relate to two things only; when more are referred to, *any* and *none*, or *any one* and *no one*, should be used in stead of them: as, "*Any* of the three," or, "*Any one* of the three;" not, "*Either* of the three."—"*None* of the four," or, "*No one* of the four;" not, "*Neither* of the four." [376]

NOTE XIV.—The adjective *whole* must not be used in a plural sense, for *all*; nor *less,* in the sense of *fewer;* nor *more* or *most,* in any ambiguous construction, where it may be either an adverb of degree, or an adjective of number or quantity: as, "Almost the *whole* inhabitants were present."—HUME: see *Priestley's Gram.,* p. 190.[377] Say, "Almost *all* the inhabitants." "No *less* than three dictionaries have been published to correct it."—*Dr. Webster.* Say, "No *fewer.*" "This trade enriched some *people more* than them."—*Murray's Gram.,* Vol. i, p. 215. This passage is not clear in its import: it may have either of two meanings. Say, "This trade enriched some *other* people, *besides* them." Or, "This trade enriched some *others* more than *it did them.*"

NOTE XV.—Participial adjectives retain the termination, but not the government of participles; when, therefore, they are followed by the objective case, a preposition must be inserted to govern it: as, "The man who is most *sparing of* his words, is generally most *deserving of* attention."

NOTE XVI.—When the figure of any adjective affects the syntax and sense of the sentence, care must be taken to give to the word or words that form, simple or compound, which suits the true meaning and construction. Examples: "He is *forehead bald,* yet he is clean."—FRIENDS' BIBLE: *Lev.,* xiii, 41. Say, "*forehead-bald.,*"—ALGER'S BIBLE, and SCOTT'S. "From such phrases as, '*New England scenery,*' convenience requires the *omission* of the hyphen."—*Sanborn's Gram.,* p. 89. This is a false notion. Without the hyphen, the phrase properly means, "*New scenery in England;*" but *New-England scenery* is scenery in New England. "'*Many coloured wings,*' means *many wings which are coloured;* but '*many-coloured wings*' means *wings of many colours.*"—*Blair's Gram.,* p. 116.

IMPROPRIETIESFORCORRECTION.

FALSE SYNT AX UNDER RULE IX.

EXAMPLES UNDER NOTE I.—AGREEMENT OF ADJECTIVES.

"I am not recommending these kind of sufferings to your liking."—BP. SHERLOCK: *Lowth's Gram.*, p. 87.

[FORMULE.—Not proper, because the adjective *these* is plural, and does not agree with its noun *kind*, which is singular. But, according to Note 1st under Rule 9th: "Adjectives that imply unity or plurality, must agree with their nouns in number." Therefore, *these* should be *this*; thus, "I am not recommending *this* kind of sufferings."]

"I have not been to London this five years."—*Webster's Philos. Gram.*, p. 152. "These kind of verbs are more expressive than their radicals."—*Dr. Murray's Hist. of Lang.*, Vol. ii, p. 163. "Few of us would be less corrupted than kings are, were we, like them, beset with flatterers, and poisoned with that vermin."—*Art of Thinking*, p. 66. "But it seems this literati had been very ill rewarded for their ingenious labours."—*Roderick Random*, Vol. ii, p. 87. "If I had not left off troubling myself about those kind of things."—*Swift*. "For these sort of things are usually join'd to the most noted fortune."—*Bacon's Essays*, p. 101. "The nature of that riches and long-suffering is, to lead to repentance."—*Barclay's Works*, iii, 380. "I fancy they are these kind of gods, which Horace mentions."—*Addison, on Medals*, p. 74. "During that eight days they are prohibited from touching the skin."—*Hope of Israel*, p. 78. "Besides, he had not much provisions left for his army."—*Goldsmith's Greece*, i, 86. "Are you not ashamed to have no other thoughts than that of amassing wealth, and of acquiring glory, credit, and dignities?"—*Ib.*, p. 192. "It distinguisheth still more remarkably the feelings of the former from that of the latter."—*Kames, El. of Crit.*, Vol. i, p. xvii. "And this good tidings of the reign shall be published through all the world."—*Campbell's Gospels, Matt.*, xxiv, 14. "This twenty years have I been with thee."—*Gen.*, xxxi, 38. "In these kind of expressions some words seem to be understood."—*Walker's Particles*, p. 179. "He thought these kind of excesses indicative of greatness."—*Hunt's Byron*, p. 117. "These sort of fellows are very numerous."—*Spect.*, No. 486. "Whereas these sort of men cannot give account of their faith."—*Barclay's Works*, i, 444. "But the question is, whether that be the words."—*Ib.*, iii, 321. "So that these sort of Expressions are not properly Optative."—*Johnson's Gram. Com.*, p. 276. "Many things are not that which they appear to be."—*Sanborn's Gram.*, p. 176. "So that every possible means are used."—*Formey's Belles-Lettres*, p. iv.

"We have strict statutes, and most biting laws,
  Which for this nineteen years we have let sleep."—*Shak.*

"They could not speak; and so I left them both,
  To bear this tidings to the bloody king."—*Id., Richard III.*

UNDERNOTEII.—OFFIXEDNUMBERS.

"Why, I think she cannot be above six foot two inches high."—*Spect.*, No. 533. "The world is pretty regular for about forty rod east and ten west."—*Ib.*, No. 535. "The standard being more than two foot above it."—BACON: *Joh. Dict., w. Standard.* "Supposing (among other Things) he saw two Suns, and two Thebes."—*Bacon's Wisdom*, p. 25. "On the right hand we go into a parlour thirty three foot by thirty nine."—*Sheffield's Works*, ii, 258. "Three pound of gold went to one shield."—*1 Kings*, x, 17. "Such an assemblage of men as there appears to have been at that sessions."—*The Friend*, x, 389. "And, truly, he hath saved me this pains."—*Barclay's Works*, ii, 266. "Within this three mile may you see it coming."—SHAK.: *Joh. Dict., w. Mile.* "Most of the churches, not all, had one or more ruling elder."—*Hutchinson's Hist. of Mass.*, i, 375. "While a Minute Philosopher, not six foot high, attempts to dethrone the Monarch of the universe."—*Berkley's Alciphron*, p. 151. "The wall is ten foot high."—*Harrison's Gram.*, p. 50. "The stalls must be ten foot broad."—*Walker's Particles*, p. 201. "A close prisoner in a room twenty foot square, being at the north side of his chamber, is at liberty to walk twenty foot southward, not to walk twenty foot northward."—LOCKE: *Joh. Dict., w. Northward*. "Nor, after all this pains and industry, did they think themselves qualified."—*Columbian Orator*, p. 13. "No less than thirteen *gypsies* were condemned at one Suffolk assizes, and executed."—*Webster's Essays*, p. 333. "The king was petitioned to appoint one, or more, person, or persons."—MACAULAY: *Priestley's Gram.*, p. 194. "He carries weight! he rides a race! 'Tis for a thousand pound!"—*Cowper's Poems*, i, 279. "They carry three tire of guns at the head, and at the stern there are two tire of guns."—*Joh. Dict., w. Galleass*. "The verses consist of two sort of rhymes."—*Formey's Belles-Lettres*, p. 112. "A present of 40 camel's load of the most precious things of Syria."—*Wood's Dict.*, Vol. i, p. 162. "A large grammar, that shall extend to every minutiæ."—*S. Barrett's Gram.*, Tenth Ed., Pref., p. iii.

"So many spots, like næves on Venus' soil,
One jewel set off with so many foil."—*Dryden*.

"For, of the lower end, two handful
It had devour'd, it was so manful."—*Hudibras*, i, 365.

UNDERNOTE III.—OF RECIPROCALS.

"That *shall* and *will* might be substituted for one another."—*Priestley's Gram.*, p. 131. "We use not *shall* and *will* promiscuously for one another."—*Brightland's Gram.*, p. 110. "But I wish to distinguish the three high ones from each other also."—*Fowle's True Eng. Gram.*, p. 13. "Or on some other relation, which two objects bear to one another."—*Blair's Rhet.*,

p. 142. "Yet the two words lie so near to one another in meaning, that in the present case, any one of them, perhaps, would have been sufficient."—*Ib.*, p. 203. "Both orators use great liberties with one another."—*Ib.*, p. 244. "That greater separation of the two sexes from one another."—*Ib.*, p. 466. "Most of whom live remote from each other."—*Webster's Essays*, p. 39. "Teachers like to see their pupils polite to each other."—*Webster's El. Spelling-Book*, p. 28. "In a little time, he and I must keep company with one another only."—*Spect.*, No. 474. "Thoughts and circumstances crowd upon each other."—*Kames, El. of Crit.*, i, 32. "They cannot see how the ancient Greeks could understand each other."—*Literary Convention*, p. 96. "The spirit of the poet, the patriot, and the prophet, vied with each other in his breast."—*Hazlitt's Lect.*, p. 112. "Athamas and Ino loved one another."—*Classic Tales*, p. 91. "Where two things are compared or contrasted to one another."—*Blair's Rhet.*, p. 119. "Where two things are compared, or contrasted, with one another."—*Murray's Gram.*, Vol. i, p. 324. "In the classification of words, almost all writers differ from each other."—*Bullions, E. Gram.*, p. iv.

"I will not trouble thee, my child. Farewell;
We'll no more meet; no more see one another."—*Shak. Lear*.

UNDER NOTE IV.—OF COMPARATIVES.

"Errours in Education should be less indulged than any."—*Locke, on Ed.*, p. iv. "This was less his case than any man's that ever wrote."—*Pref. to Waller*. "This trade enriched some people more than it enriched them." [378]—*Murray's Gram.*, Vol. i, p. 215. "The Chaldee alphabet, in which the Old Testament has reached us, is more beautiful than any ancient character known."—*Wilson's Essay*, p. 5. "The Christian religion gives a more lovely character of God, than any religion ever did."—*Murray's Key*, p. 169. "The temple of Cholula was deemed more holy than any in New Spain."—*Robertson's America*, ii, 477. "Cibber grants it to be a better poem of its kind than ever was writ."—*Pope*. "Shakspeare is more faithful to the true language of nature, than any writer."—*Blair's Rhet.*, p. 468. "One son I had —one, more than all my sons, the strength of Troy."—*Cowper's Homer*. "Now Israel loved Joseph more than all his children, because he was the son of his old age."—*Gen.*, xxxvii, 3.

UNDER NOTE V.—OF SUPERLATIVES.

"Of all other simpletons, he was the greatest."—*Nutting's English Idioms*. "Of all other beings, man has certainly the greatest reason for gratitude."—*Ibid., Gram.*, p. 110. "This lady is the prettiest of all her sisters."—*Peyton's Elements of Eng. Lang.*, p. 39. "The relation which, of all others, is by far the most fruitful of tropes, I have not yet mentioned."—*Blair's Rhet.*, p. 141. "He studied Greek the most of any nobleman."—*Walker's Particles*, p. 231. "And indeed that was the qualification of all others most wanted at that time."—*Goldsmith's Greece,* ii, 35. "Yet we deny that the knowledge of him, as outwardly crucified, is the best of all other knowledge of him."—*Barclay's Works,* i, 144. "Our ideas of numbers are of all others the most accurate and distinct."—*Duncan's Logic,* p. 35. "This indeed is of all others the case when it can be least necessary to name the agent."—*J. Q. Adams's Rhet.,* i, 231. "The period, to which you have arrived, is perhaps the most critical and important of any moment of your lives."—*Ib.,* i, 394. "Perry's royal octavo is esteemed the best of any pronouncing Dictionary yet known."—*Red Book,* p. x. "This is the tenth persecution, and of all the foregoing, the most bloody."—*Sammes's Antiquities,* Chap. xiii. "The English tongue is the most susceptible of sublime imagery, of any language in the world."—See *Bucke's Gram.,* p. 141. "Homer is universally allowed to have had the greatest Invention of any writer whatever."—*Pope's Preface to Homer.* "In a version of this particular work, which most of any other seems to require a venerable antique cast."—*Ib.* "Because I think him the best informed of any naturalist who has ever written."— *Jefferson's Notes,* p. 82. "Man is capable of being the most social of any animal."—*Sheridan's Elocution,* p. 145. "It is of all others that which most moves us."—*Ib.,* p. 158. "Which of all others, is the most necessary article."—*Ib.,* p. 166.

> "Quoth he 'this gambol thou advisest,
> Is, of all others, the unwisest.'"—*Hudibras,* iii, 316.

UNDER NOTE VI.—INCLUSIVE TERMS. "Noah and his family outlived all the people who lived before the flood."—*Webster's El. Spelling-Book,* p. 101. "I think it superior to any work of that nature we have yet had."—*Dr. Blair's Rec. in Murray's Gram.,* Vol. ii, p. 300. "We have had no grammarian who has employed so much labour and judgment upon our native language, as the author of these volumes."—*British Critic, ib.,* ii, 299. "No persons feel so much the distresses of others, as they who have experienced distress themselves."—*Murray's Key*, 8vo., p. 227. "Never was any people so much infatuated as the Jewish nation."—*Ib.*, p. 185; *Frazee's Gram.*, p. 135. "No tongue is so full of connective particles as the Greek."—*Blair's Rhet.*, p. 85. "Never sovereign was so much beloved by the people."—*Murray's Exercises*, R. xv, p. 68. "No sovereign was ever so much beloved by the people."—*Murray's Key*, p. 202. "Nothing ever affected her so much as this misconduct of her child."—*Ib.*, p. 203; *Merchant's*, 195. "Of all the figures of speech, none comes so near to painting as metaphor."—*Blair's Rhet.*, p. 142; *Jamieson's*, 149. "I know none so happy in his metaphors as Mr. Addison."—*Blair's Rhet.*, p. 150. "Of all the English authors, none is so happy in his metaphors as Addison."—*Jamieson's, Rhet.*, p. 157. "Perhaps no writer in the world was ever so frugal of his words as Aristotle."—*Blair*, p. 177; *Jamieson*, 251. "Never was any writer so happy in that concise spirited style as Mr. Pope."—*Blair's Rhet.*, p. 403. "In the harmonious structure and disposition of periods, no writer whatever, ancient or modern, equals Cicero."—*Blair*, 121; *Jamieson*, 123. "Nothing delights me so much as the works of nature."—*Murray's Gram.*, Vol. i, p. 150. "No person was ever so perplexed as he has been to-day."—*Murray's Key*, ii, 216. "In no case are writers so apt to err as in the position of the word *only*."—*Maunder's Gram.*, p. 15. "For nothing is so tiresome as perpetual uniformity."—*Blair's Rhet.*, p. 102.

"No writing lifts exalted man so high,
As sacred and soul-moving poesy."—*Sheffield*.

UNDER NOTE VII.—EXTRA COMPARISONS.

"How much more are ye better than the fowls!"—*Luke*, xii, 24. "Do not thou hasten above the Most Highest."—*2 Esdras*, iv, 34. "This word *peer* is most principally used for the nobility of the realm."—*Cowell*. "Because the same is not only most universally received," &c.—*Barclay's Works*, i, 447. "This is, I say, not the best and most principal evidence."—*Ib.*, iii, 41. "Offer unto God thanksgiving, and pay thy vows unto the Most Highest."—*The Psalter*, Ps. 1, 14. "The holy place of the tabernacle of the Most Highest."—*Ib.*, Ps. xlvi, 4. "As boys should be educated with temperance, so the first greatest lesson that should be taught them is to admire frugality."—*Goldsmith's Essays*, p. 152. "More universal terms are put for such as are more restricted."—*Brown's Metaphors*, p. 11. "This was the most unkindest cut of all."—*Dodd's Beauties of Shak.*, p. 251; *Singer's Shak.*, ii, 264. "To take the basest and most poorest shape."—*Dodd's Shak.*, p. 261. "I'll forbear: and am fallen out with my more headier will."—*Ib.*, p. 262. "The power of the Most Highest guard thee from sin."—*Percival, on Apostolic Succession*, p. 90. "Which title had been more truer, if the dictionary had been in Latin and Welch."—VERSTEGAN: *Harrison's E. Lang.*, p. 254. "The waters are more sooner and harder frozen, than more further upward, within the inlands."—*Id., ib.* "At every descent, the worst may become more worse."—H. MANN: *Louisville Examiner*, 8vo, Vol. i, p. 149.

"Or as a moat defensive to a house
Against the envy of less happier lands."—*Shakspeare.*

"A dreadful quiet felt, and worser far
Than arms, a sullen interval of war."—*Dryden.*

UNDER NOTE VIII.—ADJECTIVES CONNECTED.

"It breaks forth in its most energetick, impassioned, and highest strain."—*Kirkham's Elocution*, p. 66. "He has fallen into the most gross and vilest sort of railing."—*Barclay's Works*, iii, 261. "To receive that more general and higher instruction which the public affords."—*District School*, p. 281.

"If the best things have the perfectest and best operations."—HOOKER: *Joh. Dict.* "It became the plainest and most elegant, the most splendid and richest, of all languages."—See *Bucke's Gram.*, p. 140. "But the most frequent and the principal use of pauses, is, to mark the divisions of the sense."—*Blair's Rhet.*, p. 331; *Murray's Gram.*, 248. "That every thing belonging to ourselves is the perfectest and the best."—*Clarkson's Prize Essay*, p. 189. "And to instruct their pupils in the most thorough and best manner."—*Report of a School Committee.*

UNDER NOTE IX.—ADJECTIVES SUPERADDED.

"The Father is figured out as an old venerable man."—*Dr. Brownlee's Controversy.* "There never was exhibited such another masterpiece of ghostly assurance."—*Id.* "After the three first sentences, the question is entirely lost."—*Spect.*, No, 476. "The four last parts of speech are commonly called particles."—*Alex. Murray's Gram.*, p. 14. "The two last chapters will not be found deficient in this respect."—*Student's Manual*, p. 6. "Write upon your slates a list of the ten first nouns."—*Abbott's Teacher*, p. 85. "We have a few remains of other two Greek poets in the pastoral style, Moschus and Bion."—*Blair's Rhet.*, p. 393. "The nine first chapters of the book of Proverbs are highly poetical."—*Ib.*, p. 417. "For of these five heads, only the two first have any particular relation to the sublime."—*Ib.*, p. 35. "The resembling sounds of the two last syllables give a ludicrous air to the whole."—*Kames, El. of Crit.*, ii, 69. "The three last are arbitrary."—*Ib.*, p. 72. "But in the phrase 'She hangs the curtains,' the verb *hangs* is a transitive active verb."—*Comly's Gram.*, p. 30. "If our definition of a verb, and the arrangement of transitive or intransitive active, passive, and neuter verbs, are properly understood."—*Ib.*, 15th Ed., p. 30. "These two last lines have an embarrassing construction."—*Rush, on the Voice*, p. 160. "God was provoked to drown them all, but Noah and other seven persons."—*Wood's*

Dict., ii, 129. "The *six first* books of the Æneid are extremely beautiful."—*Formey's Belles-Lettres*, p. 27. "A few more instances only can be given here."—*Murray's Gram.*, p. 131. "A few more years will obliterate every vestige of a subjunctive form."—*Nutting's Gram.*, p. 46. "Some define them to be verbs devoid of the two first persons."—*Crombie's Treatise*, p. 205. "In such another Essay-tract as this."—*White's English Verb*, p. 302. "But we fear that not such another man is to be found."—REV. ED. IRVING: *on Horne's Psalms*, p. xxiii.

"Oh such another sleep, that I might see
But such another man!"—SHAK., *Antony and Cleopatra*.

UNDER NOTE X.—ADJECTIVES FOR ADVERBS.

"*The* is an article, relating to the noun *balm*, agreeable to Rule 11."—*Comly's Gram.*, p. 133. "*Wise* is an adjective relating to the noun *man's*, agreeable to Rule 11th."—*Ibid.*, 12th Ed., often. "To whom I observed, that the beer was extreme good."—*Goldsmith's Essays*, p. 127. "He writes remarkably elegant."—*O. B. Peirce's Gram.*, p. 152. "John behaves truly civil to all men."—*Ib.*, p. 153. "All the sorts of words hitherto considered have each of them some meaning, even when taken separate."—*Beattie's Moral Science*, i, 44. "He behaved himself conformable to that blessed example."—*Sprat's Sermons*, p. 80. "Marvellous graceful."—*Clarendon, Life*, p. 18. "The Queen having changed her ministry suitable to her wisdom."—*Swift, Exam.*, No. 21. "The assertions of this author are easier detected."—*Swift*: censured in *Lowth's Gram.*, p. 93. "The characteristic of his sect allowed him to affirm no stronger than that."—*Bentley: ibid.* "If one author had spoken nobler and loftier than an other."—*Id., ib.* "Xenophon says express."—*Id., ib.* "I can never think so very mean of him."—*Id., ib.* "To convince all that are ungodly among them, of all their ungodly deeds, which they have ungodly committed."—*Jude*, 15th: *ib.* "I think it very masterly written."—*Swift to Pope*, Let. 74: *ib.* "The whole design must refer to the golden age, which it lively represents."—*Addison, on Medals: ib.* "Agreeable to this, we read of names being blotted out of God's book."—BURDER: approved in *Webster's Impr. Gram.*, p. 107; *Frazee's*, 140; *Maltby's*, 93. "Agreeable to the law of nature, children are bound to support their indigent parents."—*Webster's Impr. Gram.*, p. 109. "Words taken independent of their meaning are parsed as nouns of the neuter gender."—*Maltby's Gr.*, 96.

"Conceit in weakest bodies strongest works."—*Beaut. of Shak.*, p. 236.

UNDER NOTE XI.—THEM FOR THOSE.

"Though he was not known by them letters, or the name Christ."—*Wm. Bayly's Works*, p. 94. "In a gig, or some of them things."—*Edgeworth's Castle Rackrent*, p. 35. "When cross-examined by them lawyers."—*Ib.*, p. 98. "As the custom in them cases is."—*Ib.*, p. 101. "If you'd have listened to them slanders."—*Ib.*, p. 115. "The old people were telling stories about them fairies, but to the best of my judgment there's nothing in it."—*Ib.*, p. 188. "And is it not a pity that the Quakers have no better authority to substantiate their principles than the testimony of them old Pharisees?"—*Hibbard's Errors of the Quakers*, p. 107.

UNDER NOTE XII.—THIS AND THAT.

"Hope is as strong an incentive to action, as fear: this is the anticipation of good, that of evil."—*Brown's Institutes*, p. 135. "The poor want some advantages which the rich enjoy; but we should not therefore account those happy, and these miserable."—*Ib.*

"Ellen and Margaret fearfully,
Sought comfort in each other's eye;
Then turned their ghastly look each one,
This to her sire, that to her son."
    Scott's *Lady of the Lake*, Canto ii, Stanza 29.

"Six youthful sons, as many blooming maids,
In one sad day beheld the Stygian shades;
These by Apollo's silver bow were slain,
Those Cynthia's arrows stretched upon the plain."
    —*Pope, Il.*, xxiv, 760.

"Memory and forecast just returns engage,
This pointing back to youth, that on to age."
    —See *Key*.

UNDER NOTE XIII.—EITHER AND NEITHER.

"These make the three great subjects of discussion among mankind; truth, duty, and interest. But the arguments directed towards either of them are generically distinct."—*Blair's Rhet.*, p. 318. "A thousand other deviations may be made, and still either of them may be correct in principle. For these divisions and their technical terms, are all arbitrary."—*R. W. Green's Inductive Gram.*, p. vi. "Thus it appears, that our alphabet is deficient, as it has but seven vowels to represent thirteen different sounds; and has no letter to represent either of five simple consonant sounds."—*Churchill's Gram.*, p. 19. "Then neither of these [five] verbs can be neuter."—*Oliver B. Peirce's Gram.*, p. 343. "And the asserter is in neither of the four already mentioned."—*Ib.*, p. 356. "As it is not in either of these four."—*Ib.*, p. 356. "See whether or not the word comes within the definition of either of the other three simple cases."—*Ib.*, p. 51. "Neither of the ten was there."—

Frazee's Gram., p. 108. "Here are ten oranges, take either of them."—*Ib.*, p. 102. "There are three modes, by either of which recollection will generally be supplied; inclination, practice, and association."—*Rippingham's Art of Speaking*, p. xxix. "Words not reducible to either of the three preceding heads."—*Fowler's E. Gram.*, 8vo, 1850, pp. 335 and 340. "Now a sentence may be analyzed in reference to either of these [four] classes."—*Ib.*, p. 577.

UNDER NOTE XIV.—WHOLE, LESS, MORE, AND MOST.

"Does not all proceed from the law, which regulates the whole departments of the state?"—*Blair's Rhet.*, p. 278. "A messenger relates to Theseus the whole particulars."—*Kames. El. of Crit.*, Vol. ii, p. 313. "There are no less than twenty dipthhongs [sic—KTH] in the English language."—*Dr. Ash's Gram.*, p. xii. "The Redcross Knight runs through the whole steps of the Christian life."—*Spectator* No. 540. "There were not less than fifty or sixty persons present."—*Teachers' Report.* "Greater experience, and more cultivated society, abate the warmth of imagination, and chasten the manner of expression."—*Blair's Rhet.*, p. 152; *Murray's Gram.*, i, 351. "By which means knowledge, much more than oratory, is become the principal requisite."—*Blair's Rhet.*, p. 254. "No less than seven illustrious cities disputed the right of having given birth to the greatest of poets."—*Lemp. Dict., n. Homer.* "Temperance, more than medicines, is the proper means of curing many diseases."—*Murray's Key*, 8vo, p. 222. "I do not suppose, that we Britons want genius, more than our neighbours."—*Ib.*, p. 215. "In which he saith, he has found no less than twelve untruths."—*Barclay's Works*, i, 460. "The several places of rendezvous were concerted, and the whole operations fixed."—HUME: see *Priestley's Gram.*, p. 190. "In these rigid opinions the whole sectaries concurred."—*Id., ib.* "Out of whose modifications have been made most complex modes."—LOCKE: *Sanborn's Gram.*, p. 148. "The Chinese vary each of their words on no less than five different tones."—*Blair's Rhet.*, p. 58. "These people, though they possess more shining qualities, are not so proud as he is, nor so vain as she."—*Murray's Key*, 8vo, p. 211. "'Tis certain, we believe ourselves more, after we have made a thorough Inquiry into the Thing."—*Brightland's Gram.*, p. 244. "As well as the whole Course and Reasons of the Operation."—*Ib.* "Those rules and principles which are of most practical advantage."—*Newman's Rhet.*, p. 4. "And there shall be no more curse."—*Rev.*, xxii, 3. "And there shall be no more death."—*Rev.*, xxi, 4. "But in recompense, we have more pleasing pictures of ancient manners."—*Blair's Rhet.*, p. 436. "Our language has suffered more injurious changes in America, since the British army landed on our shores, than it had suffered before, in the period of three centuries."—*Webster's Essays*, Ed. of 1790, p. 96. "The whole conveniences of life are derived from mutual aid and support in society."—*Kames, El. of Crit.*, Vol. i, p. 166.

UNDER NOTE XV.—PARTICIPIAL ADJECTIVES.

"To such as think the nature of it deserving their attention."—*Butler's Analogy*, p. 84. "In all points, more deserving the approbation of their readers."—*Keepsake*, 1830. "But to give way to childish sensations was unbecoming our nature."—*Lempriere's Dict., n. Zeno.* "The following extracts are deserving the serious perusal of all."—*The Friend*, Vol. v, p. 135. "No inquiry into wisdom, however superficial, is undeserving attention."—*Bulwer's Disowned*, ii, 95. "The opinions of illustrious men are deserving great consideration."—*Porter's Family Journal*, p. 3. "And resolutely keeps its laws, Uncaring consequences."—*Burns's Works*, ii, 43. "This is an item that is deserving more attention."—*Goodell's Lectures.*

"Leave then thy joys, unsuiting such an age, To a fresh comer, and resign the stage."—*Dryden.*

UNDER NOTE XVI.—FIGURE OF ADJECTIVES.

"The tall dark mountains and the deep toned seas."—*Sanborn's Gram.*, p. 278. "O! learn from him To station quick eyed Prudence at the helm."—ANON.: *Frost's El. of Gram.*, p. 104. "He went in a one horse chaise."—*Blair's Gram.*, p. 113. "It ought to be, 'in a one horse chaise.'"—*Dr. Crombie's Treatise*, p. 334. "These are marked with the above mentioned letters."—*Folker's Gram.*, p. 4. "A many headed faction."—*Ware's Gram.*, p. 18. "Lest there should be no authority in any popular grammar for the perhaps heaven inspired effort."—*Fowle's True English Gram.*, Part 2d, p. 25. "Common metre stanzas consist of four Iambic lines; one of eight, and the next of six syllables. They were formerly written in two fourteen syllable lines."—*Goodenow's Gram.*, p. 69. "Short metre stanzas consist of four Iambic lines; the third of eight, and the rest of six syllables."—*Ibid.* "Particular metre stanzas consist of six Iambic lines; the third and sixth of six syllables, the rest of eight."—*Ibid.* "Hallelujah metre stanzas consist of six Iambic lines; the last two of eight syllables, and the rest of six."—*Ibid.* "Long metre stanzas are merely the union of four Iambic lines, of ten syllables each."—*Ibid.* "A majesty more commanding than is to be found among the rest of the Old Testament poets."—*Blair's Rhet.*, p. 418.

"You sulphurous and thought executed fires, Vaunt couriers to oak cleaving thunderbolts, Singe my white head! And thou, all shaking thunder Strike flat the thick rotundity o' the world!"—*Beauties of Shak.*, p. 264.

—PRONOUNS.

The rules for the agreement of Pronouns with their antecedents are four; hence this chapter extends from the tenth rule to the thirteenth, inclusively. The *cases* of Pronouns are embraced with those of nouns, in the seven rules of the third chapter.

RULE X.—PRONOUNS.

A Pronoun must agree with its antecedent, or the noun or pronoun which it represents, in person, number, and gender:[379] as, "This is the friend *of whom I spoke*; he has just arrived."—"This is the book *which I* bought; it is an excellent work."—"*Ye*, therefore, *who* love mercy, teach *your* sons to love *it* too."—*Cowper.*

"Speak *thou, whose* thoughts at humble peace repine,
Shall Wolsey's wealth with Wolsey's end be *thine*?"—*Dr. Johnson.*

EXCEPTION FIRST.

When a pronoun stands for some person or thing *indefinite*, or *unknown to the speaker*, this rule is not *strictly* applicable; because the person, number, and gender, are rather assumed in the pronoun, than regulated by an antecedent: as, "I do not care *who* knows it."—*Steele.* "*Who* touched me?

Tell me *who* it was."—"We have no knowledge how, or by *whom,* it is inhabited."—ABBOT: *Joh. Dict.*

EXCEPTION SECOND.

The neuter pronoun *it* may be applied to a young child, or to other creatures masculine or feminine by nature, when they are not obviously distinguishable with regard to sex; as, "Which is the real friend to the *child,* the person who gives *it* the sweetmeats, or the person who, considering only *its* health, resists *its* importunities?"—*Opis.* "He loads the *animal* he is showing me, with so many trappings and collars, that I cannot distinctly view *it*"—*Murray's Gram.,* p. 301. "The *nightingale* sings most sweetly when *it* sings in the night."—*Bucke's Gram.,* p. 52.

EXCEPTION THIRD.

The pronoun *it* is often used without a definite reference to any antecedent, and is sometimes a mere expletive, and sometimes the representative of an action expressed afterwards by a verb; as, "Whether she grapple *it* with the pride of philosophy."—*Chalmers.* "Seeking to lord *it* over God's heritage."—*The Friend,* vii, 253. "*It* is not for kings, O Lemuel, *it* is not for kings *to drink* wine, nor for princes strong drink."—*Prov.,* xxxi, 4. "Having no temptation to *it,* God cannot *act unjustly* without defiling his nature."—*Brown's Divinity,* p. 11.

"Come, and trip *it* as you go, On the light fantastic toe."—*Milton.*

EXCEPTION FOURTH.

A singular antecedent with the adjective *many,* sometimes admits a plural pronoun, but never in the same clause; as, "Hard has been the fate of *many* a great *genius,* that while *they* have conferred immortality on others, *they* have wanted themselves some friend to embalm their names to posterity."—*Welwood's Pref. to Rowe's Lucan.*

"In Hawick twinkled *many a light,*
Behind him soon *they* set in night."—*W. Scott.*

EXCEPTION FIFTH.

When a plural pronoun is put by enallagè for the singular, it does not agree with its noun in number, because it still requires a plural verb; as, "*We* [Lindley Murray] *have followed* those authors, who appear to have given them the most natural and intelligible distribution."—*Murray's Gram.*, 8vo, p. 29. "*We shall close our* remarks on this subject, by introducing the sentiments of Dr. Johnson respecting it."—*Ib.* "My lord, *you know* I love *you*"—*Shakspeare.*

EXCEPTION SIXTH.

The pronoun sometimes disagrees with its antecedent in one sense, because it takes it in an other; as, "I have perused Mr. Johnson's *Grammatical Commentaries,* and find *it*[380] a very laborious, learned, and useful Work."—*Tho. Knipe,* D. D. "*Lamps* is of the plural number, because *it* means more than one."—*Smith's New Gram.*, p. 8. "*Man* is of the masculine gender, because *it* is the name of a male."—*Ib.* "The *Utica Sentinel* says *it* has not heard whether the wounds are dangerous."—*Evening Post.* (Better: "The *editor* of the Utica Sentinel says, *he* has not heard," &c.) "There is little *Benjamin* with *their* ruler."—*Psalms,* lxviii, 27.

"*Her* end when *emulation* misses, *She* turns to envy, stings, and hisses."—*Swift's Poems,* p. 415.

OBSERVATIONS ON RULE X.

OBS. 1.—Respecting a pronoun, the main thing is, that the reader perceive clearly *for what it stands*; and next, that he do not misapprehend *its relation of case*. For the sake of completeness and uniformity in parsing, it is, I think, expedient to apply the foregoing rule not only to those pronouns which have obvious antecedents expressed, but also to such as are not accompanied by the nouns for which they stand. Even those which are put for persons or things unknown or indefinite, may be said to agree with whatever is meant by them; that is, with such nouns as their own properties indicate. For the reader will naturally understand something by every pronoun, unless it be a mere expletive, and without any antecedent. For example: "It would depend upon *who* the forty were."—*Trial at Steubenville*, p. 50. Here *who* is an indefinite relative, equivalent to *what persons*; of the third person, plural, masculine; and is in the nominative case after were, by Rule 6th. For the full construction seems to be this: "It would depend upon *the persons who* the forty were." So *which*, for *which person*, or *which thing*, (if we call it a pronoun rather than an adjective,) may be said to have the properties of the noun *person* or *thing* understood; as,

"His notions fitted things so well,
That *which* was *which* he could not tell."—*Hudibras.*

OBS. 2.—The pronoun *we* is used by the speaker or writer to represent himself and others, and is therefore plural. But it is sometimes used, by a sort of fiction, in stead of the singular, to intimate that the speaker or writer is not alone in his opinions; or, perhaps more frequently, to evade the charge of egotism; for this modest assumption of plurality seems most common with those who have something else to assume: as, "And so lately as 1809, Pope Pius VII, in excommunicating his 'own dear son,' Napoleon, whom he crowned and blessed, says: '*We*, unworthy as *we* are, represent the God of peace.'"—*Dr. Brownlee.* "The coat fits *us* as well as if *we* had been melted and poured into it."—*Prentice.* Monarchs sometimes prefer *we* to *I*, in immediate connexion with a singular noun; as, "*We Alexander,* Autocrat of all the Russias."—"*We the Emperor* of China," &c.—*Economy of Human Life*, p. vi. They also employ the anomalous compound *ourself,* which is not often used by other people; as, "Witness *ourself* at Westminster, 28 day of April, in the tenth year of *our* reign. CHARLES."

> "*Cæs.* What touches *us ourself,* shall be last serv'd." —*Shak., J. C.,* Act iii, Sc. 1.

> "*Ourself* to hoary Nestor will repair." —*Pope, Iliad,* B. x, l. 65.

OBS. 3.—The pronoun *you,* though originally and properly plural, is now generally applied alike to one person or to more. Several observations upon this fashionable substitution of the plural number for the singular, will be found in the fifth and sixth chapters of Etymology. This usage, however it may seem to involve a solecism, is established by that authority against which the mere grammarian has scarcely a right to remonstrate. Alexander Murray, the schoolmaster, observes, "When language was plain and simple, the English always said *thou,* when speaking to a single person. But when an affected politeness, and a fondness for continental manners and customs began to take place, persons of rank and fashion said *you* in stead of *thou.* The innovation gained ground, and custom gave sanction to the change, and stamped it with the authority of law."—*English Gram.,* Third Edition, 1793, p. 107. This respectable grammarian acknowledged both *thou* and *you* to be of the second person singular. I do not, however, think it necessary or advisable to do this, or to encumber the conjugations, as some have done, by introducing the latter pronoun, and the corresponding form of the verb, as singular.[381] It is manifestly better to say, that the plural is used *for the singular,* by the figure *Enallagè.* For if *you* has literally become singular by virtue of this substitution, *we* also is singular for the same reason, as often as it is substituted for *I*; else the authority of innumerable authors, editors, compilers, and crowned, heads, is insufficient to make it so. And again, if *you* and the corresponding form of the verb are *literally of the second person singular*, (as Wells contends, with an array of more than sixty names of English grammarians to prove it,) then, by their own rule of concord, since *thou* and its verb are still generally retained in the same place by these grammarians, a verb that agrees with one of these nominatives, must also agree with the other; so that *you hast* and *thou have, you seest* and *thou see,* may be, so far as appears from *their* instructions, as good a concord as can be made of these words!

OBS. 4.—The putting of you for thou has introduced the anomalous compound *yourself,* which is now very generally used in stead of *thyself.* In this instance, as in the less frequent adoption of *ourself* for *myself,* Fashion so tramples upon the laws of grammar, that it is scarcely possible to frame an intelligible exception in her favour. These pronouns are essentially singular, both in form and meaning; and yet they cannot be used with *I* or *thou,* with *me* or *thee,* or with any verb that is literally singular; as, "*I ourself am.*" but, on the contrary, they must be connected only with such plural terms as are put for the singular; as, "*We ourself are* king."—"Undoubtedly *you yourself become* an innovator."—*L. Murray's Gram.,* p. 364; *Campbell's Rhet.,* 167.

"Try touch, or sight, or smell; try what you will,
You strangely *find* nought but *yourself* alone."
—*Pollok, C. of T.,* B. i, l. 162.

OBS. 5.—Such terms of address, as *your Majesty, your Highness, your Lordship, your Honour,* are sometimes followed by verbs and pronouns of the second person plural, substituted for the singular; and sometimes by words literally singular, and of the third person, with no other figure than a substitution of *who* for *which*: as, "Wherein *your Lordship, who shines* with so much distinction in the noblest assembly in the world, peculiarly *excels*"—*Dedication of Sale's Koran.* "We have good cause to give *your Highness* the first place; *who*, by a continued series of favours *have obliged* us, not only while *you moved* in a lower orb, but since the Lord hath called *your Highness* to supreme authority."—*Massachusetts to Cromwell*, in 1654.

OBS. 6.—The general usage of the French is like that of the English, *you* for *thou*; but Spanish, Portuguese, or German politeness requires that the third person be substituted for the second. And when they would be very courteous, the Germans use also the plural for the singular, as *they* for *thou*. Thus they have a fourfold method of addressing a person: as, *they*, denoting the highest degree of respect; *he*, a less degree; *you*, a degree still less; and *thou*, none at all, or absolute reproach. Yet, even among them, the last is used as a term of endearment to children, and of veneration to God! *Thou*, in English, still retains its place firmly, and without dispute, in all addresses to the Supreme Being; but in respect to the *first person*, an observant clergyman has suggested the following dilemma: "Some men will be pained, if a minister says *we* in the pulpit; and others will quarrel with him, if he says *I*."—*Abbott's Young Christian*, p. 268.

OBS. 7.—Any extensive perversion of the common words of a language from their original and proper use, is doubtless a matter of considerable moment. These changes in the use of the pronouns, being some of them evidently a sort of complimentary fictions, some religious people have made it a matter of conscience to abstain from them, and have published their reasons for so doing. But the *moral objections* which may lie against such or any other applications of words, do not come within the grammarian's province. Let every one consider for himself the moral bearing of what he utters: not forgetting the text, "But I say unto you, that *every idle word* that men shall speak, they shall give account thereof in the day of judgement: for *by thy words* thou shalt be justified, and *by thy words* thou shalt be condemned."—*Matt.*, xii, 36 and 37. What scruples this declaration *ought to* raise, it is not my business to define. But if such be God's law, what shall be the reckoning of those who make no conscience of uttering continually, or when they will, not idle words only, but expressions the most absurd, insignificant, false, exaggerated, vulgar, indecent, injurious, wicked, sophistical, unprincipled, ungentle, and perhaps blasphemous, or profane?

OBS. 8.—The agreement of pronouns with their antecedents, it is necessary to observe, is liable to be controlled or affected by several of the figures of rhetoric. A noun used figuratively often suggests two different senses, the one literal, and the other tropical; and the agreement of the pronoun must be sometimes with this, and sometimes with that, according to the nature of the trope. If the reader be unacquainted with tropes and figures, he should turn to the explanation of them in Part Fourth of this work; but almost every one knows something about them, and such as must here be named, will perhaps be made sufficiently intelligible by the examples. There seems to be no occasion to introduce under this head more than four; namely, personification, metaphor, metonymy, and synecdoche.

OBS. 9.—When a pronoun represents the name of an inanimate object *personified*, it agrees with its antecedent in the figurative, and not in the literal sense; as, "There were others whose crime it was rather to neglect *Reason* than to disobey *her*."—*Dr. Johnson*. "*Penance* dreams her life away."—*Rogers*. "Grim *Darkness* furls *his* leaden shroud."—*Id.* Here if the pronoun were made neuter, the personification would be destroyed; as, "By the progress which *England* had already made in navigation and commerce, *it* was now prepared for advancing farther."—*Robertson's America*, Vol. ii, p. 341. If the pronoun *it* was here intended to represent England, the feminine *she* would have been much better; and, if such was not the author's meaning, the sentence has some worse fault than the agreement of a pronoun with its noun in a wrong sense.

OBS. 10.—When the antecedent is applied *metaphorically,* the pronoun usually agrees with it in its literal, and not in its figurative sense; as, "Pitt was the *pillar which* upheld the state."—"The *monarch* of mountains rears *his* snowy head."—"The *stone which* the builders rejected."—*Matt.,* xxi, 42. According to this rule, *which* would be better than *whom,* in the following text: "I considered the horns, and, behold, there came up among them an other *little horn,* before *whom* there were three of the first horns plucked up by the roots."—*Daniel,* vii, 8. In *Rom.,* ix, 33, there is something similar: "Behold, I lay in Sion a *stumbling-stone* and *rock* of offence: and whosoever believeth *on him* shall not be ashamed." Here the *stone* or *rock* is a metaphor for *Christ,* and the pronoun *him* may be referred to the sixth exception above; but the construction is not agreeable, because it is not regular: it would be more grammatical, to change *on him* to *thereon.* In the following example, the noun "*wolves,*" which literally requires *which,* and not *who,* is used metaphorically for *selfish priests*; and, in the relative, the figurative or personal sense is allowed to prevail:

"*Wolves* shall succeed for teachers, grievous *wolves,*
Who all the sacred mysteries of Heaven
To their own vile advantages shall turn."
—*Milton, P. L.,* B. xii, l. 508.

This seems to me somewhat forced and catachrestical. So too, and worse, the following; which makes a *star* rise and *speak*:

"So *spake* our *Morning Star* then in *his rise,*
And *looking* round on every side *beheld*
A pathless desert, dusk with horrid shades."
—*Id., P. R.,* B. i, l. 294.

OBS. 11.—When the antecedent is put by *metonymy* for a noun of different properties, the pronoun sometimes agrees with it in the figurative, and sometimes in the literal sense; as, "When *Israel* was a child, then I loved *him*, and called my son out of Egypt. As they called *them*, so *they* went from them: [i. e., When Moses and the prophets called the *Israelites*, they often refused to hear:] *they* sacrificed unto Baalim, and burnt incense to graven images. I taught *Ephraim* also to go, taking *them* by *their* arms; but *they* knew not that I healed *them*."—*Hosea*, xi, 1, 2, 3. The mixture and obscurity which are here, ought not to be imitated. The name of a man, put for the nation or tribe of his descendants, may have a pronoun of either number, and a nation may be figuratively represented as feminine; but a mingling of different genders or numbers ought to be avoided: as, "*Moab* is spoiled, and gone up out of *her* cities, and *his* chosen young men are gone down to the slaughter."—*Jeremiah*, xlviii, 15.

"The wolf, who [say *that*] from the nightly fold,
Fierce drags the bleating *prey*, ne'er drunk *her* milk,
Nor wore *her* warming fleece."—*Thomson's Seasons.*

"That each may fill the circle mark'd by *Heaven*,
Who sees with equal eye, as God of all,
A hero perish or a sparrow fall."—*Pope's Essay on Man.*

"And *heaven* behold *its* image in his breast."—*Ib.*

"Such fate to suffering *worth* is given, *Who* long with wants and
woes has striven."—*Burns.*

OBS. 12.—When the antecedent is put by *synecdoche* for more or less than it literally signifies, the pronoun agrees with it in the figurative, and not in the literal sense; as,

"A dauntless *soul* erect, *who* smiled on death."—*Thomson*

"But to the generous still improving *mind,*
That gives the hopeless heart to sing for joy,
To *him* the long review of ordered life
Is inward rapture only to be felt."—*Id. Seasons.*

OBS. 13.—Pronouns usually *follow* the words which they represent; but this order is sometimes reversed: as, "*Whom* the cap fits, let *him* put it on."—"Hark! *they* whisper; angels say," &c.—*Pope.* "*Thou, O Lord*, art a God full of compassion."—*Old Test.* And in some cases of apposition, the pronoun naturally comes first; as, "*I Tertius*"—"*Ye lawyers*." The pronoun *it*, likewise, very often precedes the clause or phrase which it represents; as, "Is *it* not manifest, that the generality of people speak and write very badly?"—*Campbell's Rhet.*, p. 160; *Murray's Gram.*, i, 358. This arrangement is too natural to be called a transposition. The most common form of the real inversion is that of the antecedent and relative in poetry; as,

"*Who* stops to plunder at this signal hour,
The birds shall tear *him*, and the dogs devour."
—POPE: *Iliad*, xv, 400.

OBS. 14.—A pronoun sometimes represents a *phrase* or a *sentence*; and in this case the pronoun is always in the third person singular neuter: as, "Surely the Lord is in this place, and I knew *it* not."—*Gen.*, xxviii, 10. "Yet men can go on to vilify or disregard Christianity; *which* is to talk and act as if they had a demonstration of its falsehood."—*Butler's Analogy*, p. 269. "When *it* is asked wherein personal identity consists, the answer should be the same as if *it* were asked, wherein consists similitude or equality."—*Ib.*, p. 270. "Also, that the soul be without knowledge, *it* is not good."—*Prov.*, xix, 2. In this last example, the pronoun is not really necessary. "That the soul be without knowledge, *is* not good."—*Jenks's Prayers*, p. 144.

Sometimes an infinitive verb is taken as an antecedent; as, "He will not be able *to think,* without *which it* is impertinent *to read*; nor *to act*, without *which it* is impertinent *to think*."—*Bolingbroke, on History*, p. 103.

OBS. 15.—When a pronoun follows two words, having a neuter verb between them, and both referring to the same thing, it may represent either of them, but not often with the same meaning: as, 1. "I am the man, who command." Here, *who command* belongs to the subject *I*, and the meaning is, "I who command, am the man." (The latter expression places the relative nearer to its antecedent, and is therefore preferable.) 2. "I am the man who commands." Here, *who commands* belongs to the predicate *man*, and the meaning is, "I am the commander." Again: "I perceive thou art a pupil, *who possessest* good talents."—*Cooper's Pl. and Pract. Gram.*, p. 136. Here the construction corresponds not to the perception, which is, of the pupil's talents. Say, therefore, "I perceive thou art a *pupil possessing* (or, *who possesses*) good talents."

OBS. 16.—After the expletive *it,* which may be employed to introduce a noun or a pronoun of any person, number, or gender, the above-mentioned distinction is generally disregarded; and the relative is most commonly made to agree with the latter word, especially if this word be of the first or the second person: as, "*It* is no more *I that do it.*"—*Rom.*, vii, 20. "For *it* is not *ye that speak.*"—*Matt.*, x, 20. The propriety of this construction is questionable. In the following examples, the relative agrees with the *it*, and not with the subsequent nouns: "*It* is the combined *excellencies* of all the denominations *that* gives to her her winning beauty and her powerful charms."—*Bible Society's Report*, 1838, p. 89. "*It* is *purity and neatness* of expression *which is* chiefly to be studied."—*Blair's Rhet.*, p. 271. "*It* is *not the difficulty* of the language, but on the contrary the *simplicity and facility* of it, *that occasions* this neglect."—*Lowth's Gram.*, p. vi. "*It* is *a wise head and a good heart that constitutes* a great man."—*Child's Instructor*, p. 22.

OBS. 17.—The pronoun *it* very frequently refers to something mentioned subsequently in the sentence; as, "*It* is useless *to complain* of what is irremediable." This pronoun is a necessary expletive at the commencement of any sentence in which the verb is followed by a phrase or a clause which, by transposition, might be made the subject of the verb; as, "*It is impossible to please every one.*"—*W. Allen's Gram.* "*It* was requisite *that the papers should be* sent."—*Ib.* The following example is censured by the Rev. Matt. Harrison: "*It is really curious, the course* which balls will sometimes take."—*Abernethy's Lectures.* "This awkward expression," says the critic, "might have been avoided by saying, 'The course which balls will sometimes take is really curious.'"—*Harrison, on the English Language*, p. 147. If the construction is objectionable, it may, in this instance, be altered thus: "It is really curious, *to observe* the course which balls will sometimes take!" So, it appears, we may avoid a *pleonasm* by an *addition.* But he finds a worse example: saying, "Again, in an article *from* the 'New Monthly,' No. 103, we meet with the same form of expression, *but with an aggravated aspect:*—'It is incredible, the number of apothecaries' shops, presenting themselves.' It would be quite as easy to say, 'The number of apothecaries' shops, presenting themselves, is incredible.' "—*Ib.*, p. 147. This, too, may take an infinitive, "*to tell,*" or "*to behold;*" for there is no more extravagance in doubting one's eyes, than in declaring one's own statement "incredible." But I am not sure that the original form is not allowable. In the following line, we seem to have something like it:

"It curled not Tweed alone, that breeze."—*Sir W. Scott.*

OBS. 18.—*Relative* and *interrogative* pronouns are placed at or near the beginning of their own clauses; and the learner must observe that, through all their cases, they almost invariably retain this situation in the sentence, and are found before their verbs even when the order of the construction would reverse this arrangement: as, "He *who* preserves me, to *whom* I owe my being, *whose* I am, and *whom* I serve, is eternal."—*Murray*, p. 159. "He *whom* you seek."—*Lowth*.

"The good must merit God's peculiar care;
But *who*, but God, can tell us *who* they are?"—*Pope*.

OBS. 19.—A *relative* pronoun, being the representative of some antecedent word or phrase, derives from this relation its person, number, and gender, but not its case. By taking an other relation of case, it helps to form an other clause; and, by retaining the essential meaning of its antecedent, serves to connect this clause to that in which the antecedent is found. No relative, therefore, can ever be used in an independent simple sentence, or be made the subject of a subjunctive verb, or be put in apposition with any noun or pronoun; but, like other connectives, this pronoun belongs at the head of a clause in a compound sentence, and excludes conjunctions, except when two such clauses are to be joined together, as in the following example: "I should be glad, at least, of an easy companion, *who* may tell me his thoughts, *and* to *whom* I may communicate mine."—*Goldsmith's Essays*, p. 196.

OBS. 20.—The two *special* rules commonly given by the grammarians, for the construction of relatives, are not only unnecessary,[382] but faulty. I shall notice them only to show my reasons for discarding them. With whom they originated, it is difficult to say. Paul's Accidence has them, and if Dean Colet, the supposed writer, did not take them from some earlier author, they must have been first taught by *him*, about the year 1510; and it is certain that they have been copied into almost every grammar published since. The first one is faulty, because, "*When there cometh no nominative case between the relative and the verb, the relative shall* [not always] *be the nominative case to the verb*;" as may be seen by the following examples: "Many are the works of human industry, *which* to begin and finish are [say *is*] hardly granted to the same man."—*Dr. Johnson's Adv. to Dict.* "They aim at his removal; *which* there is reason to fear they will effect."—"*Which* to avoid, I cut them off."—*Shak., Hen. IV.* The second rule is faulty, because, "*When there cometh a nominative case between the relative and the verb, the relative shall* [not always] *be such case as the verb will have after it*;" as may be seen by the following examples: "The author has not advanced any instances, *which* he does not think *are* pertinent."—*Murray's Gram.*, i, 192. "*Which* we have reason to think *was* the case with the Greek and Latin."—*Ib.*, 112. "Is this your son, *who* ye say *was born* blind?"—*John*, ix, 19. The case of the relative cannot be accurately determined by any rules of mere location. It may be nominative to a verb afar off, or it may be objective with a verb immediately following; as, "*Which* I do not find that there ever *was*."—*Knight, on the Greek Alphabet*, p. 31. "And our chief reason for believing *which* is that our ancestors did so before us."—*Philological Museum*, i, 641. Both these particular rules are useless, because the general rules for the cases, as given in chapter third above, are applicable to relatives, sufficient to all the purpose, and not liable to any exceptions.

OBS. 21.—In syntactical parsing, each word, in general, is to be resolved by some *one* rule; but the parsing of a pronoun commonly requires *two*; one for its agreement with the noun or nouns for which it stands, and an other for its case. The rule of agreement will be one of the four which are embraced in this present chapter; and the rule for the case will be one of the seven which compose chapter third. So that the whole syntax of pronouns requires the application of eleven different rules, while that of nouns or verbs is embraced in six or seven, and that of any other part of speech, in one only. In respect to their cases, relatives and interrogatives admit of every construction common to nouns, or to the personal pronouns, except apposition. This is proved by the following examples:

1. Nominatives by Rule 2d: "I *who* write;—Thou *who* writest;—He *who* writes;—The animal *which* runs."—*Dr. Adam.* "He *that spareth* his rod, hateth his son."—*Solomon.* "He *who* does any thing *which* he knows is wrong, ventures on dangerous ground."—"*What* will become of us without religion?"—*Blair.* "Here I determined to wait the hand of death; *which,* I hope, when at last it comes, *will fall* lightly upon me."—*Dr. Johnson.* "*What is* sudden and unaccountable, *serves* to confound."—*Crabb.* "They only are wise, *who are* wise to salvation."—*Goodwin.*

2. Nominatives by Rule 6th: (i.e., words parsed as nominatives after the verbs, though mostly transposed:) "*Who* art thou?"—*Bible.* "*What* were we?"—*Ib.* "Do not tell them *who* I am."—"Let him be *who* he may, he is not the honest fellow *that* he seemed."—"The general conduct of mankind is neither *what* it was designed, nor *what* it ought to be."

3. Nominatives absolute by Rule 8th: "There are certain bounds to imprudence, *which being transgressed,* there remains no place for repentance in the natural course of things."—*Bp. Butler.* "*Which being so,* it need not be any wonder, why I should."—*Walker's Particles, Pref.,* p. xiv. "He offered an apology, *which not being admitted,* he became submissive."—*Murray's Key,* p. 202. This construction of the relative is a Latinism, and very seldom used by the best *English* writers.

4. Possessives by Rule 4th: "The chief man of the island, *whose* name was Publius."—*Acts.* "Despair, a cruel tyrant, from *whose* prisons none can escape."—*Dr. Johnson.* "To contemplate on Him *whose* yoke is easy and *whose* burden is light."—*Steele.*

5. Objectives by Rule 5th: "Those *whom* she persuaded."—*Dr. Johnson.* "The cloak *that* I left at Troas."—*St. Paul.* "By the things *which* he suffered."—*Id.* "A man *whom* there is reason to suspect."—"*What* are we to do?"—*Burke.* "Love refuses nothing *that* love sends."—*Gurnall.* "The first

thing, says he, is, to choose some maxim or point of morality; to inculcate *which*, is to be the design of his work."—*Blair's Rhet.*, p. 421. "*Whomsoever* you please to appoint."—*Lowth.* "*Whatsover* [sic—KTH] he doeth, shall prosper."—*Bible.* "*What* we are afraid to do before men, we should be afraid to think before God."—*Sibs.* "Shall I hide from Abraham that thing *which* I do?"—*Gen.*, xviii, 32. "Shall I hide from Abraham *what* I am going to do?"—"Call imperfection *what* thou fanciest such."—*Pope.*

6. Objectives by Rule 6th: (i.e., pronouns parsed as objectives after neuter verbs, though they stand before them:) "He is not the man *that* I took him to be."—"*Whom* did you suppose me to be?"—"If the lad ever become *what* you wish him to be."

7. Objectives by Rule 7th: "To *whom* shall we go?"—*Bible.* "The laws by *which* the world is governed, are general."—*Bp. Butler.* "*Whom* he looks upon as his defender."—*Addison.* "That secret heaviness of heart *which* unthinking men are subject to."—*Id.* "I cannot but think the loss of such talents as the man of *whom* I am speaking was master of, a more melancholy instance."—*Steele.* "Grammar is the solid foundation upon *which* all other science rests."—*Buchanan's Eng. Synt.*, p. xx.

OBS. 22.—In familiar language, the relative of the objective case is frequently understood; as, "The man [*whom*] I trust."—*Cowper.* "Here is the letter [*which*] I received." So in the following sentences: "This is the man they hate. These are the goods they bought. Are these the Gods they worship? Is this the woman you saw?"—*Ash's Gram.*, p. 96. This ellipsis seems allowable only in the familiar style. In grave writing, or deliberate discourse, it is much better to express this relative. The omission of it is often attended with some obscurity; as, "The next error [*that*] I shall mention [,] is a capital one."—*Kames, El. of Crit.*, ii, 157. "It is little [*that*] we know of the divine perfections."—*Scougal*, p. 94. "The faith [*which*] we give to memory, may be thought, on a superficial view, to be resolvable into consciousness, as well as that [*which*] we give to the immediate impressions of sense."—*Campbell's Rhet.*, p. 53. "We speak that [*which*] we do know, and testify that [*which*] we have seen."—*John*, iii, 11. The omission of a relative in the nominative case, is almost always inelegant; as, "This is the worst thing [*that*] could happen."—"There were several things [*which*] brought it upon me."—*Pilgrim's Progress*, p. 162. The latter ellipsis may occur after *but* or *than*, and it is also sometimes allowed in poetry; as, [There is] "No person of reflection but [who] must be sensible, that an incident makes a stronger impression on an eye-witness, than when heard at second hand."—*Kames, El. of Crit.*, ii, 257.

"In this 'tis God directs, in that 'tis man."—*Pope, on Man.*

"Abuse on all he lov'd, or lov'd him, spread."—*Id., to Arbuthnot.*

"There's nothing blackens like the ink of fools."—*Id., to Augustus.*

OBS. 23.—The *antecedent* is sometimes suppressed, especially in poetry; as, "Who will, may be a judge."—*Churchill.* "How shall I curse [*him* or *them*] whom God hath not cursed?"—*Numbers*, xxiii, 8. "There are, indeed, [some persons] who seem disposed to extend her authority much farther."—*Campbell's Philosophy of Rhet.*, p. 187.

[He] "Who lives to nature, rarely can be poor;
[He] Who lives to fancy, never can be rich."—*Young.*

"Serious should be an author's final views;
[They] Who write for pure amusement, ne'er amuse."—*Id.*

OBS. 24.—*Which*, as well as *who*, was formerly applied to persons; as, "Our *Father which* art in heaven."—*Bible*. "Pray for *them which* despitefully use you."—*Luke*, vi, 28. And, as to the former example here cited, some British critics, still preferring the archaism, have accused "The Americans" of "poor criticism," in that they "have changed *which* into *who*, as being more consonant to the rules of Grammar." Falsely imagining, that *which* and *who*, with the same antecedent, can be of different *genders*, they allege, that, "The use of the *neuter* pronoun carried with it a certain vagueness and sublimity, not inappropriate in reminding us that our worship is addressed to a Being, infinite, and superior to all distinctions applicable to material objects."—*Men and Manners in America*: quoted and endorsed by the REV. MATT. HARRISON, in his treatise on the English Language, p. 191. This is all fancy; and, in my opinion, absurd. It is just like the religious prejudice which could discern "a singular propriety" in "the double superlative *most highest*."—*Lowth's Gram.*, p. 28. But *which* may still be applied to a young child, if sex and intelligence be disregarded; as, "The *child which* died." Or even to adults, when they are spoken of without regard to a distinct personality or identity; as, "*Which* of you will go?"—"Crabb knoweth not *which* is *which*, himself or his parodist."—*Leigh Hunt*.

OBS. 25.—A proper name taken merely as a name, or an appellative taken in any sense not strictly personal, must be represented by *which*, and not by *who*; as, "Herod—*which* is but an other name for cruelty."—"In every prescription of duty, God proposeth himself as a rewarder; *which* he is only to those that please him."—*Dr. J. Owen*. *Which* would perhaps be more proper than *whom*, in the following passage: "They did not destroy the *nations*, concerning *whom* the Lord commanded them."—*Psalms*, cvi, 34. Dr. Blair has preferred it in the following instance: "My lion and my pillar are sufficiently interpreted by the mention of *Achilles* and the *minister*, *which* I join to them."—*Lectures*, p. 151. He meant, "*whose names I connect with theirs*;" and not, that he joined the *person* of Achilles to a lion, or that of a minister to a pillar.

OBS. 26.—When two or more relative clauses pertain to the same antecedent, if they are connected by a conjunction, the same relative ought to be employed in each, agreeably to the doctrine of the seventh note below; but if no conjunction is expressed or understood between them, the pronouns ought rather to be different; as, "There are many things *that* you can speak of, *which* cannot be seen."—*R W. Green's Gram.*, p. 11. This distinction is noticed in the fifth chapter of Etymology, Obs. 29th, on the Classes of Pronouns. Dr. Priestley says, "Whatever relative *be* used, in a *series* of clauses, relating to the same antecedent, the same ought to be used in them all. 'It is remarkable, that *Holland*, against *which* the war was undertaken, *and that,* in the very beginning, was reduced to the brink of destruction, lost nothing.'—*Universal History*, Vol. 25, p. 117. It ought to have been, *and which in the very beginning.*"—*Priestley's Gram.*, p. 102. L. Murray, (as I have shown in the Introduction, Ch. x, ¶ 22,) assumes all this, without references; adding as a salvo the word "*generally*," which merely impairs the certainty of the rule:—"the same relative ought *generally* to be used in them all."—*Octavo Gram.*, p. 155. And, of *who* and *that*, Cobbett says: "Either may do; but both *never* ought to be relatives of the same antecedent in the same sentence."—*Gram.*, ¶ 202. The inaccuracy of these rules is as great as that of the phraseology which is corrected under them. In the following sentence, the first relative only is restrictive, and consequently the other may be different: "These were the officers *that* were called *Homotimoi*, and *who* signalized themselves afterwards so gloriously upon all occasions."—*Rollin's Hist.*, ii, 62. See also in *Rev.*, x, 6th, a similar example without the conjunction.

OBS. 27.—In conversation, the possessive pronoun *your* is sometimes used in a droll way, being shortened into *your* in pronunciation, and nothing more being meant by it, than might be expressed by the article *an* or *a*: as, "Rich honesty dwells, like *your* miser, sir, in a poor house; as, *your* pearl in *your* foul oyster."—*Shakspeare*.

NOTES TO RULE X.

NOTE 1.—A pronoun should not be introduced in connexion with words that belong more properly to the antecedent, or to an other pronoun; as, "And then there is good use for *Pallas her* glass."—*Bacon's Wisdom*, p. 22. Say—"for *Pallas's* glass."

    "My *banks they* are furnish'd with bees,
Whose murmur invites one to sleep."—*Shenstone*, p. 284.

This last instance, however, is only an example of *pleonasm*; which is allowable and frequent in *animated discourse*, but inelegant in any other. Our grammarians have condemned it too positively. It occurs sundry times in the Bible; as, "Know ye that the LORD *he* is God."—*Psalms*, c, 3.

NOTE II.—A change of number in the second person, or even a promiscuous use of *ye* and *you* in the same case and the same style, is inelegant, and ought to be avoided; as, "*You* wept, and I for *thee*"—"Harry, said my lord, don't cry; I'll give *you* something towards *thy* loss."—*Swift's Poems*, p. 267. "*Ye* sons of sloth, *you* offspring of darkness, awake from your sleep."—*Brown's Metaphors*, p. 96. Our poets have very often adopted the former solecism, to accommodate their measure, or to avoid the harshness of the old verb in the second person singular: as, "*Thy* heart is yet blameless, O fly while *you may*!"—*Queen's Wake*, p. 46.

    "Oh! Peggy, Peggy, when *thou* goest to brew,
Consider well what *you're* about to do."—*King's Poems*, p. 594.

    "As in that lov'd Athenian bower,
You *learn'd* an all-commanding power,
Thy mimic soul, O nymph endear'd!
Can well recall what then it heard."—*Collins, Ode to Music.*

NOTE III.—The relative *who* is applied only to persons, and to animals or things personified; and *which,* to brute animals and inanimate things spoken of literally: as, "The *judge who* presided;"—"The old *crab who* advised the young one;"—"The *horse which* ran away;"—"The *book which* was given me."

NOTE IV.—Nouns of multitude, unless they express persons directly as such, should not be represented by the relative *who*: to say, "The *family whom* I visited," would hardly be proper; *that* would here be better. When such nouns are strictly of the neuter gender, *which* may represent them; as, "The *committees which* were appointed." But where the idea of rationality is predominant, *who* or *whom* seems not to be improper; as, "The conclusion of the Iliad is like the exit of a great man out of *company whom* he has entertained magnificently."—*Cowper.* "A law is only the expression of the desire of a *multitude who* have power to punish."—*Brown's Philosophy of the Mind.*

NOTE V.—In general, the pronoun must so agree with its antecedent as to present the same idea, and never in such a manner as to confound the name with the thing signified, or any two things with each other. Examples: "*Jane* is in the nominative case, because *it* leads the sentence."—*Infant School Gram.*, p. 30. Here *it* represents *the word "Jane"* and not *the person Jane.* "What mark or sign is put after *master* to show that *he* is in the possessive case? Spell *it*"—*Ib.*, p. 32. Here *the word "master"* is most absurdly confounded with *the man*; and that to accommodate grammar to a child's comprehension!

NOTE VI.—The relative *that* may be applied either to persons or to things. In the following cases, it is more appropriate than *who, whom,* or *which*; and ought to be preferred, unless it be necessary to use a preposition before the relative:—(1.) After an adjective of the superlative degree, when the relative clause is restrictive;[383] as, "He was the *first that* came."—"He was the *fittest* person *that* could then be found."—*Campbell's Rhet.*, p. 422. "The Greeks were the *greatest* reasoners *that* ever appeared in the world."—BEATTIE: *Murray's Gram.*, p. 127. (2.) After the adjective *same*, when the relative clause is restrictive; as, "He is the *same* man *that* you saw before."— *Priestley's Gram.*, p. 101; *Murray's*, 156; *Campbell's Rhet.*, 422. (3.) After the antecedent *who*; as, "Who *that* is a sincere friend to it, can look with indifference upon attempts to shake the foundation of the fabric?"—*Washington.* (4.) After two or more antecedents that demand a relative adapted both to persons and to things; as, "He spoke largely of the *men and things that* he had seen."—"When some particular *person* or *thing* is spoken of, *that* ought to be more distinctly marked."— *Murray's Gram.*, p. 51. (5.) After an unlimited antecedent which the relative clause is designed to restrict; as, "*Thoughts that* breathe, and *words that* burn."—*Gray.* "Music *that accords* with the present tone of mind, is, on that account, doubly agreeable."—*Kames, El. of Crit.*, ii, 311. "For Theocritus descends sometimes into *ideas that* are gross and mean."—*Blair's Rhet.*, p. 393. (6.) After any antecedent introduced by the expletive *it*; as, "*It* is *you that* suffer."—"It was I, and not he, *that* did it."—*Churchill's Gram.*, p. 142. "It was not he[384] *that* they were so angry with."—*Murray's Exercises*, R. 17. "*It* was not *Gavius* alone *that* Verres meant to insult."—*Blair's Rhet.*, p. 325. (7.) And, in general, wherever the propriety of *who* or *which* is doubtful; as, "The little *child that* was placed in the midst."

NOTE VII.—When two or more relative clauses connected by a conjunction have a similar dependence in respect to the antecedent, the same pronoun must be employed in each; as, "O thou, *who* art, and *who* wast, and *who* art to come!"—"And they shall spread them before the sun, and the moon, and all the host of heaven, *whom* they have loved, and *whom* they have served, and after *whom* they have walked, and *whom* they have sought, and *whom* they have worshiped."—*Jer.*, viii, 2. NOTE VIII.—The relative, and the preposition governing it, should not be omitted, when they are necessary to the sense intended, or to a proper connexion of the parts of the sentence; as, "He is still in the situation you saw him." Better thus: "He is still in the situation in *which* you saw him."

NOTE IX.—After certain nouns, of time, place, manner, or cause, the conjunctive adverbs *when, where, whither, whence, how*, and *why*, are a sort of special relatives; but no such adverb should be used where a preposition and a relative pronoun would better express the relation of the terms: as, "A cause *where* justice is so much concerned." Say, "A cause *in which*." See Etymology, Obs. 6th, 7th, and 8th, on the Classes of Adverbs.

NOTE X.—Where a pronoun or a pronominal adjective will not express the meaning clearly, the noun must be repeated, or inserted in stead of it: as, "We see the beautiful variety of colour in the rainbow, and are led to consider the cause of *it*." Say,—"the cause of *that variety*;" because the *it* may mean *the variety, the colour*, or *the rainbow*.

NOTE XI.—To prevent ambiguity or obscurity, the relative should, in general, be placed as near as possible to the antecedent. The following sentence is therefore faulty: "He is like a beast of prey, that is void of compassion." Better thus: "He that is void of compassion, is like a beast of prey."

NOTE XII.—The pronoun *what* should never be used in stead of the conjunction *that*; as, "Think no man so perfect but *what* he may err." This is a vulgar fault. Say,—"but *that* he may err."

NOTE XIII.—A pronoun should never be used to represent an *adjective*, —except the pronominal adjectives, and others taken substantively; because a pronoun can neither express a concrete quality as such, nor convert it properly into an abstract: as, "Be *attentive*; without *which* you will learn nothing." Better thus: "Be attentive; *for without attention* you will learn nothing."

NOTE XIV.—Though the relative which may in some instances stand for a phrase or a sentence, it is seldom, if ever, a fit representative of an indicative assertion; as, "The man opposed me, *which* was anticipated."—*Nixon's Parser*, p. 127. Say,—"*but his opposition* was anticipated." Or: "The man opposed me, *as* was anticipated." Or:—"*as I expected he would.*" Again: "The captain disobeys orders, *which* is punished."—*Ib.*, p. 128. This is an other factitious sentence, formed after the same model, and too erroneous for correction: none but a conceited grammatist could ever have framed such a construction.

NOTE XV.—The possessive pronouns, *my, thy, his, her, its,* &c., should be inserted or repeated as often as the sense or construction of the sentence requires them; their omission, like that of the articles, can scarcely in any instance constitute a proper ellipsis: as, "Of Princeton and vicinity."—Say, "Of Princeton and *its* vicinity." "The man and wife."—Say, "The man and *his* wife." "Many verbs vary both their signification and construction."—*Adam's Gram.*, p. 170; *Gould's*, 171. Say,—"and *their* construction."

NOTE XVI.—In the correcting of any discord between the antecedent and its pronoun, if the latter for any sufficient reason is most proper as it stands, the former must be changed to accord with it: as, "Let us discuss what relates to *each particular* in *their* order:—*its* order."— *Priestley's Gram.*, p. 193. Better thus: "Let us discuss what relates to *the several particulars,* in *their* order." For the order of things implies plurality.

IMPROPRIETIES FOR CORRECTION.

FALSE SYNTAX UNDER RULE X. UNDER THE RULE ITSELF.—OF AGREEMENT

"The subject is to be joined with his predicate."—BP. WILKINS: *Lowth's Gram.*, p. 42.

[FORMULE.—Not proper, because the pronoun *his* is of the masculine gender, and does not correctly represent its antecedent noun *subject*, which is of the third person, singular, *neuter*. But, according to Rule 10th, "A pronoun must agree with its antecedent, or the noun or pronoun which it represents, in person, number, and gender." Therefore, *his* should be *its*; thus, "The subject is to be joined with *its* predicate."]

"Every one must judge of their own feelings."—*Byron's Letters.* "Every one in the family should know their duty."—*Wm. Penn.* "To introduce its possessor into 'that way in which it should go.'"—*Infant School Gram.*, p. v. "Do not they say, every true believer has the Spirit of God in them?"— *Barclay's Works*, iii, 388. "There is none in their natural state righteous, no not one."—*Wood's Dict. of Bible*, ii, 129. "If ye were of the world, the world would love his own."—*John*, xv, 19. "His form had not yet lost all her original brightness."—*Milton.* "No one will answer as if I were their friend or companion."—*Steele*, Spect., No. 534. "But in lowliness of mind let each esteem other better than themselves."— *Philippians*, ii, 3. "And let none of you imagine evil in your hearts against his neighbour."—*Zechariah*, viii, 17. "For every tree is known by his own fruit."—*Luke*, vi, 44. "But she fell to laughing, like one out of their right mind."—*Castle Rackrent*, p. 51. "Now these systems, so far from having any tendency to make men better, have a manifest tendency to make him worse."—*Wayland's Moral Science*, p. 128. "And nobody else would make that city their refuge any more."—*Josephus's Life*, p. 158. "What is quantity, as it respects syllables or words? It is that time which is occupied in pronouncing it."—*Bradley's Gram.*, p. 108. "In such expressions the adjective so much resembles an adverb in its meaning, that they are usually parsed as such."—*Bullions, E. Gram.*, p. 103. "The tongue is like a race-horse; which runs the faster the less weight it carries."—ADDISON: *Joh. Dict.; Murray's Key*, Rule 8. "As two thoughtless boys were trying to see which could lift the greatest weight with their jaws, one of them had several of his firm-set teeth wrenched from their sockets."—*Newspaper*. "Everybody nowadays publishes memoirs; everybody has recollections which they think worthy of recording."—*Duchess D'Abrantes*, p. 25. "Every body trembled for themselves or their friends."—*Goldsmith's Greece*, i, 171.

"A steed comes at morning: no rider is there;
But its bridle is red with the sign of despair."—*Campbell*.

UNDER NOTE I.—PRONOUNS WRONG OR NEEDLESS.

"Charles loves to study; but John, alas! he is very idle."—*Merchant's School Gram.*, p. 22. "Or what man is there of you, whom if his son ask bread, will he give him a stone?"—*Matt.*, vii, 9. "Who, in stead of going about doing good, they are perpetually intent upon doing mischief."—*Tillotson*. "Whom ye delivered up, and denied him in the presence of Pontius Pilate."—*Acts*, iii, 13. "Whom, when they had washed, they laid her in an upper chamber."—*Acts*, ix, 37. "Then Manasseh knew that the Lord he was God."—*2 Chron.*, xxxiii, 13. "Whatever a man conceives clearly, he may, if he will be at the trouble, put it into distinct propositions, and express it clearly to others."—*Murray's Gram.*, 8vo, p. 293. "But to that point of time which he has chosen, the painter being entirely confined, he cannot exhibit various stages of the same action."—*Blair's Rhet.*, p. 52. "It is without any proof at all what he subjoins."—*Barclay's Works*, i, 301. "George Fox his Testimony concerning Robert Barclay."—*Ib.*, i, 111. "According to the author of the Postscript his advice."—*Ib.*, iii, 263. "These things seem as ugly to the Eye of their Meditations, as those Æthiopians pictur'd in Nemesis her Pitcher."—*Bacon's Wisdom of the Ancients*, p. 49. "Moreover, there is always a twofold Condition propounded with Sphynx her Ænigma's."—*Ib.*, p. 73. "Whoever believeth not therein, they shall perish."—*Sale's Koran*, p. 20. "When, at Sestius his entreaty, I had been at his house."—*Walker's Particles*, p. 59.

"There high on Sipylus his shaggy brow,
She stands, her own sad monument of woe."
—*Pope's Homer*, B. xxiv, l. 777.

UNDER NOTE II.—CHANGE OF NUMBER.

"So will I send upon you famine, and evil beasts, and they shall bereave thee."—*Ezekiel*, v, 17. "Why do you plead so much for it? why do ye preach it up?"—*Barclay's Works*, i, 180. "Since thou hast decreed that I shall bear man, your darling."—*Edward's First Lesson in Gram.*, p. 106. "You have my book and I have thine; i.e. thy book."—*Chandler's Gram.*, 1821, p. 22. "Neither art thou such a one as to be ignorant of what you are."—*Bullions, Lat. Gram.*, p. 70. "Return, thou backsliding Israel, saith the Lord, and I will not cause mine anger to fall upon you."—*Jeremiah*, iii, 12. "The

Almighty, unwilling to cut thee off in the fullness of iniquity, has sent me to give you warning."—*Art of Thinking*, p. 278. "Wert thou born only for pleasure? were you never to do any thing?"—*Collier's Antoninus*, p. 63. "Thou shalt be required to go to God, to die, and give up your account."—BARNES'S NOTES: *on Luke*, xii, 20. "And canst thou expect to behold the resplendent glory of the Creator? would not such a sight annihilate you?"—*Milton*. "If the prophet had commanded thee to do some great thing, would you have refused?"—*Common School Journal*, i, 80. "Art thou a penitent? Evince your sincerity by bringing forth fruits meet for repentance."—*Christian's Vade-Mecum*, p. 117. "I will call thee my dear son: I remember all your tenderness."— *Classic Tales*, p. 8. "So do thou, my son: open your ears, and your eyes."—*Wright's Athens*, p. 33. "I promise you, this was enough to discourage thee."—*Pilgrim's Progress*, p. 446. "Ere you remark an other's sin, Bid thy own conscience look within."—*Gay*. "Permit that I share in thy woe, The privilege can you refuse?"—*Perfect's Poems*, p. 6. "Ah! Strephon, how can you despise Her who without thy pity dies?"—*Swift's Poems*, p. 340.

"Thy verses, friend, are Kidderminster stuff,
And I must own, you've measur'd out enough."—*Shenstone*.

"This day, dear Bee, is thy nativity;
Had Fate a luckier one, she'd give it ye."—*Swift*.

UNDER NOTE III.—WHO AND WHICH.

"Exactly like so many puppets, who are moved by wires."—*Blair's Rhet.*, p. 462. "They are my servants, which I brought forth out of the land of Egypt."—*Leviticus*, xxv, 42. "Behold I and the children which God hath given me."—*Heb.*, ii, 13; *Webster's Bible, and others*. "And he sent Eliakim which was over the household, and Shebna the scribe."—*2 Kings*, xix, 2.

"In a short time the streets were cleared of the corpses who filled them."—*M'Ilvaine's Led.*, p. 411. "They are not of those which teach things which they ought not, for filthy lucre's sake."—*Barclay's Works*, i, 435. "As a lion among the beasts of the forest, as a young lion among the flocks of sheep; who, if he go through, both treadeth down and teareth in pieces."—*Micah*, v, 8. "Frequented by every fowl whom nature has taught to dip the wing in water."—*Rasselas*, p. 10. "He had two sons, one of which was adopted by the family of Maximus."—*Lempriere, w. Æmytius.* "And the ants, who are collected by the smell, are burned by fire."—*The Friend*, xii, 49. "They being the agents, to which this thing was trusted."—*Nixon's Parser*, p. 139. "A packhorse who is driven constantly forwards and backwards to market."—LOCKE: *Joh. Dict.* "By instructing children, the affection of which will be increased."—*Nixon's Parser*, p. 136. "He had a comely young woman which travelled with him."—*Hutchinson's Hist.*, i, 29. "A butterfly, which thought himself an accomplished traveller, happened to light upon a beehive."—*Inst.*, p. 143. "It is an enormous elephant of stone, who disgorges from his uplifted trunk a vast but graceful shower."—*Zenobia*, i, 150. "He was met by a dolphin, who sometimes swam before him, and sometimes behind him."—*Edward's First Lessons in Gram.*, p. 34.

"That Cæsar's horse, who, as fame goes,
Had corns upon his feet and toes,
Was not by half so tender-hooft,
Nor trod upon the ground so soft."—*Hudibras*, p. 6.

UNDER NOTE IV.—NOUNS OF MULTITUDE.

"He instructed and fed the crowds who surrounded him."—*Murray's Exercises*, p. 52. "The court, who gives currency to manners, ought to be exemplary."—*Ibid.* "Nor does he describe classes of sinners who do not exist."—*Anti-Slavery Magazine*, i, 27. "Because the nations among whom they took their rise, were not savage."—*Murray's Gram.*, p. 113. "Among nations who are in the first and rude periods of society."—*Blair's Rhet.*, p. 60. "The martial spirit of those nations, among whom the feudal government prevailed."—*Ib.*, p. 374. "France who was in alliance with Sweden."—*Smollett's Voltaire*, vi, 187. "That faction in England who most powerfully opposed his arbitrary pretensions."—*Mrs. Macaulay's Hist.*, iii, 21. "We may say, the crowd, *who* was going up the street.'"—*Cobbett's Gram.*, ¶ 204. "Such members of the Convention who formed this Lyceum, as have subscribed this Constitution."—*New-York Lyceum*.

UNDER NOTE V.—CONFUSION OF SENSES.

"The possessor shall take a particular form to show its case."—*Kirkham's Gram.*, p. 53. "Of which reasons the principal one is, that no Noun, properly so called, implies its own Presence."—*Harris's Hermes*, p. 76. "Boston is a proper noun, which distinguishes it from other cities."—*Sanborn's Gram.*, p. 22. "Conjunction means union, or joining together. It is used to join or unite either words or sentences."—*Ib.*, p. 20. "The word *interjection* means *thrown among*. It is interspersed among other words to express sudden or strong emotion."—*Ib.*, p. 21. "*In deed*, or in very deed, may better be written separately, as they formerly were."—*Cardell's Gram.*, 12mo, p. 89. "*Alexander*, on the contrary, is a particular name, and is restricted to distinguish him alone."—*Jamieson's Rhet.*, p. 25. "As an indication that nature itself had changed her course."—*Hist. of America*, p. 9. "Of removing from the United States and her territories the free people of colour."—*Jenifer*. "So that *gh* may be said not to have their proper sound."—*Webster's El. Spelling-Book*, p. 10. "Are we to welcome the loathsome harlot, and introduce it to our children?"—*Maturin's Sermons*, p. 167. "The first question is this, 'Is reputable, national, and present use, which, for brevity's sake, I shall hereafter simply denominate good use, always uniform in her decisions?"—*Campbell's Rhet.*, p. 171. "Time is always masculine, on account of its mighty efficacy. Virtue is feminine from its beauty, and its being the object of love."—*Murray's Gram.*, p. 37; *Blair's*, 125; *Sanborn's*, 189; *Emmons's*, 13; *Putnam's*, 25; *Fisk's*, 57; *Ingersoll's*, 26; *Greenleaf's*, 21. See also *Blair's Rhet.*, p. 76. "When you speak to a person or thing, it is in the second person."—*Bartlett's Manual*, Part ii, p. 27. "You now know the noun, for it means name."—*Ibid.* "*T.* What do you see? *P.* A book. *T.* Spell it."—*R. W. Green's Gram.*, p. 12. "*T.* What do you see now? *P.* Two books. *T.* Spell them."—*Ibid.* "If the United States lose her rights as a nation."—*Liberator*, Vol. ix, p. 24. "When a person or thing is addressed or spoken to, it is in the second person."—*Frost's El. of Gram.*, p. 7. "When a person or thing is spoken of, it is in the third person."—*Ibid.* "The ox, that ploughs the ground, has the same plural termination also, *oxen*."—*Bucke's Classical Gram.*, p. 40.

"Hail, happy States! thine is the blissful seat,
  Where nature's gifts and art's improvements meet."
          EVERETT: *Columbian Orator*, p. 239.

UNDER NOTE VI.—THE RELATIVE THAT.

(1.) "This is the most useful art which men possess."—*Murray's Key*, 8vo, p. 275. "The earliest accounts which history gives us concerning all nations, bear testimony to these facts."—*Blair's Rhet.*, p. 379; *Jamieson's*, 300. "Mr. Addison was the first who attempted a regular inquiry" [into the pleasures of taste.]—*Blair's Rhet.*, p. 28. "One of the first who introduced it was Montesquieu."—*Murray's Gram.*, p. 125. "Massillon is perhaps the most eloquent writer of sermons which modern times have produced."—*Blair's*

Rhet., p. 289. "The greatest barber who ever lived, is our guiding star and prototype."—*Hart's Figaro*, No. 6.

(2.) "When prepositions are subjoined to nouns, they are generally the same which are subjoined to the verbs, from which the nouns are derived."—*Priestley's Gram.*, p. 157. "The same proportions which are agreeable in a model, are not agreeable in a large building."—*Kames, EL of Crit.*, ii, 343. "The same ornaments, which we admire in a private apartment, are unseemly in a temple."—*Murray's Gram.*, p. 128. "The same whom John saw also in the sun."—*Milton. P. L.*, B. iii, l. 623.

(3.) "Who can ever be easy, who is reproached with his own ill conduct?"—*Thomas à Kempis*, p. 72. "Who is she who comes clothed in a robe of green?"—*Inst.*, p. 143. "Who who has either sense or civility, does not perceive the vileness of profanity?"

(4.) "The second person denotes the person or thing which is spoken to."—*Compendium in Kirkham's Gram.* "The third person denotes the person or thing which is spoken of."—*Ibid.* "A passive verb denotes action received or endured by the person or thing which is its nominative."—*Ibid, and Gram.*, p. 157. "The princes and states who had neglected or favoured the growth of this power."—*Bolingbroke, on History*, p. 222. "The nominative expresses the name of the person, or thing which acts, or which is the subject of discourse."—*Hiley's Gram.*, p. 19. (5.) "Authors who deal in long sentences, are very apt to be faulty."—*Blair's Rhet.*, p. 108. "Writers who deal in long sentences, are very apt to be faulty."—*Murray's Gram.*, p. 313. "The neuter gender denotes objects which are neither male nor female."—*Merchant's Gram.*, p. 26. "The neuter gender denotes things which have no sex."—*Kirkham's Compendium.* "Nouns which denote objects neither male nor female, are of the neuter gender."—*Wells's Gram.*, 1st Ed., p. 49. "Objects and ideas which have been long familiar, make too faint an impression to give an agreeable exercise to our faculties."—*Blair's Rhet.*, p. 50. "Cases which custom has left dubious, are certainly within the grammarian's province."—*Murray's Gram.*, p. 164. "Substantives which end in *ery,* signify action or habit."—*Ib.*, p. 132. "After all which can be done to render the definitions and rules of grammar accurate," &c.—*Ib.*, p. 36. "Possibly, all which I have said, is known and taught."—*A. B. Johnson's Plan of a Dict.*, p. 15.

(6.) "It is a strong and manly style which should chiefly be studied."— *Blair's Rhet.*, p. 261. "It is this which chiefly makes a division appear neat and elegant."—*Ib.*, p. 313. "I hope it is not I with whom he is displeased."—*Murray's Key*, R. 17. "When it is this alone which renders the sentence obscure."—*Campbell's Rhet.*, p. 242. "This sort of full and ample assertion, *'it is this which,'* is fit to be used when a proposition of importance is laid down."—*Blair's Rhet.*, p. 197. "She is the person whom I understood it to have been." *See Murray's Gram.*, p. 181. "Was it thou, or the wind, who shut the door?"—*Inst.*, p. 143. "It was not I who shut it."— *Ib.*

(7.) "He is not the person who it seemed he was."—*Murray's Gram.*, p. 181; *Ingersoll's*, p. 147. "He is really the person who he appeared to be."— *Same*. "She is not now the woman whom they represented her to have been."—*Same*. "An only child, is one who has neither brother nor sister; a child alone, is one who is left by itself"—*Blair's Rhet.*, p. 98; *Jamieson's*, 71; *Murray's Gram.* 303.

UNDER NOTE VII.—RELATIVE CLAUSES CONNECTED.

(1.) "A Substantive, or Noun, is the name of a thing; of whatever we conceive in any way to subsist, or of which we have any notion."—*Lowth's Gram.*, p. 14. (2.) "A Substantive or noun is the name of any thing that exists, or of which we have any notion."—*L. Murray's Gram.*, p. 27; *Alger's*, 15; *Bacon's*, 9; *E. Dean's*, 8; *A. Flint's*, 10; *Folker's*, 5; *Hamlin's*, 9; *Ingersoll's*, 14; *Merchant's*, 25; *Pond's*, 15; *S. Putnam's*, 10; *Rand's*, 9; *Russell's*, 9; *T. Smith's*, 12; and others. (3.) "A substantive or noun is the name of any person, place, or thing that exists, or of which we can have an idea."—*Frost's El. of E. Gram.*, p. 6. (4.) "A noun is the name of anything that exists, or of which we form an idea."—*Hallock's Gram.*, p. 37. (5.) "A Noun is the name of any person, place, object, or thing, that exists, or which we may conceive to exist."—*D. C. Allen's Grammatic Guide*, p. 19. (6.) "The name of every thing that exists, or of which we can form any notion, is a noun."—*Fisk's Murray's Gram.*, p. 56. (7.) "An allegory is the representation of some one thing by an other that resembles it, and which is made to stand for it."—*Murray's Gram.*, p. 341. (8.) "Had he exhibited such sentences as contained ideas inapplicable to young minds, or which were of a trivial or injurious nature."—*Murray's Gram.*, Vol. ii, p. v. (9.) "Man would have others obey him, even his own kind; but he will not obey God, that is so much above him, and who made him."—*Penn's Maxims*. (10.) "But what we may consider here, and which few Persons have taken Notice of, is," &c.—*Brightland's Gram.*, p. 117. (11.) "The Compiler has not inserted such verbs as are irregular only in familiar writing or discourse, and which are improperly terminated by *t*, instead of *ed*."—*Murray's Gram.*, p. 107; *Fisk's*, 81; *Hart's*, 68; *Ingersoll's*, 104; *Merchant's*, 63. (12.) "The remaining parts of speech, which are called the indeclinable parts, or that admit of no variations, will not detain us long."—*Blair's Rhet.*, p. 84.

UNDER NOTE VIII.—THE RELATIVE AND PREPOSITION.

"In the temper of mind he was then."—*Addison, Spect.*, No. 54. "To bring them into the condition I am at present."—*Spect.*, No. 520. "In the posture I lay."—*Swift's Gulliver*. "In the sense it is sometimes taken."—*Barclay's*

Works, i, 527. "Tools and utensils are said to be *right*, when they serve for the uses they were made."—*Collier's Antoninus*, p. 99. "If, in the extreme danger I now am, I do not imitate the behaviour of those," &c.—*Goldsmith's Greece*, i, 193. "News was brought, that Darius was but twenty miles from the place they then were."—*Ib.*, ii, 113. "Alexander, upon hearing this news, continued four days in the place he then was."—*Ib.*, ii, 113. "To read, in the best manner it is now taught."—*L. Murray's Gram.*, p. 246. "It may be expedient to give a few directions as to the manner it should be studied."—*Hallock's Gram.*, p. 9. "Participles are words derived from verbs, and convey an idea of the acting of an agent, or the suffering of an object, with the time it happens."—*Alex. Murray's Gram.*, p. 50.

"Had I but serv'd my God with half the zeal
I serv'd my king, he would not in mine age
Have left me naked to mine enemies."—*Beauties of Shak.*, p. 173.

UNDER NOTE IX.—ADVERBS FOR RELATIVES.

"In compositions where pronunciation has no place."—*Blair's Rhet.*, p. 101. "They framed a protestation, where they repeated their claims."—*Hume's Hist.* "Which have reference to Substances, where Sex never had existence."—*Harris's Hermes*, p. 43. "Which denote substances where sex never had existence."—*Murray's Gram.*, p. 38; *Fisk's*, 57. "There is no rule given how truth may be found out."—*Walker's Particles*, p. 160. "The nature of the objects whence they are taken."—*Blair's Rhet.*, p. 165. "That darkness of character, where we can see no heart."—*Murray's Key*, 8vo, p. 236. "The states where they negotiated."—*Formey's Belles-Lettres*, p. 159. "Till the motives whence men act be known."—*Beattie's Moral Science*, p. 262. "He assigns the principles whence their power of pleasing flows."—*Blair's Rhet.*, p. 19. "But I went on, and so finished this History in that form as it now appears."—*Sewel's Preface*, p. v. "By prepositions we express the cause why, the instrument by which, wherewith, or the manner how a thing is done."—*Alex. Murray's Gram.*, p. 128; *John Burn's*, 121. "They are not such in the language whence they are derived."—*Town's Analysis*, p. 13. "I find it very hard to persuade several, that their passions are affected by words from whence they have no ideas."—*Burke, on the Sublime*, p. 95. "The known end, then, why we are placed in a state of so much affliction, hazard, and difficulty, is our improvement in virtue and piety."—*Butler's Anal.*, p. 109.

"Yet such his acts, as Greeks unborn shall tell,
And curse the battle where their fathers fell."
—*Pope, Il.*, B. x, I. 61.

UNDER NOTE X.—REPEAT THE NOUN.

"Youth may be thoughtful, but it is not very common."—*Webster's El. Spelling-Book*, p. 85. "A proper name is that given to one person or thing."—*Bartlett's School Manual*, ii, 27. "A common name is that given to many things of the same sort."—*Ibid.* "This rule is often violated; some instances of which are annexed."—*Murray's Gram.*, p. 149; *Ingersoll's*, 237. "This is altogether careless writing. It renders style often obscure, always embarrassed and inelegant."—*Blair's Rhet.*, p. 106. "Every inversion which is not governed by this rule, will be disrelished by every one of taste."—*Kames, El. of Crit.*, ii, 62. "A proper diphthong is that in which both the vowels are sounded."—*Murray's Gram.*, p. 9; *Alger's*, 11; *Bacon's*, 8; *Merchant's*, 9; *Hiley's*, 3; and others. "An improper Diphthong is one in which only one of the two Vowels is sounded."—*Lennie's Gram.*, p. 5. "Abraham, Isaac, Jacob, and his descendants, are called Hebrews."—*Wood's Dict.* "Every word in our language, of more than one syllable, has one of them distinguished from the rest in this manner."—*Murray's Gram.*, p. 236. "Two consonants proper to begin a word must not be separated; as, fa-ble, sti-fle. But when they come between two vowels, and are such as cannot begin a word, they must be divided; as, ut-most, un-der."—*Ib.*, p. 22. "Shall the intellect alone feel no pleasures in its energy, when we allow them to the grossest energies of appetite and sense?"—*Harris's Hermes*, p. 298; *Murray's Gram.*, 289. "No man hath a propensity to vice as such: on the contrary, a wicked deed disgusts him, and makes him abhor the author."—*Kames, El. of Crit.*, i, 66. "The same that belong to nouns, belong also to pronouns."—*Greenleaf's Gram.*, p. 8. "What is Language? It is the means of communicating thoughts from one to another."—*O. B. Peirce's Gram.*, p. 15. "A simple word is that which is not made up of more than one."—*Adam's Gram.*, p. 4; *Gould's*, p. 4. "A compound word is that which is made up of two or more words."—*Ib.* "When a conjunction is to be supplied, it is called Asyndeton."—*Adam's Gram.*, p. 235.

UNDER NOTE XI.—PLACE OF THE RELATIVE.

"It gives a meaning to words, which they would not have."—*Murray's Gram.*, p. 244. "There are many words in the English language, that are sometimes used as adjectives, and sometimes as adverbs."—*Ib.*, p. 114. "Which do not more effectually show the varied intentions of the mind, than the auxiliaries do which are used to form the potential mood."—*Ib.*, p. 67. "These accents make different impressions on the mind, which will be the subject of a following speculation."—*Kames, El. of Crit.*, ii, 108. "And others very much differed from the writer's words, to whom they were ascribed."—*Pref. to Lily's Gram.*, p. xii. "Where there is nothing in the sense which requires the last sound to be elevated, an easy fall will be proper."—*Murray's Gram.*, Vol. i, p. 250; *Bullions's E. Gram.*, 167. "There is an ellipsis of the verb in the last clause, which, when you supply, you find it necessary to use the adverb not."—*Campbell's Rhet.*, p. 176; *Murray's Gram.*, 368. "*Study* is singular number, because its nominative *I* is, with which it agrees."—*Smith's New Gram.*, p. 22. "John is the person, or, thou art who is in error."—*Wright's Gram.*, p. 136. "For he hath made him to be sin for us, who knew no sin."—*2 Cor.*, v, 21.

"Take that of me, my friend, who have the power
To seal the accuser's lips."—*Beauties of Shakspeare*, p. 268.

UNDER NOTE XII.—WHAT FOR THAT.

"I had no idea but what the story was true."—*Browns Inst.*, p. 144. "The post-boy is not so weary but what he can whistle."—*Ib.* "He had no intimation but what the men were honest."—*Ib.* "Neither Lady Haversham nor Miss Mildmay will ever believe, but what I have been entirely to blame."—See *Priestley's Gram.*, p. 93. "I am not satisfied, but what the integrity of our friends is more essential to our welfare than their knowledge of the world."—*Ibid.* "There is, indeed, nothing in poetry, so entertaining or descriptive, but what a didactic writer of genius may be allowed to introduce in some part of his work."—*Blair's Rhet.*, p. 401. "Brasidas, being bit by a mouse he had catched, let it slip out of his fingers: 'No creature, (says he,) is so contemptible but what may provide for its own safety, if it have courage.'"—PLUTARCH: *Kames, El. of Crit.*, Vol. i, p. 81.

UNDER NOTE XIII.—ADJECTIVES FOR ANTECEDENTS.

"In narration, Homer is, at all times, remarkably concise, which renders him lively and agreeable."—*Blair's Rhet.*, p. 435. "It is usual to talk of a nervous, a feeble, or a spirited style; which are plainly the characters of a writer's manner of thinking."—*Ib.*, p. 92. "It is too violent an alteration, if any alteration were necessary, which none is."—*Knight, on the Greek Alphabet*, p. 134. "Some men are too ignorant to be humble, without which, there can be no docility."—*Berkley's Alciphron*, p. 385. "Judas declared him innocent; which he could not be, had he in any respect deceived the disciples."—*Porteus.* "They supposed him to be innocent, which he certainly was not."—*Murray's Gram.*, Vol. i, p. 50; *Emmons's*, 25. "They accounted him honest, which he certainly was not."—*Fetch's Comp. Gram.*, p. 89. "Be accurate in all you say or do; for it is important in all the concerns of life."—*Brown's Inst.*, p. 145. "Every law supposes the transgressor to be wicked; which indeed he is, if the law is just."—*Ib.* "To be pure in heart, pious, and benevolent, which all may be, constitutes human happiness."—*Murray's Gram.*, p. 232. "To be dexterous in danger, is a virtue; but to court danger to show it, is weakness."—*Penn's Maxims.*

UNDER NOTE XIV.—SENTENCES FOR ANTECEDENTS.

"This seems not so allowable in prose; which the following erroneous examples will demonstrate."—*Murray's Gram.*, p. 175. "The accent is laid upon the last syllable of a word; which is favourable to the melody."—*Kames, El. of Crit.*, ii, 86. "Every line consists of ten syllables, five short and five long; from which there are but two exceptions, both of them rare."—*Ib.*, ii, 89. "The soldiers refused obedience, which has been explained."—*Nixon's Parser*, p. 128. "Cæsar overcame Pompey, which was lamented."—*Ib.* "The crowd hailed William, which was expected."—*Ib.* "The tribunes resisted Scipio, which was anticipated."—*Ib.* "The censors reproved vice, which was admired."—*Ib.* "The generals neglected discipline, which has been proved."—*Ib.* "There would be two nominatives to the verb was, which is improper."—*Adam's Lat. Gram.*, p. 205; *Gould's*, 202. "His friend bore the abuse very patiently; which served to increase his rudeness: it produced, at length, contempt and insolence."—*Murray's*

Gram., Vol. i, p. 50; *Emmons's*, 25. "Almost all compounded sentences, are more or less elliptical; some examples of which may be seen under the different parts of speech."—*Murray's Gram.*, p. 217; *Guy's*, 90; *R G. Smith's*, 180; *Ingersoll's*, 153; *Fisk's*, 144; *J. M. Putnam's*, 137; *Weld's*, 190, *Weld's Imp. Ed.*, 214.

UNDER NOTE XV.—REPEAT THE PRONOUN.

"In things of Nature's workmanship, whether we regard their internal or external structure, beauty and design are equally conspicuous."—*Kames, El. of Crit.*, i, 269. "It puzzles the reader, by making him doubt whether the word ought to be taken in its proper or figurative sense."—*Ib.*, ii, 231. "Neither my obligations to the muses, nor expectations from them, are so great."—*Cowley's Preface.* "The Fifth Annual Report of the Anti-Slavery Society of Ferrisburgh and vicinity."—*Liberator*, ix, 69. "Meaning taste in its figurative as well as proper sense."—*Kames, El. of Crit.*, ii, 360. "Every measure in which either your personal or political character is concerned."—*Junius*, Let. ix. "A jealous, righteous God has often punished such in themselves or offspring."—*Extracts*, p. 179. "Hence their civil and religious history are inseparable."—*Milman's Jews*, i, 7. "Esau thus carelessly threw away both his civil and religious inheritance."—*Ib.*, i, 24. "This intelligence excited not only our hopes, but fears likewise."—*Jaudon's Gram.*, p. 170. "In what manner our defect of principle and ruling manners have completed the ruin of the national spirit of union."—*Brown's Estimate*, i, 77. "Considering her descent, her connexion, and present intercourse."—*Webster's Essays*, p. 85. "His own and wife's wardrobe are packed up in a firkin."—*Parker and Fox's Gram.*, Part i, p. 73.

UNDER NOTE XVI.—CHANGE THE ANTECEDENT.

"The sound of *e* and *o* long, in their due degrees, will be preserved, and clearly distinguished."—*Murray's Gram.*, 8vo, p. 242. "If any person should be inclined to think," &c., "the author takes the liberty to suggest to them," &c.—*Ib., Pref.*, p. iv. "And he walked in all the ways of Asa his father; he turned not aside from it."—*1 Kings*, xxii, 43. "If ye from your hearts forgive not every one his brother their trespasses."—*Matt.*, xviii, 35. "Nobody ever fancied they were slighted by him, or had the courage to think themselves his betters."—*Collier's Antoninus*, p. 8. "And Rebekah took goodly raiment of her eldest son Esau, which were with her in the house, and put them upon Jacob her younger son."—*Gen.*, xxvii, 15. "Where all the attention of man is given to their own indulgence."—*Maturin's Sermons*, p. 181. "The idea of a *father* is a notion superinduced to the substance, or man—let man be what it will."—*Locke's Essay*, i, 219. "Leaving every one to do as they list."—*Barclay's Works*, i, 460. "Each body performed his part handsomely."—*J. Flint's Gram.*, p. 15. "This block of marble rests on two layers of stone, bound together with lead, which, however, has not prevented the Arabs from forcing out several of them."—*Parker and Fox's Gram.*, Part i, p. 72.

> "Love gives to every power a double power,
> Above their functions and their offices."—*Shakspeare.*

RULE XI.—PRONOUNS.

When the antecedent is a collective noun conveying the idea of plurality, the Pronoun must agree with it in the plural number: as, "The *council* were divided in *their* sentiments."—"The Christian *world* are beginning to awake out of *their* slumber."—*C. Simeon.* "Whatever Adam's *posterity* lost through him, that and more *they* gain in Christ."—*J. Phipps.*

"To this, one pathway gently-winding leads,
  Where march a train with baskets on their heads."
    —*Pope, Iliad*, B. xviii, l. 657.

OBSERVATIONS ON RULE XI.

OBS. 1.—The collective noun, or noun of multitude, being a name that signifies many, may in general be taken in either of two ways, according to the intention of the user: that is, either with reference to the *aggregate* as one thing, in which sense it will accord with the neuter pronoun *it* or *which*; or with reference to the *individuals*, so as to accord with a plural pronoun *they, their, them,* or *who*, masculine, or feminine, as the individuals of the assemblage may happen to be. The noun itself, being literally singular both in form and in fact, has not unfrequently some article or adjective before it that implies unity; so that the interpretation of it in a plural sense by the pronoun or verb, was perhaps not improperly regarded by the old grammarians as an example of the figure *syllepsis*:.as, "Liberty should reach every individual of *a people*, as *they* all share one common nature."—*Spectator*, No. 287.

   "Thus urg'd the chief; *a generous troop appears,*
  Who spread their bucklers and *advance their* spears."
    —*Pope, Iliad*, B. xi, l. 720.

OBS. 2.—Many of our grammarians say, "When a noun of multitude is preceded by a definitive word, which clearly limits the sense to an aggregate with an idea of unity, it requires a verb and pronoun to agree with it in the singular number."—*Murray's Gram.*, p. 153; *Ingersoll's*, 249; Fisk's, 122; *Fowler's*, 528. But this principle, I apprehend, cannot be sustained by an appeal to general usage. The instances in practice are not few, in which both these senses are clearly indicated with regard to the same noun; as, "*Each House* shall keep a journal of *its* proceedings, and from time to time publish the same, excepting such parts as may in *their* judgement require secrecy."—*Constitution of the United States*, Art. i, Sec. 5. "I mean *that part* of mankind *who are known* by the name of women's men, or beaux."—*Addison, Spect.*, No. 536. "A *set* of men *who are* common enough in the world."—*Ibid.* "It is vain for *a people* to expect to be free, unless *they* are first willing to be virtuous."—*Wayland's Moral Science*, p. 397. "For *this people's* heart is waxed gross, and *their* ears are dull of hearing, and *their* eyes *they* have closed."—*Matt.*, xiii, 15. "*This enemy* had now enlarged *their* confederacy, and made *themselves* more formidable than before."—*Life of Antoninus*, p. 62.

"Thus from the tents the fervent *legion swarms*;
So loud *their* clamour, and so keen *their* arms."
—*Pope, Iliad*, B. xvi, l. 320.

OBS. 3.—Most collective nouns of the neuter gender, may take the regular plural form, and be represented by a pronoun in the third person, plural, neuter; as, "The *nations* will enforce *their* laws." This construction comes under Rule 10th, as does also the singular, "The *nations* will enforce *its* laws;" for, in either case, the agreement is entirely literal. Half of Murray's Rule 4th is therefore needless. To Rule 11th above, there are properly no exceptions; because the number of the pronoun is itself the index to the sense in which the antecedent is therein taken. It does not follow, however, but that there may be violations of the rule, or of the notes under it, by the adoption of one number when the other would be more correct, or in better taste. A collection of things inanimate, as a fleet, a heap, a row, a tier, a bundle, is seldom, if ever, taken distributively, with a plural pronoun. For a further elucidation of the construction of collective nouns, see Rule 15th, and the observations under it.

NOTES TO RULE XI.

NOTE I.—A collective noun conveying the idea of unity, requires a pronoun in the third person, singular, neuter; as, "When a legislative *body* makes laws, *it* acts for *itself* only; but when *it* makes grants or contracts, *it* acts as a party."—*Webster's Essays,* p. 40. "A civilized *people* has no right to violate *its* solemn obligations, because the other party is uncivilized."—*Wayland's Moral Science,* p. 314.

NOTE II.—When a collective noun is followed by two or more words which must each in some sense agree with it, uniformity of number is commonly preferable to diversity, and especially to such a mixture as puts the singular both before and after the plural; as, "*That* ingenious nation *who have done* so much honour to modern literature, *possesses,* in an eminent degree, the talent of narration."—*Blair's Rhet.,* p. 364. Better: *"which has done."*

IMPROPRIETIES FOR CORRECTION.

FALSE SYNTAX UNDER RULE XI.

UNDER THE RULE ITSELF.—THE IDEA OF PLURALITY.

"The jury will be confined till it agrees on a verdict."—*Brown's Inst.,* p. 145.

[FORMULE.—Not proper, because the pronoun *it* is of the singular number, and does not correctly represent its antecedent *jury,* which is a collective noun conveying rather the idea of plurality. But, according to Rule 11th, "When the antecedent is a collective noun conveying the idea of plurality, the pronoun must agree with it in the plural number." Therefore, it should be *they*; thus, "The jury will be confined till *they* agree on a verdict."]

"And mankind directed its first cares towards the needful."—*Formey's Belles-Lettres*, p. 114. "It is difficult to deceive a free people respecting its true interest."—*Life of Charles XII*, p. 67. "All the virtues of mankind are to be counted upon a few fingers, but his follies and vices are innumerable."—*Swift*. "Every sect saith, 'Give me liberty:' but give it him, and to his power, he will not yield it to any body else."—*Oliver Cromwell*. "Behold, the people shall rise up as a great lion, and lift up himself as a young lion."—*Numbers, xxiii*, 24. "For all flesh had corrupted his way upon the earth."—*Gen.*, vi, 12. "There happened to the army a very strange accident, which put it in great consternation."—*Goldsmith*.

UNDER NOTE I.—THE IDEA OF UNITY.

"The meeting went on in their business as a united body."—*Foster's Report*, i, 69. "Every religious association has an undoubted right to adopt a creed for themselves."—*Gould's Advocate*, iii, 405. "It would therefore be extremely difficult to raise an insurrection in that State against their own government."—*Webster's Essays*, p. 104. "The mode in which a Lyceum can apply themselves in effecting a reform in common schools."—*New York Lyceum*. "Hath a nation changed their gods, which are yet no gods?"—*Jeremiah*, ii, 11. "In the holy scriptures each of the twelve tribes of Israel is often called by the name of the patriarch, from whom they descended."—*J. Q. Adams's Rhet.*, ii, 331.

UNDER NOTE II.—UNIFORMITY OF NUMBER.

"A nation, by the reparation of their own wrongs, achieves a triumph more glorious than any field of blood can ever give."—*J. Q. Adams*. "The English nation, from which we descended, have been gaining their liberties inch by inch."—*Webster's Essays*, p. 45. "If a Yearly Meeting should undertake to alter its fundamental doctrines, is there any power in the society to prevent their doing so?"—*Foster's Report*, i, 96. "There is a generation that curseth their father, and doth not bless their mother."—*Proverbs*, xxx, 11. "There is a generation that are pure in their own eyes, and yet is not washed from their filthiness."—*Ib.*, xxx, 12. "He hath not beheld iniquity in Jacob, neither hath he seen perverseness in Israel: the Lord his God is with him, and the shout of a king is among them."—*Numb.*, xxiii, 21. "My people hath forgotten me, they have burnt incense to vanity."—*Jer.*, xviii, 15. "When a quarterly meeting hath come to a judgment respecting any difference, relative to any monthly meeting belonging to them," &c.—*Extracts*, p. 195; *N. E. Discip.*, p. 118. "The number of such compositions is every day increasing, and appear to be limited only by the pleasure or conveniency of the writer."—*Booth's Introd. to Dict.*, p. 37. "The church of Christ hath the same power now as ever, and are led by the same Spirit into the same practices."—*Barclay's Works*, i, 477. "The army, whom the chief had thus abandoned, pursued meanwhile their miserable march."—*Lockhart's Napoleon*, ii, 165.

RULE XII.—PRONOUNS.

When a Pronoun has two or more antecedents connected by *and*, it must agree with them jointly in the plural, because they are taken together: as, "*Minos* and *Thales* sung to the lyre the laws which *they* composed."—STRABO: *Blair's Rhet.*, p. 379. "*Saul* and *Jonathan* were lovely and pleasant in *their* lives, and in *their* death *they* were not divided."—*2 Sam.*, i, 23.

"*Rhesus* and *Rhodius* then unite their rills, Caresus roaring down the stony hills."—*Pope, Il.*, B. xii, l. 17.

EXCEPTION FIRST.

When two or more antecedents connected by and serve merely to describe one person or thing, they are either in apposition or equivalent to one name, and do not require a plural pronoun; as, "This great *philosopher* and *statesman* continued in public life till *his* eighty-second year."—"The same *Spirit, light,* and *life, which enlighteneth,* also sanctifieth, and there is not an other."—*Penington.* "My *Constantius and Philetus* confesseth me two years older when I writ *it.*"—*Cowley's Preface.* "Remember these, O *Jacob* and *Israel!* for *thou* art my servant."—*Isaiah,* xliv, 21. "In that *strength* and *cogency which renders* eloquence powerful."—*Blair's Rhet.,* p. 252.

EXCEPTION SECOND.

When two antecedents connected by *and* are emphatically distinguished, they belong to different propositions, and, if singular, do not require a plural pronoun; as, "The *butler,* and not the *baker,* was restored to *his* office."—"The *good man,* and the *sinner too,* shall have *his* reward."—"*Truth,* and *truth only,* is worth seeking for *its* own sake."—"It is *the sense* in which the word is used, and *not the letters* of which it is composed, *that determines* what is the part of speech to which it belongs."—*Cobbett's Gram.,* ¶ 130.

EXCEPTION THIRD.

When two or more antecedents connected by *and* are preceded by the adjective *each, every,* or *no,* they are taken separately, and do not require a plural pronoun; as, "*Every plant* and *every tree* produces others after *its* own kind."—"It is the cause of *every reproach* and *distress* which *has attended* your government."—*Junius,* Let. xxxv. But if the latter be a collective noun, the pronoun may be plural; as, "*Each minister* and *each church* act according to *their* own impressions."—*Dr. M'Cartee.*

OBSERVATIONS ON RULE XII.

OBS. 1.—When the antecedents are of *different persons*, the first person is preferred to the second, and the second to the third; as, "*John*, and *thou*, and *I*, are attached to *our* country."—"*John* and *thou* are attached to *your* country."—"The Lord open some light, and show both *you* and *me our* inheritance!"—*Baxter*. "*Thou* and thy *sons* with thee *shall bear* the iniquity of *your* priesthood."—*Numbers*, xviii, 1.

> "For all are friends in heaven; all faithful friends;
> And many friendships in the days of Time
> Begun, are lasting here, and growing still:
> So grows *ours* evermore, both *theirs and mine*."
> —*Pollok, C. of T.,* B. v, l. 335.

OBS 2.—The *gender* of pronouns, except in the third person singular, is distinguished only by their antecedents. In expressing that of a pronoun which has antecedents of *different* genders, the masculine should be preferred to the feminine, and the feminine to the neuter. The parser of English should remember, that this is a principle of General Grammar.

OBS 3.—When two words are taken separately as nominatives, they ought not to be united in the same sentence as antecedents. In the following example, therefore, *them* should be *it*: "The first has a lenis, and the other an asper over *them*."—*Printer's Gram.*, p. 246. Better thus: "The first has a lenis *over it*, and the other an asper."

OBS. 4.—Nouns that stand as nominatives or antecedents, are sometimes taken conjointly when there is no conjunction expressed; as, "The historian, the orator, the philosopher, *address themselves* primarily to the understanding: *their* direct aim is, to inform, to persuade, to instruct."— *Blair's Rhet.*, p. 377. The copulative *and* may here be said to be understood, because the verb and the pronouns are plural; but it seems better *in general*, either to introduce the connective word, or to take the nouns disjunctively: as, "They have all the copiousness, the fervour, the inculcating method, that *is* allowable and graceful in an orator; perhaps too much of it for a writer."—*Blair's Rhet.*, p. 343. To this, however, there may be exceptions, —cases in which the plural form is to be preferred,—especially in poetry; as,

"Faith, justice, heaven itself, now quit their hold,
When to false fame the captive heart is sold."—*Brown, on Satire.*

OBS. 5.—When two or more antecedents connected by *and* are nominally alike, one or more of them may be *understood*; and, in such a case, the pronoun must still be plural, as agreeing with all the nouns, whether expressed or implied: as, "But intellectual and moral culture ought to go hand in hand; *they* will greatly help each other."—*Dr. Weeks.* Here *they* stands for *intellectual culture* and *moral culture.* The following example is incorrect: "The Commanding and Unlimited *mode* may be used in an absolute sense, or without a name or substitute on which *it* can depend."—*O. B. Peirce's Gram.*, p. 80. Change *it* to *they*, or *and* to *or*. See Note 6th to Rule 16th.

IMPROPRIETIES FOR CORRECTION.

FALSE SYNTAX UNDER RULE XII.

PRONOUNS WITH ANTECEDENTS CONNECTED BY AND.

"Discontent and sorrow manifested itself in his countenance."—*Brown's Inst.*, p. 146.

[FORMULE—Not proper, because the pronoun *itself* is of the singular number, and does not correctly represent its two antecedents *discontent* and *sorrow*, which are connected by *and*, and taken conjointly. But, according to Rule 12th, "When a pronoun has two or more antecedents connected by *and*, it must agree with then, jointly in the plural, because they are taken together." Therefore, *itself* should be *themselves*; thus, "Discontent and sorrow manifested *themselves* in his countenance."]

"Both conversation and public speaking became more simple and plain, such as we now find it."—*Blair's Rhet.*, p. 59. "Idleness and ignorance, if it be suffered to proceed, &c."—JOHNSON: *Priestley's Gram.*, p. 186. "Avoid questions and strife; it shows a busy and contentious disposition."—*Wm. Penn.* "To receive the gifts and benefits of God with thanksgiving, and witness it blessed and sanctified to us by the word and prayer, is owned by us."—*Barclays Works*, i, 213. "Both minister and magistrate are compelled to choose between his duty and his reputation."—*Junius*, p. 9. "All the sincerity, truth, and faithfulness, or disposition of heart or conscience to approve it, found among rational creatures, necessarily originate from God."—*Brown's Divinity*, p. 12. "Your levity and heedlessness, if it continue, will prevent all substantial improvement."—*Brown's Inst.*, p. 147. "Poverty and obscurity will oppress him only who esteems it oppressive."—*Ib.* "Good sense and refined policy are obvious to few, because it cannot be discovered but by a train of reflection."—*Ib.* "Avoid haughtiness of behaviour, and affectation, of manners: it implies a want of solid merit."—*Ib.* "If love and unity continue, it will make you partakers of one an other's joy."—*Ib.* "Suffer not jealousy and distrust to enter: it will destroy, like a canker, every germ of friendship."—*Ib.* "Hatred and animosity are inconsistent with Christian charity; guard, therefore, against the slightest indulgence of it."—*Ib.* "Every man is entitled to liberty of conscience, and freedom of opinion, if he does not pervert it to the injury of others."—*Ib.*

"With the azure and vermilion
Which is mix'd for my pavilion."—*Byron's Manfred*, p. 9.

RULE XIII.—PRONOUNS.

When a Pronoun has two or more antecedents connected by *or* or *nor*, it must agree with them singly, and not as if taken together: as; "*James* or *John* will favour us with *his* company."—"Neither *wealth* nor *honour* can secure the happiness of *its* votaries."

"What *virtue* or what mental *grace*,
But men unqualified and base
Will boast *it* their possession?"—*Cowper, on Friendship.*

OBSERVATIONS ON RULE XIII.

OBS. 1.—When two or more singular antecedents are connected by *or* or *nor*, the pronoun which represents them, ought in general to be singular, because *or* and *nor* are disjunctives; and, to form a complete concord, the nouns ought also to be of the same person and gender, that the pronoun may agree in all respects with each of them. But when *plural* nouns are connected in this manner, the pronoun will of course be plural, though it still agrees with the antecedents singly; as, "Neither *riches* nor *honours* ever satisfy *their* pursuers." Sometimes, when different numbers occur together, we find the plural noun put last, and the pronoun made plural after both, especially if this noun is a mere substitute for the other; as,

"What's justice to a man, or laws,
That never comes within *their* claws."—*Hudibras.*

OBS. 2.—When antecedents of different persons, numbers, or genders, are connected by *or* or *nor*, they cannot very properly be represented by any pronoun that is not applicable to each of them. The following sentences are therefore inaccurate; or at least they contradict the teachings of their own authors: "Either *thou or I* am greatly mistaken, in *our* judgment on this subject."—*Murray's Key*, p. 184 "Your character, which *I, or any other writer*, may now value *ourselves* by (upon) drawing."—SWIFT: *Lowth's Gram.*, p. 96. "Either *you or I* will be in *our* place in due time."—*Coopers Gram.*, p. 127. But different pronouns may be so connected as to refer to such antecedents taken separately; as, "By requiring greater labour from such *slave or slaves*, than *he or she or they* are able to perform."—*Prince's Digest.* Or, if the gender only be different, the masculine may involve the feminine by implication; as, "If a man smite the eye of his *servant*, or the eye of his *maid*, that it perish, he shall let *him* go free for *his* eye's sake."—*Exodus*, xxi, 26.

OBS. 3.—It is however very common to resort to the plural number in such instances as the foregoing, because our plural pronouns are alike in all the genders; as, "When either *man or woman* shall separate *themselves* to vow a vow of a Nazarite."—*Numbers*, vi, 2. "Then shalt thou bring forth *that man or that woman* unto thy gates, and shalt stone them with stones, till *they* die."—*Deut.*, xvii, 5. "Not on outward charms could *he or she* build *their* pretensions to please."—*Opie, on Lying*, p. 148. "Complimenting either *man or woman* on agreeable qualities which *they* do not possess, in hopes of imposing on *their* credulity."—*Ib.*, p. 108. "*Avidien*, or his *wife*, (no matter which,) *sell their* presented partridges and fruits."—*Pope*, Sat. ii, l. 50. "Beginning with Latin *or* Greek hexameter, *which are* the same."—*Kames, El. of Crit.*, i, 79.

"Did ever *Proteus, Merlin,* any *witch,*
Transform *themselves* so strangely as the rich?"
—*Pope,* Ep. i, l. 152.

OBS. 4.—From the observations and examples above, it may be perceived, that whenever there is a difference of person, number, or gender, in antecedents connected disjunctively, there is an inherent difficulty respecting the form of the pronoun personal. The best mode of meeting this inconvenience, or of avoiding it by a change of the phraseology, may be different on different occasions. The disjunctive connexion of explicit pronouns is the most correct, but it savours too much of legal precision and wordiness to be always eligible. Commonly an ingenious mind may invent some better expression, and yet avoid any syntactical anomaly. In Latin, when nouns are connected by the conjunctions which correspond to *or* or *nor,* the pronoun or verb is so often made plural, that no such principle as that of the foregoing Rule, or of Rule 17th, is taught by the common grammars of that language. How such usage can be logically right, however, it is difficult to imagine. Lowth, Murray, Webster, and most other English grammarians, teach, that, "The conjunction disjunctive has an effect contrary to that of the copulative; and, as the verb, noun, or pronoun, is referred to the preceding terms taken separately, it must be in the singular number."—*Lowth's Gram.,* p. 75; *L. Murray's,* 151; *Churchill's,* 142; *W. Allen's,* 133; *Lennie's,* 83; *and many others.* If there is any allowable exception to this principle, it is for the adoption of the plural when the concord cannot be made by any one pronoun singular; as, "If I value my friend's *wife or son* upon account of *their* connexion with him."—*Kames, El. of Crit.,* i, 73. "Do not drink wine nor strong drink, *thou nor thy sons* with thee, when *ye* go into the tabernacle of the congregation."—*Levit.,* x, 8. These examples, though they do not accord with the preceding rule, seem not to be susceptible of any change for the better. There are also some other modes of expression, in which nouns that are connected disjunctively, may afterwards be represented together; as "*Foppery* is a sort of folly much more contagious THAN *pedantry*; but as *they* result alike from affectation, *they* deserve alike to be proscribed."—*Campbell's Rhet.*, p. 217.

IMPROPRIETIES FOR CORRECTION.

FALSE SYNTAX UNDER RULE XIII.

PRONOUNS WITH ANTECEDENTS CONNECTED BY OR OR NOR.

"Neither prelate nor priest can give their flocks any decisive evidence that you are lawful pastors."—*Dr. Brownlee.*

[FORMULE.—Not proper, because the pronoun *their* is of the plural number, and does not correctly represent its two antecedents *prelate* and *priest*, which are connected by *nor*, and taken disjunctively. But, according to Rule 13th, "When a pronoun has two or more antecedents connected by *or* or *nor*, it must agree with them singly, and not as if taken together." Therefore, *their* should be *his*; thus, "Neither prelate nor priest can give *his* flocks any decisive evidence that you are lawful pastors."]

"And is there a heart of parent or of child, that does not beat and burn within them?"—*Maturin's Sermons*, p. 367. "This is just as if an eye or a foot should demand a salary for their service to the body."—*Collier's Antoninus*, p. 178. "If thy hand or thy foot offend thee, cut them off, and cast them from thee."—*Matt.*, xviii, 8. "The same might as well be said of Virgil, or any great author, whose general character will infallibly raise many casual additions to their reputation."—*Pope's Pref. to Homer.* "Either James or John, one of them, will come."—*Smith's New Gram.*, p. 37. "Even a rugged rock or barren heath, though in themselves disagreeable, contribute by contrast to the beauty of the whole."—*Kames, El. of Crit.*, i, 185. "That neither Count Rechteren nor Monsieur Mesnager had behaved themselves right in this affair."—*Spect.*, No. 481. "If an Aristotle, a Pythagoras, or a Galileo, suffer for their opinions, they are 'martyrs.'"—*Gospel its own Witness*, p. 80. "If an ox gore a man or a woman, that they die; then the ox shall be surely stoned."—*Exodus*, xxi, 28. "She was calling out to one or an other, at every step, that a Habit was ensnaring them."—DR. JOHNSON: *Murray's Sequel*, 181. "Here is a Task put upon Children, that neither this Author, nor any other have yet undergone themselves."—*Johnson's Gram. Com.*, p. 162. "Hence, if an adjective or participle be subjoined to the verb, when of the singular number, they will agree both in gender and number with the collective noun."—*Adam's Lat. Gram.*, p. 154; *Gould's*, 158. "And if you can find a diphthong, or a triphthong, be pleased to point them out too."—*Bucke's Classical Gram.*, p. 16. "And if you can find a diphthong, or a triphthong, a trissyllable, or a polysyllable, point them respectively out."—*Ib.*, p. 25. "The false refuges in which the atheist or the sceptic have intrenched themselves."—*Christian Spect.*, viii, 185. "While the man or woman thus assisted by art expects their charms will be imputed to nature alone."—*Opie*, 141. "When you press a watch, or pull a clock, they answer your question with precision; for they repeat exactly the hour of the day, and tell you neither more nor less than you desire to know."—*Bolingbroke, on History*, p. 102.

"Not the Mogul, or Czar of Muscovy,
Not Prester John, or Cham of Tartary,
Are in their houses Monarch more than I."
—KING: *Brit. Poets*, Vol. iii, p. 613.

—VERBS.

In this work, the syntax of Verbs is embraced in six consecutive rules, with the necessary exceptions, notes, and observations, under them; hence this chapter extends from the fourteenth to the twentieth rule in the series.

RULE XIV.—FINITE VERBS.

Every finite Verb must agree with its subject, or nominative, in person and number: as, "I *know*; thou *knowst,* or *knowest*; he *knows,* or *knoweth*"—"The bird *flies*; the birds *fly*."

"Our fathers' fertile *fields* by slaves *are till'd,*
And *Rome* with dregs of foreign lands *is fill'd*."
—*Rowe's Lucan,* B. vii, l. 600.

OBSERVATIONS ON RULE XIV.

OBS. 1.—To this general rule for the verb, there are properly *no exceptions*;[385] and all the special rules that follow, which prescribe the concord of verbs in particular instances, virtually accord with it. Every *finite verb,* (that is, every verb *not in the infinitive mood,*) must have some noun, pronoun, or phrase equivalent, known as the *subject* of the being, action, or passion;[386] and with this subject, whether expressed or understood, the verb must agree in person and number. The infinitive mood, as it does not unite with a nominative to form an assertion, is of course exempt from any such agreement. These may be considered principles of Universal Grammar. The Greeks, however, had a strange custom of using a plural noun of the neuter gender, with a verb of the third person singular; and in both Greek and Latin, the infinitive mood with an accusative before it was often equivalent to a finite verb with its nominative. In English we have *neither of these usages*; and plural nouns, even when they denote no absolute plurality, (as *shears, scissors, trowsers, pantaloons, tongs,*) require plural verbs or pronouns: as, "Your *shears come* too late, to clip the bird's wings."—SIDNEY: *Churchill's Gram.*, p. 30.

OBS. 2.—When a book that bears a plural title, is spoken of as one thing, there is sometimes presented an *apparent exception* to the foregoing rule; as, "The *Pleasures* of Memory *was published* in the year 1792, and became at once popular."—*Allan Cunningham.* "The '*Sentiments* of a Church-of-England Man' *is written* with great coolness, moderation, ease, and perspicuity."—*Johnson's Life of Swift.* "The '*Pleasures* of Hope' *is* a splendid poem; *it* was written for perpetuity."—*Samuel L. Knapp.* In these instances, there is, I apprehend, either an agreement of the verb, by the figure *syllepsis*, with the mental conception of the thing spoken of; or an improper ellipsis of the common noun, with which each sentence ought to commence; as, "The *poem* entitled,"—"The *work* entitled," &c. But the plural title sometimes controls the form of the verb; as, "My Lives are reprinting."—*Dr. Johnson.*

OBS. 3.—In the figurative use of the present tense for the past or imperfect, the vulgar have a habit of putting the third person singular with the pronoun *I*; as, "*Thinks I* to myself."—*Rev. J. Marriott.* "O, *says I*, Jacky, are you at that work?"—*Day's Sandford and Merton.* "Huzza! huzza! Sir Condy Rackrent forever, was the first thing *I hears* in the morning."—*Edgeworth's Castle Rackrent*, p. 97. This vulgarism is to be avoided, not by a simple omission of the terminational *s*, but rather by the use of the literal preterit: as, "*Thought* I to myself;"—"O, *said* I;"—"The first thing I *heard*." The same mode of correction is also proper, when, under like circumstances, there occurs a disagreement in number; as, "After the election was over, there *comes shoals* of people from all parts."—*Castle Rackrent*, p. 103. "Didn't ye hear it? *says they* that were looking on."—*Ib.*, p. 147. Write, "there *came*,"—"*said they*."

OBS. 4.—It has already been noticed, that the article *a*, or a singular adjective, sometimes precedes an arithmetical number with a plural noun; as, "*A thousand years* in thy sight *are* but as yesterday."—*Psalms*, xc, 4. So we might say, "*One* thousand years *are*,"—"*Each* thousand years *are*"—"*Every* thousand years *are*," &c. But it would not be proper to say, "A thousand years *is*," or, "Every thousand years *is*;" because the noun *years* is plainly plural, and the anomaly of putting a singular verb after it, is both needless and unauthorized. Yet, to this general rule for the verb, the author of a certain "English Grammar *on the Productive System*," (a strange perversion of Murray's compilation, and a mere catch-penny work, now extensively used in New England,) is endeavouring to establish, by his own bare word, the following exception: "*Every* is sometimes associated with a plural noun, in which case the verb must be singular; as, 'Every hundred years *constitutes* a century.'"—*Smith's New Gram.*, p. 103. His *reason* is this; that the phrase containing the nominative, "*signifies a single period of time*, and is, therefore, *in reality* singular."—*Ib.* Cutler also, a more recent writer, seems to have imbibed the same notion; for he gives the following sentence as an example of "false construction: Every hundred years *are* called a century."—*Cutler's Grammar and Parser*, p. 145. But, according to this argument, no plural verb could ever be used with any *definite number* of the parts of time; for any three years, forty years, or threescore years and ten, are as single a period of time, as "every hundred years," "every four years," or "every twenty-four hours." Nor is it true, that, "*Every* is sometimes associated with a plural noun;" for "*every years*" or "*every hours,*" would be worse than nonsense. I, therefore, acknowledge no such exception; but, discarding the principle of the note, put this author's pretended *corrections* among my quotations of *false syntax.*

OBS. 5.—Different verbs always have different subjects, expressed or understood; except when two or more verbs are connected in the same construction, or when the same word is repeated for the sake of emphasis. But let not the reader believe the common doctrine of our grammarians, respecting either the ellipsis of nominatives or the ellipsis of verbs. In the text, "The man was old and crafty," Murray sees no connexion of the ideas of age and craftiness, but thinks the text a *compound sentence,* containing two nominatives and two verbs; i.e., "The man was old, and *the man was* crafty." [387] And all his other instances of "the ellipsis of the verb" are equally fanciful! See his *Octavo Gram.,* p. 219; *Duodecimo,* 175. In the text, "God loves, protects, supports, and rewards the rights," there are four verbs in *the same construction,* agreeing with the same nominative, and governing the same object; but Buchanan and others expound it, "God loves, and God protects, and God supports, and God rewards the righteous."—*English Syntax,* p. 76; *British Gram.,* 192. This also is fanciful and inconsistent. If the nominative is here "*elegantly understood* to each verb," so is the objective, which they do not repeat. "And again," they immediately add, "the *verb* is often understood to its noun or nouns; as, He dreams of gibbets, halters, racks, daggers, &c. i.e. He dreams of gibbets, and he dreams of halters, &c."—*Same works and places.* In none of these examples is there any occasion to suppose an ellipsis, if we admit that two or more words *can* be connected in the same construction!

OBS. 6.—Verbs in the imperative mood commonly agree with the pronoun *thou, ye,* or *you,* understood after them; as, "*Heal [ye]* the sick, *cleanse [ye]* the lepers, *raise [ye]* the dead, *cast [ye]* out devils."—*Matt.,* x,

8. "*Trust* God and *be doing,* and *leave* the rest with him."—*Dr. Sibs.* When the doer of a thing must first proceed to the place of action, we sometimes use *go* or *come* before an other verb, without any conjunction between the two; as, "Son, *go work* to-day in my vineyard."—*Matt.,* xxi, 28. "*Come see* a man who [has] told me all things that ever I did."—*John,* iv, 29. "He ordered his soldiers to *go murder* every child about Bethlehem, or near it."—*Wood's Dict. of Bible, w. Herod.* "Take a present in thine hand, and *go meet* the man of God."—*2 Kings,* viii, 8. "I will *go see* if he be at home."—*Walker's Particles,* p. 169.

OBS. 7.—The *place* of the verb has reference mainly to that of the subject with which it agrees, and that of the object which it governs; and as the arrangement of these, with the instances in which they come before or after the verb, has already been noticed, the position of the latter seems to require no further explanation. See Obs. 2d under Rule 2d, and Obs. 2d under Rule 5th.

OBS. 8.—The infinitive mood, a phrase, or a sentence, (and, according to some authors, the participle in *ing,* or a phrase beginning with this participle,) is sometimes the proper subject of a verb, being equivalent to a nominative of the third person singular; as, "To play *is* pleasant."—*Lowth's Gram.,* p. 80. "To write well, *is* difficult; to speak eloquently, *is* still more difficult."—*Blair's Rhet.,* p. 81. "To take men off from prayer, *tends* to irreligiousness, *is granted.*"—*Barclay's Works,* i, 214. "To educate a child perfectly, *requires* profounder thought, greater wisdom, than to govern a state."—*Channing's Self-Culture,* p. 30. "To determine these points, *belongs* to good sense."—*Blair's Rhet.,* p. 321. "How far the change would contribute to his welfare, *comes* to be considered."—*Id., Sermons.* "That too much care does hurt in any of our tasks, *is* a doctrine so flattering to indolence, that we ought to receive it with extreme caution."—*Life of Schiller,* p. 148. "That there is no disputing about taste, *is* a saying so generally received as to have become a proverb."—*Kames, El. of Crit.*, ii, 360. "For what purpose they embarked, *is* not yet known."—"To live in sin and yet to believe the forgiveness of sin, *is* utterly impossible."—*Dr. J. Owen.*

"There shallow draughts intoxicate the brain,
But drinking largely *sobers* us again."—*Pope.*

OBS. 9.—The same meaning will be expressed, if the pronoun *it* be placed before the verb, and the infinitive, phrase, or santance, after it; as, "*It* is pleasant *to play*,"—"*It* is difficult *to write well*;" &c. The construction of the following sentences is rendered defective by the omission of this pronoun: "Why do ye that which [*it*] is not lawful to do on the sabbath days?"—*Luke*, vi, 2. "The show-bread, which [*it*] is not lawful to eat, but for the priests only."—*Ib.*, vi, 4. "We have done that which [*it*] was our duty to do."—*Ib.*, xvii, 10. Here the relative *which* ought to be in the objective case, governed by the infinitives; but the omission of the word *it* makes this relative the nominative to *is* or *was*, and leaves *to do* and *to eat* without any regimen. This is not ellipsis, but error. It is an accidental gap into which a side piece falls, and leaves a breach elsewhere. The following is somewhat like it, though what falls in, appears to leave no chasm: "From this deduction, [*it*] *may be easily seen* how it comes to pass, that personification makes so great a figure."—*Blair's Rhet.*, p. 155. "Whether the author had any meaning in this expression, or what it was, [*it*] *is not easy* to determine."—*Murray's Gram.*, Vol. i, p. 298. "That warm climates should accelerate the growth of the human body, and shorten its duration, [*it*] *is very reasonable* to believe."—*Ib.*, p. 144. These also need the pronoun, though Murray thought them complete without it.

OBS. 10.—When the infinitive mood is made the subject of a finite verb, it is most commonly used to express action or state in the abstract; as, "*To be* contents his natural desire."—*Pope.* Here *to be* stands for simple *existence*; or if for the existence *of the Indian,* of whom the author speaks, that relation is merely implied. "*To define ridicule,* has puzzled and vexed every critic."—*Kames, El. of Crit.,* i, 300. Here "*to define*" expresses an action quite as distinct from any agent, as would the participial noun; as, "The *defining of* ridicule," &c. In connexion with the infinitive, a concrete quality may also be taken as an abstract; as, "*To be good* is *to be happy.*" Here *good* and *happy* express the quality of *goodness* and the state of *happiness* considered abstractly; and therefore these adjectives do not relate to any particular noun. So also the passive infinitive, or a perfect participle taken in a passive sense; as, "*To be satisfied with a little,* is the greatest wisdom."—"*To appear discouraged,* is the way to become so." Here the *satisfaction* and the *discouragement* are considered abstractly, and without reference to any particular person. (See Obs. 12th and 13th on Rule 6th.) So too, apparently, the participles *doing* and *suffering,* as well as the adjective *weak,* in the following example:

> "Fallen Cherub, to be *weak* is miserable, *Doing* or *suffering.*"—*Milton's Paradise Lost.*

OBS. 11.—When the action or state is to be expressly limited to one class of beings, or to a particular person or thing, without making the verb finite; the noun or pronoun may be introduced before the infinitive by the preposition *for:* as, "*For men to search* their own glory, is not glory."—*Prov.,* xxv, 27. "*For a prince to be reduced* by villany [sic—KTH] to my distressful circumstances, is calamity enough."—*Translation of Sallust.* "*For holy persons to be humble,* is as hard, as *for a prince to submit* himself to be guided by tutors."—TAYLOR: *Priestley's Gram.,* p. 132; *Murray's,*

184. But such a limitation is sometimes implied, when the expression itself is general; as, "*Not to know me,* argues thyself unknown."—*Milton.* That is, "*For thee* not to know me." The phrase is put far, "*Thy ignorance of me;*" for an other's ignorance would be no argument in regard to the individual addressed. "*I, to bear this,* that never knew but better, *is* some burden."—*Beauties of Shak.,* p. 327. Here the infinitive *to bear,* which is the subject of the verb *is,* is limited in sense by the pronoun *I,* which is put absolute in the nominative, though perhaps *improperly;* because, "*For me to bear this,*" &c., will convey the same meaning, in a form much more common, and perhaps more grammatical. In the following couplet, there is an ellipsis of the infinitive; for the phrase, "fool with fool," means, "*for* fool *to contend* with fool," or, "for one fool to contend with an other:"

"Blockheads with reason wicked wits abhor,
But *fool with fool* is barb'rous civil war."
—*Pope, Dunciad,* B. iii, l. 175.

OBS. 12.—The objective noun or pronoun thus introduced by *for* before the infinitive, was erroneously called by Priestley, "*the subject of the affirmation;*" (*Gram.,* p. 132;) and Murray, Ingersoll, and others, have blindly copied the blunder. See *Murray's Gram.,* p. 184; *Ingersoll's,* 244. Again, Ingersoll says, "The infinitive mood, or part of a sentence, is sometimes the subject of a verb, *and is, therefore, its* NOMINATIVE."—*Conversations on English Gram.,* p. 246. To this erroneous deduction, the phraseology used by Murray and others too plainly gives countenance: "The infinitive mood, or part of a sentence, is sometimes put *as the nominative case* to the verb."—*Murray's Gram.,* p. 144; *Fisk's,* 123; *Kirkham's,* 188; *Lennie's,* 99; *Bullions's,* 89; and many more. Now the objective before the infinitive may not improperly be called *the subject* of this form of the verb, as the nominative is, of the finite; but to call it "the subject *of the affirmation,*" is plainly absurd; because no infinitive, in English, ever expresses an affirmation. And again, if a whole phrase or sentence is made the subject of a *finite* verb, or of an affirmation, no one word contained in it, can singly claim this title. Nor can the whole, by virtue of this relation, be said to be "in the *nominative case*;" because, in the nature of things, neither phrases nor sentences are capable of being declined by cases.

OBS. 13.—Any phrase or sentence which is made the subject of a finite verb, must be taken in the sense of *one thing*, and be spoken of as *a whole*; so that the verb's agreement with it, in the third person singular, is not an exception to Rule 14th, but a construction in which the verb may be parsed by that rule. For any one thing merely spoken of, is of the third person singular, whatever may be the nature of its parts. Not every phrase or sentence, however, is fit to be made the subject of a verb;—that is, if its own import, and not the mere expression, is the thing whereof we affirm. Thus Dr. Ash's example for this very construction, "a *sentence* made the subject of a verb," is, I think, a palpable solecism: "The King and Queen appearing in public *was* the cause of my going."—*Ash's Gram.*, p. 52. What is here before the verb *was*, is *no* "*sentence*;" but a mere phrase, and such a one as we should expect to see used independently, if any regard were had to its own import. The Doctor would tell us what "was *the cause* of his going:" and here he has two nominatives, which are equivalent to the plural *they*; q.d., "*They* appearing in public *was* the cause." But such a construction is not English. It is an other sample of the false illustration which grammar receives from those who *invent* the proof-texts which they ought to *quote*.

OBS. 14.—One of Murray's examples of what he erroneously terms "*nominative sentences*," i.e., "sentences or clauses constituting the subject of an affirmation," is the following: "A desire to excel others in learning and virtue [,] *is* commendable."—*Gram.*, 8vo, p. 144. Here the verb *is* agrees regularly with the noun *desire*, and with that only; the whole text being merely a simple sentence, and totally irrelevant to the doctrine which it accompanies.[388] But the great "Compiler" supposes the adjuncts of this noun to be parts of the nominative, and imagines the verb to agree with all that precedes it. Yet, soon after, he expends upon the ninth rule of Webster's Philosophical Grammar a whole page of useless criticism, to show that the adjuncts of a noun are not to be taken as parts of the nominative; and that, when objectives are thus subjoined, "the assertion grammatically respects the first nouns only."—*Ib.*, p. 148. I say *useless*, because the truth of the doctrine is so very plain. Some, however, may imagine an example like the following to be an exception to it; but I do not, because I think the true nominative suppressed:

"By force they could not introduce these gods;
For *ten to one* in former days *was* odds."—*Dryden's Poems*, p. 38.

OBS. 15.—Dr. Webster's ninth rule is this: "When the nominative consists of several words, and the last of the names is in the plural number, the verb is commonly in the plural also; as, 'A part of the exports *consist* of raw silk.' 'The number of oysters *increase*.' GOLDSMITH. 'Such as the train of our ideas *have lodged* in our memories.' LOCKE. 'The greater part of philosophers *have acknowledged* the excellence of this government.' ANACHARSIS."—*Philos. Gram.*, p. 146; *Impr. Gram.*, 100. The last of these examples Murray omits; the second he changes thus: "A number of men and women *were* present." But all of them his reasoning condemns as ungrammatical. He thinks them wrong, upon the principle, that the verbs, being plural, do not agree with the first nouns only. Webster, on the contrary, judges them all to be right; and, upon this same principle, conceives that his rule must be so too. He did not retract or alter the doctrine after he saw the criticism, but republished it verbatim, in his "Improved Grammar," of 1831. Both err, and neither convinces the other.

OBS. 16.—In this instance, as Webster and Murray both teach erroneously, whoever follows either, will be led into many mistakes. The fact is, that some of the foregoing examples, though perhaps not all, are perfectly right; and hundreds more, of a similar character, might be quoted, which no true grammarian would presume to condemn. But what have these to do with the monstrous absurdity of supposing objective adjuncts to be "parts of the actual nominative?" The words, "*part,*" "*number,*" "*train*" and the like, are *collective nouns*; and, as such, they often have plural verbs in agreement with them. To say, "A *number* of men and women *were* present," is as correct as to say, "A very great *number* of our words *are* plainly derived from the Latin."—*Blair's Rhet.*, p. 86. Murray's criticism, therefore, since it does not exempt these examples from the censure justly laid upon Webster's rule, will certainly mislead the learner. And again the rule, being utterly wrong in principle, will justify blunders like these: "The truth of the narratives *have* never been disputed;"—"The virtue of these men and women *are* indeed exemplary."—*Murray's Gram.*, p. 148. In one of his notes, Murray suggests, that the article *an* or *a* before a collective noun must confine the verb to the singular number; as, "A *great number* of men and women *was* collected."—*Ib.*, p. 153. But this doctrine he sometimes forgot or disregarded; as, "But if *a number* of interrogative or exclamatory sentences *are thrown* into one general group."—*Ib.*, p. 284; *Comly*, 166; *Fisk*, 160; *Ingersoll*, 295.

OBS. 17.—Cobbett, in a long paragraph, (the 245th of his English Grammar,) stoutly denies that any *relative pronoun* can ever be the nominative to a verb; and, to maintain this absurdity, he will have the relative and its antecedent to be always alike in *case*, the only thing in which they are always independent of each other. To prove his point, he first frames these examples: "The men *who are* here, the man *who is* here; the cocks *that crow*, the cock *that crows*;" and then asks, "Now, if the relative be the nominative, why do the verbs *change*, seeing that here is no change in the relative?" He seems ignorant of the axiom, that two things severally equal to a third, are also equal to each other: and accordingly, to answer his own question, resorts to a new principle: "The verb is continually varying. Why does it vary? Because it *disregards the relative* and goes and finds the antecedent, and accommodates its number to that."—*Ibid.* To this wild doctrine, one erratic Irishman yields a full assent; and, in one American grammatist, we find a partial and unintentional concurrence with it.[389] But the fact is, the relative agrees with the antecedent, and the verb agrees with the relative: hence all three of the words are alike in person and number. But between the case of the relative and that of the antededent [sic—KTH], there never is, or can be, in our language, any sort of connexion or interference. The words belong to different clauses; and, if both be nominatives, they must be the subjects of different verbs: or, if the noun be sometimes put absolute in the nominative, the pronoun is still left to its own verb. But Cobbett concludes his observation thus: "You will observe, therefore, that, when I, in the etymology and syntax as relating to relative pronouns, speak of relatives as being in the nominative case, I mean, that they relate to nouns or to personal pronouns, *which are in that case. The same observation applies to the other cases.*"—*Ib.*, ¶ 245. This suggestion betrays in the critic an unaccountable ignorance of his subject.

OBS. 18.—Nothing is more certain, than that the relatives, *who, which, what, that,* and *as,* are often nominatives, and the only subjects of the verbs which follow them: as, "The Lord will show *who are* his, and *who is* holy."—*Numbers,* xvi, 5. "Hardly is there any person, but *who,* on such occasions, *is disposed* to be serious."—*Blair's Rhet.,* p. 469. "Much of the merit of Mr. Addison's Cato depends upon that moral turn of thought *which distinguishes* it."—*Ib.,* 469. "Admit not a single word but *what is* necessary."—*Ib.,* p. 313. "The pleader must say nothing but *what is* true; and, at the same time, he must avoid saying any thing *that will hurt* his cause."—*Ib.*, 313. "I proceed to mention such *as appear* to me most material."—*Ib.*, p. 125. After *but* or *than*, there is sometimes an ellipsis of the relative, and perhaps also of the antecedent; as, "There is no heart *but must feel* them."—*Blair's Rhet.*, p. 469. "There is no one *but must be* sensible of the extravagance."—*Ib.*, p. 479. "Since we may date from it a more general and a more concerted opposition to France *than there had been* before."—*Bolingbroke, on Hist.*, p. 213. That is, "than *what* there had been before;"—or, "than *any opposition which* there had been before." "John has more fruit *than can be gathered* in a week."—*O. B. Peirce's Gram.*, pp. 196 and 331. I suppose this sentence to mean, "John has more fruit than *what* can be gathered in a week." But the author of it denies that it is elliptical, and seems to suppose that *can be gathered* agrees with *John.* Part of his comment stands thus: "The above sentence—'John has more fruit than can be gathered in a week'—in every respect full and *perfect*—must, to be *grammatical*! according to *all* the 'old theories,' stand, John has more fruit than *that fruit is which, or which fruit* can be gathered in a week!!!"—*Ib.*, 331. What shall be done with the headlong critic who thus mistakes exclamation points for arguments, and multiplies his confidence in proportion to his fallacies and errors?

OBS. 19.—In a question, the nominative *I* or *thou* put after the verb, controls the agreement, in preference to the interrogative *who, which*, or *what*, put before it; as, "*Who am I? What am I? Who art thou? What art thou?*" And, by analogy, this seems to be the case with all plurals; as, "*Who are we? Who are you? Who are they? What are these*?" But sometimes the interrogative pronoun is the only nominative used; and then the verb, whether singular or plural, must agree with this nominative, in the third person, and not, as Cobbett avers, with an antecedent understood: as, "*Who is* in the house? *Who are* in the house? *Who strikes* the iron? *Who strike* the iron? *Who was* in the street? *Who were* in the street?"—*Cobbett's Gram.*, ¶ 245. All the interrogative pronouns may be used in either number, but, in examples like the following, I imagine the singular to be more proper than the plural: "*What have become* of our previous customs?"—*Hunt's Byron*, p. 121. "And *what have become* of my resolutions to return to God?"—*Young Christian*, 2d Ed., p. 91. When two nominatives of different properties come after the verb, the first controls the agreement, and neither the plural number nor the most worthy person is always preferred; as, "*Is it I? Is it thou? Is it they*?"

OBS. 20.—The verb after a relative sometimes has the appearance of disagreeing with its nominative, because the writer and his reader disagree in their conceptions of its mood. When a relative clause is subjoined to what is itself subjunctive or conditional, some writers suppose that the latter verb should be put in the subjunctive mood; as, "If there be any intrigue *which stand* separate and independent."—*Blair's Rhet.*, p. 457. "The man also would be of considerable use, who should vigilantly attend to every illegal practice *that were beginning* to prevail."—*Campbell's Rhet.*, p. 171. But I have elsewhere shown, that relatives, in English, are not compatible with the subjunctive mood; and it is certain, that no other mood than the indicative or the potential is commonly used after them. Say therefore, "If there be any intrigue *which stands*," &c. In assuming to himself the other text, Murray's says, "*That* man also would be of considerable use, who should vigilantly attend to every illegal practice that *was* beginning to prevail."—*Octavo Gram.*, p. 366. But this seems too positive. The potential imperfect would be better: viz., "that *might begin* to prevail."

OBS. 21.—The termination *st* or *est,* with which the second person singular of the verb is formed in the indicative present, and, for the solemn style, in the imperfect also; and the termination *s* or *es,* with which the third person singular is formed in the indicative present, and only there; are signs of the mood and tense, as well as of the person and number, of the verb. They are not applicable to a future uncertainty, or to any mere supposition in which we would leave the time indefinite and make the action hypothetical; because they are commonly understood to fix the time of the verb to the present or the past, and to assume the action as either doing or done. For this reason, our best writers have always omitted those terminations, when they intended to represent the action as being doubtful and contingent as well as conditional. And this omission constitutes the whole *formal* difference between the indicative and the subjunctive mood. The *essential* difference has, by almost all grammarians, been conceived to extend somewhat further; for, if it were confined strictly within the limits of the literal variation, the subjunctive mood would embrace only two or three words in the whole formation of each verb. After the example of Priestley, Dr. Murray, A. Murray, Harrison, Alexander, and others, I have given to it all the persons of the two simple tenses, singular and plural; and, for various reasons, I am decidedly of the opinion, that these are its most proper limits. The perfect and pluperfect tenses, being past, cannot express what is really contingent or uncertain; and since, in expressing conditionally what may or may not happen, we use the subjunctive present as embracing the future indefinitely, there is no need of any formal futures for this mood. The comprehensive brevity of this form of the verb, is what chiefly commends it. It is not an elliptical form of the future, as some affirm it to be; nor equivalent to the indicative present, as others will have it; but a *true subjunctive*, though its distinctive parts are chiefly confined to the second and third persons singular of the simple verb: as, "Though *thou wash* thee with nitre."—*Jer.*, ii, 22. "It is just, O great king! that a *murderer perish*."— *Corneille*. "This single *crime*, in my judgment, *were* sufficient to condemn him."—*Duncan's Cicero*, p. 82. "Beware that *thou bring* not my son thither."—BIBLE: *Ward's Gram.*, p. 128. "See [that] *thou tell* no man."— *Id., ib.* These examples can hardly be resolved into any thing else than the subjunctive mood.

NOTES TO RULE XIV.

NOTE I.—When the nominative is a relative pronoun, the verb must agree with it in person and number, according to the pronoun's agreement with its true antecedent or antecedents. Example of error: "The second book [of the Æneid] is one of the greatest masterpieces *that ever was executed* by any hand."—*Blair's Rhet.*, p. 439. Here the true antecedent is *masterpieces*, and not the word *one*; but *was executed* is singular, and "by any *hand*" implies but one agent. Either say, "It is one of the greatest *masterpieces that* ever *were executed*;" or else, "It is *the greatest masterpiece that ever was executed by any hand*." But these assertions differ much in their import.

NOTE II.—"The adjuncts of the nominative do not control its agreement with the verb; as, Six months' *interest was* due. The *progress* of his forces *was* impeded."—*W. Allen's Gram.*, p. 131. "The *ship*, with all her furniture, was destroyed."—*Murray's Gram.*, p. 150. "All *appearances* of modesty *are* favourable and prepossessing."—*Blair's Rhet.*, p. 308. "The *power* of relishing natural enjoyments *is* soon gone."—*Fuller, on the Gospel*, p. 135. "*I*, your master, *command* you (not *commands*)"— *Latham's Hand-Book*, p. 330.[390]

NOTE III.—Any phrase, sentence, mere word, or other sign, taken as one whole, and made the subject of an assertion, requires a verb in the third person singular; as, "To lie *is* base."—*Adam's Gram.*, p. 154. "When, to read and write, *was* of itself an honorary distinction."—*Hazlitt's Lect.*, p. 40. "To admit a God and then refuse to worship him, *is* a modern and inconsistent practice."—*Fuller, on the Gospel*, p. 30. "*We is* a personal pronoun."—*L. Murray's Gram.*, p. 227. "*Th has* two sounds."—*Ib.*, p. 161. "The *'s is annexed* to each."—*Bucke's Gram.*, p. 89. "*Ld. stands* for *lord*."— *Webster's American Dict.*, 8vo.

NOTE IV.—The pronominal adjectives, *each, one,[391] either,* and *neither,* are always in the third person singular; and, when they are the leading words in their clauses, they require verbs and pronouns to agree with them accordingly: as, "*Each* of you *is* entitled to *his* share."—"Let no *one* deceive *himself.*"

NOTE V.—A neuter or a passive verb between two nominatives should be made to agree with that which precedes it;[392] as, "Words *are* wind:" except when the terms are transposed, and the proper subject is put after the verb by *question* or *hyperbaton*; as, "His pavilion *were* dark *waters* and thick *clouds* of the sky."—*Bible.* "Who *art thou*?"—*Ib.* "The wages of sin *is death.*"—*Ib. Murray, Comly,* and others. But, of this last example, Churchill says, "*Wages are* the subject, of which it is affirmed, that *they are* death."— *New Gram.,* p. 314. If so, *is* ought to be *are*; unless Dr. Webster is right, who imagines *wages* to be *singular,* and cites this example to prove it so. See his *Improved Gram.,* p. 21.

NOTE VI.—When the verb cannot well be made singular, the nominative should be made plural, that they may agree: or, if the verb cannot be plural, let the nominative be singular. Example of error: "For *every one* of them *know* their several duties."—*Hope of Israel,* p. 72. Say, "For *all* of them know their several duties."

NOTE VII.—When the verb has different forms, that form should be adopted, which is the most consistent with present and reputable usage in the style employed: thus, to say familiarly, "The clock *hath stricken*;"—"Thou *laughedst* and *talkedst,* when thou *oughtest* to have been silent;"—"He *readeth* and *writeth,* but he *doth* not cipher," would be no better, than to use *don't, won't, can't, shan't,* and *didn't,* in preaching.

NOTE VIII.—Every finite verb not in the imperative mood, should have a separate nominative expressed; as, "*I came, I saw, I conquered*:" except when the verb is repeated for the sake of emphasis, or connected to an other in the same construction, or put after *but* or *than*; as, "Not an eminent orator has lived *but is* an example of it."—*Ware*. "Where more is meant *than meets* the ear."—*Milton's Allegro*. (See Obs. 5th and Obs. 18th above.)

"They *bud, blow, wither, fall,* and *die*."—*Watts*.

"That evermore his teeth they *chatter,*
Chatter, chatter, chatter still."—*Wordsworth*.

NOTE IX.—A future contingency is best expressed by a verb in the subjunctive present; and a mere supposition, with indefinite time, by a verb in the subjunctive imperfect; but a conditional circumstance assumed as a fact, requires the indicative mood:[393] as, "If thou *forsake* him, he will cast thee off forever."—*Bible*. "If it *were* not so, I would have told you."—*Ib.* "If thou *went*, nothing would be gained."—"Though he *is* poor, he is contented."—"Though he *was* rich, yet for your sakes he became poor."—*2 Cor.*, viii, 9.

NOTE X.—In general, every such use or extension of the subjunctive mood, as the reader will be likely to mistake for a discord between the verb and its nominative, ought to be avoided as an impropriety: as, "We are not sensible of disproportion, till the difference between the quantities compared *become* the most striking circumstance."—*Kames, El. of Crit.*, ii, 341. Say rather, "*becomes*;" which is indicative. "Till the general preference of certain forms *have been declared*."—*Priestley's Gram., Pref.*, p. xvii. Say, "*has been declared*;" for "*preference*" is here the nominative, and Dr. Priestley himself recognizes no other subjunctive tenses than the present and the imperfect; as, "If thou *love*, If thou *loved*."—*Ib.*, p. 16.

IMPROPRIETIES FOR CORRECTION.

FALSE SYNTAX UNDER RULE XIV.

UNDER THE RULE ITSELF.—VERB AFTER THE NOMINATIVE.

"Before you left Sicily, you was reconciled to Verres."—*Duncan's Cicero*, p. 19.

[FORMULE.—Not proper, because the passive verb *was reconciled* is of the singular number, and does not agree with its nominative *you*, which is of the second person plural. But, according to Rule 14th, "Every finite verb must agree with its subject, or nominative, in person and number." Therefore, *was reconciled* should be *were reconciled*; thus, "Before you left Sicily, you *were reconciled* to Verres."]

"Knowing that you was my old master's good friend."—*Spect.*, No. 517. "When the judge dare not act, where is the loser's remedy?"—*Webster's Essays*, p. 131. "Which extends it no farther than the variation of the verb extend."—*Murray's Gram.*, 8vo, Vol. i, p. 211. "They presently dry without hurt, as myself hath often proved."—*Roger Williams*. "Whose goings forth hath been from of old, from everlasting."—*Keith's Evidences*. "You was paid to fight against Alexander, not to rail at him."—*Porter's Analysis*, p. 70. "Where more than one part of speech is almost always concerned."—*Churchill's Gram., Pref.*, p. viii. "Nothing less than murders, rapines, and conflagrations, employ their thoughts."—*Duncan's Cicero*, p. 175. "I wondered where you was, my dear."—*Lloyd's Poems*, p. 185. "When thou most sweetly sings."—*Drummond of Hawthornden*. "Who dare, at the present day, avow himself equal to the task?"—*Music of Nature*, p. 11. "Every body are very kind to her, and not discourteous to me."—*Byron's Letters*. "As to what thou says respecting the diversity of opinions."—*The Friend*, Vol. ix, p. 45. "Thy nature, immortality, who knowest?"—*Everest's Gram.*, p. 38. "The natural distinction of sex in animals gives rise to what, in grammar, is called genders."—*Ib.*, p. 51. "Some pains has likewise been taken."—*Scott's Pref. to Bible.* "And many a steed in his stables were seen."—*Penwarne's Poems*, p. 108. "They was forced to eat what never was esteemed food."—*Josephus's Jewish War*, B. i, Ch. i, §7. "This that yourself hath spoken, I desire that they may take their oaths upon."—*Hutchinson's Mass.*, ii, 435. "By men whose experience best qualify them to judge."—*Committee on Literature, N. Y. Legislature.* "He dare venture to kill and destroy several other kinds of fish."—*Johnson's Dict, w. Perch.* "If a gudgeon meet a roach, He dare not venture to approach."—SWIFT: *Ib., w. Roach.* "Which thou endeavours to establish unto thyself."—*Barclay's Works*, i, 164. "But they pray together much oftener than thou insinuates."—*Ib.*, i, 215. "Of people of all denominations, over whom thou presideth."—*The Friend*, Vol. v, p. 198. "I can produce ladies and gentlemen whose progress have been astonishing."—*Chazotte, on Teaching Lang.*, p. 62. "Which of these two kinds of vice are more criminal?"—*Brown's Estimate*, ii, 115. "Every twenty-four hours affords to us the vicissitudes of day and night."—*Smith's New Gram.*, p. 103. "Every four years adds another day."—*Ib.* "Every error I could find, Have my busy muse employed."—*Swift's Poems*, p. 335. "A studious scholar deserve the approbation of his teacher."—*Sanborn's Gram.*, p. 226. "Perfect submission to the rules of a school indicate good breeding."—*Ib.*, p. 37. "A comparison in which more than two is concerned."—*Bullions, E. Gram.*, p. 114. "By the facilities which artificial language afford them."—*O. B. Peirce's Gram.*, p. 16. "Now thyself hath lost both lop and top."—SPENSER: *Joh. Dict., w. Lop.* "Glad tidings is brought to the poor."—*Campbell's Gospels: Luke*, vii, 23. "Upon which, all that is pleasurable, or affecting in elocution, chiefly depend."—*Sheridan's Elocution*, p. 129. "No pains has been spared to render this work complete."—*Bullions, Lat. Gram., Pref.*, p. iv. "The United States contains more than a twentieth part of the land of this globe."—DE WITT CLINTON: *Cobb's N. Amer. Reader*, p. 173. "I am mindful that myself is (or am) strong."—*Fowler's E. Gram.*, § 500. "Myself *is* (not *am*) weak; thyself *is* (not *art*) weak."—*Ib.*, §479.

"How pale each worshipful and reverend guest
Rise from a clergy or a city feast!"—*Pope*, Sat. ii, l. 75.

UNDER THE RULE ITSELF.—VERB BEFORE THE NOMINATIVE.

"Where was you born? In London."—*Buchanan's Syntax*, p. 133. "There is frequent occasions for commas."—*Ingersoll's Gram.*, p. 281. "There necessarily follows from thence, these plain and unquestionable consequences."—*Priestley's Gram.*, p. 191. "And to this impression contribute the redoubled effort."—*Kames, El. of Crit.*, ii, 112. "Or if he was, was there no spiritual men then?"—*Barclay's Works*, iii, 86. "So by these two also is signified their contrary principles."—*Ib.*, iii, 200. "In the motions made with the hands, consist the chief part of gesture in speaking."—*Blair's Rhet.*, p. 336. "Dare he assume the name of a popular magistrate?"—*Duncan's Cicero*, p. 140. "There was no damages as in England, and so Scott lost his wager."—*Byron*. "In fact there exists such resemblances."—*Kames, El. of Crit.*, ii, 64. "To him giveth all the prophets witness."—*Crewdson's Beacon*, p. 79. "That there was so many witnesses and actors."—*Addison's Evidences*, p. 37. "How does this man's definitions stand affected?"—*Collier's Antoninus*, p. 136. "Whence comes all the powers and prerogatives of rational beings?"—*Ib.*, p. 144. "Nor does the Scriptures cited by thee prove thy intent."—*Barclay's Works*, i, 155. "Nor do the Scripture cited by thee prove the contrary."—*Ib.*, i, 211. "Why then cite thou a Scripture which is so plain and clear for it?"—*Ib.*, i, 163. "But what saith the Scriptures as to respect of persons among Christians?"—*Ib.*, i, 404. "But in the mind of man, while in the savage state, there seems to be hardly any ideas but what enter by the senses."—*Robertson's America*, i,

289. "What sounds have each of the vowels?"—*Griscom's Questions*. "Out of this has grown up aristocracies, monarchies, despotisms, tyrannies."—*Brownson's Elwood*, p. 222. "And there was taken up, of fragments that remained to them, twelve baskets."— *Luke*, ix, 17. "There seems to be but two general classes."—*Day's Gram.*, p. 3. "Hence arises the six forms of expressing time."—*Ib.*, p. 37. "There seems to be no other words required."—*Chandler's Gram.*, p. 28. "If there is two, the second increment is the syllable next the last."—*Bullions, Lat. Gram.*, 12th Ed., p. 281. "Hence arises the following advantages."—*Id., Analyt. and Pract. Gram.*, 1849, p. 67. "There is no data by which it can be estimated."—*J. C. Calhoun's Speech*, March 4, 1850. "To this class belong the Chinese [language], in which we have nothing but naked roots."—*Fowler's E. Gram.*, 8vo, 1850, p. 27. "There was several other grotesque figures that presented themselves."— *Spect.*, No. 173. "In these consist that sovereign good which ancient sages so much extol."—*Percival's Tales*, ii, 221. "Here comes those I have done good to against my will."—*Shak., Shrew*. "Where there is more than one auxiliary."—*O. B. Peirce's Gram.*, p. 80.

"On me to cast those eyes where shine nobility."
—SIDNEY: *Joh. Dict.*

"Here's half-pence in plenty, for one you'll have twenty."
—*Swift's Poems*, p. 347.

"Ah, Jockey, ill advises thou, I wis,
To think of songs at such a time as this."
—*Churchill*, p. 18.

UNDER NOTE I.—THE RELATIVE AND VERB.

"Thou who loves us, wilt protect us still."—*Alex. Murray's Gram.*, p. 67. "To use that endearing language, Our Father, who is in heaven"—*Bates's Doctrines*, p. 103. "Resembling the passions that produceth these actions."—*Kames, El. of Crit.*, i, 157. "Except *dwarf, grief, hoof, muff*, &c. which takes *s* to make the plural."—*Ash's Gram.*, p. 19. "As the cattle that goeth before me and the children be able to endure."— *Gen.* xxxiii, 14 "Where is the man who dare affirm that such an action is mad?"—*Werter.* "The ninth book of Livy affords one of the most beautiful exemplifications of historical painting, that is any where to be met with."—*Blair's Rhet.*, p. 360. "In some studies too, that relate to taste and fine writing, which is our object," &c.—*Ib.*, p. 349. "Of those affecting situations, which makes man's heart feel for man."—*Ib.*, p. 464. "We see very plainly, that it is neither Osmyn, nor Jane Shore, that speak."—*Ib.*, p. 468. "It should assume that briskness and ease, which is suited to the freedom of dialogue."—*Ib.*, p. 469. "Yet they grant, that none ought to be admitted into the ministry, but such as is truly pious."—*Barclay's Works*, iii, 147. "This letter is one of the best that has been written about Lord Byron."—*Hunt's Byron*, p. 119. "Thus, besides what was sunk, the Athenians took above two hundred ships."—*Goldsmith's Greece*, i, 102. "To have made and declared such orders as was necessary."—*Hutchinson's Hist.*, i, 470. "The idea of such a collection of men as make an army."—*Locke's Essay*, p. 217. "I'm not the first that have been wretched."—*Southern's In. Ad.*, Act 2. "And the faint sparks of it, which is in the angels, are concealed from our view."—*Calvin's Institutes*, B. i, Ch. 11. "The subjects are of such a nature, as allow room for much diversity of taste and sentiment."—*Blair's Rhet.*, *Pref.*, p. 5. "It is in order to propose examples of such perfection, as are not to be found in the real examples of society."—*Formey's Belles-Lettres*, p. 16. "I do not believe that he would amuse himself with such fooleries as has been attributed to him."—*Ib.*, p. 218. "That shepherd, who first taughtst the chosen seed."— *O. B. Peirce's Gram.*, p. 238. "With respect to the vehemence and warmth which is allowed in popular eloquence."— *Blair's Rhet.*, p. 261. "Ambition is one of those passions that is never to be satisfied."—*Home's Art of Thinking*, p. 36. "Thou wast he that leddest out and broughtest in Israel."—*2 Samuel*, v, 2; and *1 Chron.*, xi, 2. "Art thou the man of God that camest from Judah?"—*1 Kings*, xiii, 14.

> "How beauty is excell'd by manly grace
> And wisdom, which alone is truly fair."—*Milton*, B. iv, l. 490.

> "What art thou, speak, that on designs unknown,
> While others sleep, thus range the camp alone?"—*Pope, Il.*, x, 90.

UNDER NOTE II.—NOMINATIVE WITH ADJUNCTS.

"The literal sense of the words are, that the action had been done."—*Dr. Murray's Hist. of Lang.*, i, 65. "The rapidity of his movements were beyond example."—*Wells's Hist.*, p. 161. "Murray's Grammar, together with his Exercises and Key, have nearly superseded every thing else of the kind."—EVAN'S REC.: *Murray's Gram.*, 8vo, ii, 305. "The mechanism of clocks and watches were totally unknown."—HUME: *Priestley's Gram.*, p. 193. "The *it*, together with the verb *to be*, express states of being."—*Cobbett's Eng. Gram.*, ¶ 190. "Hence it is, that the profuse variety of objects in some natural landscapes, neither breed confusion nor fatigue."—*Kames, El. of Crit.*, i, 266. "Such a clatter of sounds indicate rage and ferocity."—*Music of Nature*, p. 195. "One of the fields make threescore square yards, and the other only fifty-five."—*Duncan's Logic*, p. 8. "The happy effects of this fable is worth attending to."—*Bailey's Ovid*, p. x. "Yet the glorious serenity of its parting rays still linger with us."—*Gould's Advocate.* "Enough of its form and force are retained to render them uneasy."—*Maturin's Sermons*, p. 261. "The works of nature, in this respect, is extremely regular."—*Dr. Pratt's Werter.* "No small addition of exotic and foreign words and phrases have been made by commerce."—*Bicknell's Gram.*, Part ii, p. 10. "The dialect of some nouns are taken notice of in the notes."—*Milnes, Greek Gram.*, p. 255. "It has been said, that a discovery of the full resources of the arts, afford the means of debasement, or of perversion."—*Rush, on the Voice*, p. xxvii. "By which means the Order of the Words are disturbed."—*Holmes's Rhet.*, B. i, p. 57. "The twofold influence of these and the others require the asserter to be in the plural form."—*O. B. Peirce's Gram.*, p. 251. "And each of these afford employment."—*Percival's Tales*, Vol. ii, p. 175. "The pronunciation of the vowels are best explained under the rules relative to the consonants."—*Coar's Gram.*, p. 7. "The judicial power of these courts extend to all cases in law and equity."—*Hall and Baker's School Hist.*, p. 286. "One of you have stolen my money."—*Rational Humorist*, p. 45. "Such redundancy of epithets, instead of pleasing, produce satiety and disgust."—*Kames, El. of Crit.*, ii, 256. "It has been alleged, that a compliance with the rules of Rhetoric, tend to cramp the mind."—*Hiley's Gram.*, 3d Ed., p. 187. "Each of these are presented to us in different relations"—*Hendrick's Gram.*, 1st Ed., p. 34. "The past tense of these verbs, *should, would, might, could,* are very indefinite with respect to time."—*Bullions, E. Gram.*, 2d Ed., p. 33; 5th Ed., p. 31. "The power of the words, which are said to govern this mood, are distinctly understood."—*Chandler's Gram.*, Ed. of 1821, p. 33.

"And now, at length, the fated term of years
The world's desire have brought, and lo! the God appears."
—*Dr. Lowth, on "the Genealogy of Christ."*

"Variety of Numbers still belong
To the soft Melody of Ode or Song."
—*Brightland's Gram.*, p. 170.

UNDER NOTE III.—COMPOSITE OR CONVERTED SUBJECTS.

"Many are the works of human industry, which to begin and finish are hardly granted to the same man."—*Johnson, Adv. to Dict.* "To lay down rules for these are as inefficacious."—*Dr. Pratt's Werter*, p. 19. "To profess regard, and to act *differently*, discover a base mind."—*Murray's Key*, ii, p. 206. See also *Bullions's E. Gram.*, 82 and 112; *Lennie's*, 58. "To magnify to the height of wonder things great, new, and admirable, extremely please the mind of man."—*Fisher's Gram.*, p. 152. "In this passage, *according as* are used in a manner which is very common."—*Webster's Philosophical Gram.*, p. 183. "A *cause de* are called a preposition; *a cause que*, a conjunction."—DR. WEBSTER: *Knickerbocker*, 1836. "To these are given to speak in the name of the Lord."—*The Friend*, vii, 256. "While *wheat* has no plural, *oats* have seldom any singular."—*Cobbett's E. Gram.* ¶ 41. "He cannot assert that *ll* are inserted in *fullness* to denote the sound of *u*."—*Cobb's Review of Webster*, p. 11. "*ch* have the power of *k*."—*Gould's Adam's Gram.*, p. 2. "*ti*, before a vowel, and unaccented, have the sound of *si* or *ci*."—*Ibid.* "In words derived from the French, as *chagrin, chicanery*, and *chaise, ch* are sounded like *sh*."—*Bucke's Gram.*, p. 10. "But in the word *schism, schismatic*, &c., the *ch* are silent."—*Ibid.* "*Ph* are always sounded like *f*, at the beginning of words."—*Bucke's Gram.* "*Ph* have the sound of *f* as in *philosophy*."—*Webster's El. Spelling-Book*, p. 11. "*Sh* have one sound only as in *shall*."—*Ib.* "*Th* have two sounds."—*Ib.* "*Sc* have the sound of *sk*, before *a, o, u*, and *r*."—*Ib.* "Aw, have the sound of *a* in hall."—*Bolles's Spelling-Book*, p. vi. "Ew, sound like *u*."—*Ib.* "Ow, when both sounded, have the sound of *ou*."—*Ib.* "Ui, when both pronounced in one syllable sound like *wi* in *languid*."—*Ib.*

"*Ui* three several Sorts of Sound express,
As *Guile, rebuild, Bruise* and *Recruit* confess."
—*Brightland's Gram.*, p. 34.

UNDER NOTE IV.—EACH, ONE, EITHER, AND NEITHER.

"When each of the letters which compose this word, have been learned."—*Dr. Weeks, on Orthog.*, p. 22. "As neither of us deny that both Homer and Virgil have great beauties."—*Blair's Rhet.*, p. 21. "Yet neither of them are remarkable for precision."—*Ib.*, p. 95. "How far each of the three great epic poets have distinguished themselves."—*Ib.*, p. 427. "Each of these produce a separate agreeable sensation."—*Ib.*, p. 48. "On the Lord's day every one of us Christians keep the sabbath."—*Tr. of Irenæus.* "And each of them bear the image of purity and holiness."—*Hope of Israel*, p. 81. "Were either of these meetings ever acknowledged or recognized?"—*Foster's Report*, i, 96. "Whilst neither of these letters exist in the Eugubian inscription."—*Knight, on Greek Alph.*, p. 122. "And neither of them are properly termed indefinite."—*Wilson's Essay on Gram.*, p. 88. "As likewise of the several subjects, which have in effect each their verb."—*Lowth's Gram.*, p. 120. "Sometimes when the word ends in *s*, neither of the signs are used."—*Alex. Murray's Gram.*, p. 21. "And as neither of these manners offend the ear."—*Walker's Dict., Pref.*, p. 5. "Neither of these two Tenses are confined to this signification only."—*Johnson's Gram. Com.*, p. 339. "But neither of these circumstances are intended here."—*Tooke's Diversions*, ii, 237. "So that all are indebted to each, and each are dependent upon all."—*Am. Bible Society's Rep.*, 1838, p. 89. "And yet neither of them express any more action in this case than they did in the other."—*Bullions, E. Gram.*, p. 201. "Each of these expressions denote action."—*Hallock's Gram.*, p. 74. "Neither of these moods seem to be defined by distinct boundaries."—*Butler's Practical Gram.*, p. 66. "Neither of these solutions are correct."—*Bullions, Lat. Gram.*, p. 236. "Neither bear any sign of case at all."—*Fowler's E. Gram.*, 8vo, 1850, §217.

"Each in their turn like Banquo's monarchs stalk."—*Byron.*

"And tell what each of them by th'other lose."—*Shak., Cori.*, iii, 2.

UNDER NOTE V.—VERB BETWEEN TWO NOMINATIVES.

"The quarrels of lovers is a renewal of love."—*Adam's Lat. Gram.*, p. 156; *Alexander's*, 49; *Gould's*, 159; *Bullions's*, 206. "Two dots, one placed above the other, is called *Sheva*."—*Dr. Wilson's Heb. Gram.*, p. 43. "A few centuries, more or less, is a matter of small consequence."—*Ib.* p. 31. "Pictures were the first step towards the art of writing. Hieroglyphicks was the second step."—*Parker's English Composition*, p. 27. "The comeliness of youth are modesty and frankness; of age, condescension and dignity."—*Murray's Key*, 8vo, p. 166. "Merit and good works is the end of man's motion."—*Lord Bacon.* "Divers philosophers hold that the lips is parcel of the mind."—*Shakspeare.* "The clothing of the natives were the skins of wild beasts."—*Indian Wars*, p. 92. "Prepossessions in favor of our nativ town, is not a matter of surprise."—*Webster's Essays*, p. 217. "Two shillings and six pence is half a crown, but not a half crown."—*Priestley's Gram.*, p. 150; *Bicknell's*, ii, 53. "Two vowels, pronounced by a single impulse of the voice, and uniting in one sound, is called a dipthong."—*Cooper's Pl. and Pr. Gram.*, p. 1. "Two or more sentences united together is called a Compound Sentence."—*P. E. Day's District School Gram.*, p. 10. "Two or more words rightly put together, but not completing an entire proposition, is called a Phrase."—*Ibid.* "But the common Number of Times are five."—*The British Grammar*, p. 122. "Technical terms, injudiciously introduced, is another source of darkness in composition."—*Jamieson's Rhet.*, p. 107. "The United States is the great middle division of North America."—*Morse's Geog.*, p. 44. "A great cause of the low state of industry were the restraints put upon it."—HUME: *Murray's Gram.*, p. 145; *Ingersoll's*, 172; *Sanborn's*, 192; *Smith's*, 123; and others. "Here two tall ships becomes the victor's prey."—*Rowe's Lucan*, B. ii, l. 1098. "The expenses incident to an outfit is surely no object."—*The Friend*, Vol. iii., p. 200.

"Perhaps their loves, or else their sheep,
  Was all that did their silly thoughts so busy keep."—*Milton*.

UNDER NOTE VI.—CHANGE THE NOMINATIVE.

"Much pains has been taken to explain all the kinds of words."—*Infant School Gram.* p. 128. "Not less [*time*] than three years are spent in attaining this faculty."—*Music of Nature*, p. 28. "Where this night are met in state Many a friend to gratulate His wish'd presence."—*Milton's Comus*. l. 948. "Peace! my darling, here's no danger, Here's no oxen near thy bed."—*Watts*. "But every one of these are mere conjectures, and some of them very unhappy ones."—*Coleridge's Introduction*, p. 61. "The old theorists, calling the Interrogatives and Repliers, *adverbs*, is only a part of their regular system of naming words."—*O. B. Peirce's Gram.*, p. 374. "Where a series of sentences occur, place them in the order in which the facts occur."—*Ib.*, p. 264. "And that the whole in conjunction make a regular chain of causes and effects."—*Kames, El. of Crit.*, ii, 275. "The origin of the Grecian, and Roman republics, though equally involved in the obscurities and uncertainties of fabulous events, present one remarkable distinction."—*Adam's Rhet.*, i, 95. "In these respects, mankind is left by nature an unformed, unfinished creature."—*Butler's Analogy*, p. 144. "The scripture are the oracles of God himself."—HOOKER: *Joh. Dict., w. Oracle.* "And at our gates are all manner of pleasant fruits."—*Solomon's Song*, vii, 13. "The preterit of *pluck, look*, and *toss* are, in speech, pronounced *pluckt, lookt, tosst.*"—*Fowler's E. Gram.*, 1850, §68.

"Severe the doom that length of days impose,
  To stand sad witness of unnumber'd woes!"—*Melmoth*.

UNDER NOTE VII.—ADAPT FORM TO STYLE.

1. *Forms not proper for the Common or Familiar Style.*

"Was it thou that buildedst that house?"—*Inst.*, p. 151. "That boy writeth very elegantly."—*Ib.* "Couldest not thou write without blotting thy book?"—*Ib.* "Thinkest thou not it will rain to-day?"—*Ib.* "Doth not your cousin intend to visit you?"—*Ib.* "That boy hath torn my book."—*Ib.* "Was it thou that spreadest the hay?"—*Ib.* "Was it James, or thou, that didst let him in?"—*Ib.* "He dareth not say a word."—*Ib.* "Thou stoodest in my way and hinderedst me."—*Ib.*

"Whom see I?—Whom seest thou now?—Whom sees he?—Whom lovest thou most?—What dost thou to-day?—What person seest thou teaching that boy?—He hath two new knives.—Which road takest thou?—What child teaches he?"—*Ingersoll's Gram.*, p. 66. "Thou, who makest my shoes, sellest many more."—*Ib.*, p. 67.

"The English language hath been much cultivated during the last two hundred years. It hath been considerably polished and refined."—*Lowth's Gram., Pref.*, p. iii. "This *stile* is ostentatious, and doth not suit grave writing."—*Priestley's Gram.*, p. 82. "But custom hath now appropriated *who* to persons, and *which* to things."—*Ib.*, p. 97. "The indicative mood sheweth or declareth; as, *Ego amo*, I love: or else asketh a question; as, *Amas tu*? Dost thou love?"—*Paul's Accidence*, Ed. of 1793, p. 16. "Though thou canst not do much for the cause, thou mayst and shouldst do something."—*Murray's Gram.*, p. 143. "The support of so many of his relations, was a heavy task; but thou knowest he paid it cheerfully."—*Murray's Key*, R. 1, p. 180. "It may, and often doth, come short of it."—*Campbell's Rhetoric*, p. 160.

""Twas thou, who, while thou seem'dst to chide,
    To give me all thy pittance tried."—*Mitford's Blanch*, p. 78.

2. *Forms not proper for the Solemn or Biblical Style.*

"The Lord has prepaid his throne in the heavens; and his kingdom rules over all."—See *Key*. "Thou answer'd them, O Lord our God: thou was a God that forgave them, though thou took vengeance of their inventions."—See *Key*. "Then thou spoke in vision to thy Holy One, and said, I have laid help upon one that is mighty."—See *Key*. "So then, it is not of him that wills, nor of him that rules, but of God that shows mercy; who dispenses his blessings, whether temporal or spiritual, as seems good in his sight."—See *Key*.

    "Thou, the mean while, was blending with my thought;
    Yea, with my life, and life's own secret joy."—*Coleridge*.

UNDER NOTE VIII.—EXPRESS THE NOMINATIVE.

"Who is here so base, that would be a bondman?"—*Beauties of Shakspeare*, p. 249. "Who is here so rude, that would not be a Roman?"—*Ib.* "There is not a sparrow falls to the ground without his notice."—*Murray's Gram.*, p. 300. "In order to adjust them so, as shall consist equally with the perspicuity and the strength of the period."—*Ib.*, p. 324; *Blair's Rhet.*, 118. "But, sometimes, there is a verb comest in."—*Cobbett's English Gram.*, ¶248. "Mr. Prince has a genius would prompt him to better things."—*Spectator*, No. 466. "It is this removes that impenetrable mist."—*Harris's Hermes*, p. 362. "By the praise is given him for his courage."—*Locke, on Education*, p. 214. "There is no man would be more welcome here."—*Steele, Spect.*, No. 544. "Between an antecedent and a consequent, or what goes before, and immediately follows."—*Blair's Rhet.*, p. 141. "And as connected with what goes before and follows."— *Ib.*, p. 354. "There is no man doth a wrong for the wrong's sake."—*Lord Bacon.* "All the various miseries of life, which people bring upon themselves by negligence and folly, and might have been avoided by proper care, are instances of this."— *Butler's Analogy*, p. 108. "Ancient philosophers have taught many things in favour of morality, so far at least as respect justice and goodness towards our fellow-creatures."—*Gospel its own Witness*, p. 56. "Indeed, if there be any such, have been, or appear to be of us, as suppose, there is not a wise man among us all, nor an honest man, that is able to judge betwixt his brethren; we shall not covet to meddle in their matter."—*Barclay's Works*, i, 504. "There were that drew back; there were that made shipwreck of faith: yea, there were that brought in damnable heresies."—*Ib.*, i, 466. "The nature of the cause rendered this plan altogether proper, and in similar situations is fit to be imitated."—*Blair's Rhet.*, p. 274. "This is an idiom to which our language is strongly inclined, and was formerly very prevalent."— *Churchill's Gram.*, p. 150. "His roots are wrapped about the heap, and seeth the place of stones."—*Job*, viii, 17.

"New York, Fifthmonth 3d, 1823.

"Dear friend, Am sorry to hear of thy loss; but hope it may be retrieved. Should be happy to render thee any assistance in my power. Shall call to see thee to-morrow morning. Accept assurances of my regard. A. B."

"New York, May 3d, P. M., 1823.

"Dear Sir, Have just received the kind note favoured me with this morning; and cannot forbear to express my gratitude to you. On further information, find have not lost so much as at first supposed; and believe shall still be able to meet all my engagements. Should, however, be happy to see you. Accept, dear sir, my most cordial thanks. C. D."—See *Brown's Institutes*, p. 151.

"Will martial flames forever fire thy mind,
And never, never be to Heaven resign'd?"—*Pope, Odys.*, xii, 145.

UNDER NOTE IX.—APPLICATION OF MOODS.

First Clause of the Note.—For the Subjunctive Present.

"He will not be pardoned, unless he repents."—*Brown's Institutes*, p. 191.

[FORMULE.—Not proper, because the verb *repents*, which is here used to express a future contingency, is in the indicative mood. But, according to the first clause of Note 9th to Rule 14th, "A future contingency is best expressed by a verb in the subjunctive present." Therefore, *repents* should be *repent*; thus, "He will not be pardoned, unless he *repent*."]

"If thou findest any kernelwort in this marshy meadow, bring it to me."—*Neef's Method of Teaching*, p. 258. "If thou leavest the room, do not forget to shut that drawer."—*Ib.*, p. 246. "If thou graspest it stoutly, thou wilt not be hurt."—*Ib.*, p. 196. "On condition that he comes, I will consent to stay."—*Murray's Exerc.*, p. 74. "If he is but discreet, he will succeed."—*Inst.*, p. 191. "Take heed that thou speakest not to Jacob."—*Ib.* "If thou castest me off, I shall be miserable."— *Ib.* "Send them to me, if thou pleasest."—*Ib.* "Watch the door of thy lips, lest thou utterest folly."—*Ib.* "Though a liar speaks the truth, he will hardly be believed."—*Common School Manual*, ii, 124. "I will go unless I should be ill."—*Murray's Gram.*, p. 300. "If the word or words understood are supplied, the true construction will be apparent."— *Murray's Exercises in Parsing*, p. 21. "Unless thou shalt see the propriety of the measure, we shall not desire thy support."—

Murray's Key, p. 209. "Unless thou shouldst make a timely retreat, the danger will be unavoidable."—*Ib.,* p. 209. "We may live happily, though our possessions are small."—*Ib.,* p. 202. "If they are carefully studied, they will enable the student to parse all the exercises."—*Ib., Note,* p. 165. "If the accent is fairly preserved on the proper syllable, this drawling sound will never be heard."—*Murray's Gram.,* p. 242. "One phrase may, in point of sense, be equivalent to another, though its grammatical nature is essentially different."—*Ib.,* p. 108. "If any man obeyeth not our word by this epistle, note that man."—*Dr. Webster's Bible.* "Thy skill will be the greater, if thou hittest it."—*Putnam's Analytical Reader,* p. 204. "Thy skill will be the greater if thou hit'st it."—*Cobb's N. A. Reader,* p. 321. "We shall overtake him though he should run."—*Priestley's Gram.,* p. 113; *Murray's,* 207; *Smith's,* 173. "We shall be disgusted if he gives us too much."—*Blair's Rhet.,* p. 388.

"What is't to thee, if he neglect thy urn,
Or without spices lets thy body burn?"—DRYDEN: *Joh. Dict., w. What.*

Second Clause of Note IX.—For the Subjunctive Imperfect.

"And so would I, if I was he."—*Brown's Institutes,* p. 191.

[FORMULE.—Not proper, because the verb *was,* which is here used to express a mere supposition, with indefinite time, is in the indicative mood. But, according to the second clause of Note 9th to Rule 14th, "A mere supposition, with indefinite time, is best expressed by a verb in the subjunctive imperfect." Therefore, *was* should be *were;* thus, "And so would I, if I *were* he."]

"If I was a Greek, I should resist Turkish despotism."—*Cardell's Elements of Gram.,* p. 80. "If he was to go, he would attend to your business."—*Ib.,* p. 81. "If thou feltest as I do, we should soon decide."—

Inst., p. 191. "Though thou sheddest thy blood in the cause, it would but prove thee sincerely a fool."—*Ib.* "If thou lovedst him, there would be more evidence of it."—*Ib.* "If thou couldst convince him, he would not act accordingly."—*Murray's Key*, p. 209. "If there was no liberty, there would be no real crime."—*Formey's Belles-Lettres*, p. 118. "If the house was burnt down, the case would be the same."—*Foster's Report*, i, 89. "As if the mind was not always in action, when it prefers any thing!"—*West, on Agency*, p. 38. "Suppose I was to say, 'Light is a body.'"—*Harris's Hermes*, p. 78. "If either oxygen or azote was omitted, life would be destroyed."—*Gurney's Evidences*, p. 155. "The verb *dare* is sometimes used as if it was an auxiliary."—*Priestley's Gram.*, p. 132. "A certain lady, whom I could name, if it was necessary."—*Spectator*, No. 536. "If the *e* was dropped, *c* and *g* would assume their hard sounds."—*Buchanan's Syntax*, p. 10. "He would no more comprehend it, than if it was the speech of a Hottentot."—*Neef's Sketch*, p. 112. "If thou knewest the gift of God," &c.—*John*, iv, 10. "I wish I was at home."—*O. B. Peirce's Gram.*, p. 260. "Fact alone does not constitute right; if it does, general warrants were lawful."—*Junius*, Let. xliv, p. 205. "Thou look'st upon thy boy as though thou guessest it."—*Putnam's Analytical Reader*, p. 202. "Thou look'st upon thy boy as though thou guessedst it."—*Cobb's N. A. Reader*, p. 320. "He fought as if he had contended for life."—*Hiley's Gram.*, p. 92. "He fought as if he had been contending for his life."—*Ib.*, 92.

"The dewdrop glistens on thy leaf,
  As if thou seem'st to shed a tear;
 As if thou knew'st my tale of grief,
  Felt all my sufferings severe."—*Alex. Letham.*

Last Clause of Note IX.—For the Indicative Mood.

"If he know the way, he does not need a guide."—*Brown's Institutes*, p. 191.

[FORMULE.—Not proper, because the verb *know*, which is used to express a conditional circumstance assumed as a fact, is in the subjunctive mood. But, according to the last clause of Note 9th to Rule 14th, "A conditional circumstance assumed as a fact, requires the indicative mood." Therefore, *know* should be *knows*; thus, "If he *knows* the way, he does not need a guide."]

"And if there be no difference, one of them must be superfluous, and ought to be rejected."—*Murray's Gram.*, p. 149. "I cannot say that I admire this construction, though it be much used."—*Priestley's Gram.*, p. 172. "We are disappointed, if the verb do not immediately follow it."—*Ib.*, p. 177. "If it were they who acted so ungratefully, they are doubly in fault."—*Murray's Key*, 8vo, p. 223. "If art become apparent, it disgusts the reader."—*Jamieson's Rhet.*, p. 80. "Though perspicuity be more properly a rhetorical than a grammatical quality, I thought it better to include it in this book."—*Campbell's Rhet.*, p. 238. "Although the efficient cause be obscure, the final cause of those sensations lies open."—*Blair's Rhet.*, p. 29. "Although the barrenness of language, and the want of words be doubtless one cause of the invention of tropes."—*Ib.*, p. 135. "Though it enforce not its instructions, yet it furnishes us with a greater variety."—*Ib.*, p. 353. "In other cases, though the idea be one, the words remain quite separate"—*Priestley's Gram.*, p. 140. "Though the Form of our language be more simple, and has that peculiar Beauty."—*Buchanan's Syntax*, p. v. "Human works are of no significancy till they be completed."—*Kames, El. of Crit.*, i, 245. "Our disgust lessens gradually till it vanish altogether."—*Ib.*, i, 338. "And our relish improves by use, till it arrive at perfection."—*Ib.*, i, 338. "So long as he keep himself in his own proper element."—COKE: *ib.*, i, 233. "Whether this translation were ever published or not I am wholly ignorant."—*Sale's Koran*, i, 13. "It is false to affirm, 'As it is day, it is light,' unless it actually be day."—*Harris's Hermes*, p. 246. "But we may at midnight affirm, 'If it be day, it is light.'"—*Ibid.* "If the Bible be true, it is a volume of unspeakable interest."—*Dickinson.* "Though he were a son, yet learned he obedience by the things which he suffered."—*Heb.*, v, 8. "If David then call him Lord, how is he his son?"—*Matt.*, xxii, 45.

"'Tis hard to say, if greater want of skill
  Appear in writing or in judging ill."—*Pope, Ess. on Crit.*

UNDER NOTE X.—FALSE SUBJUNCTIVES.

"If a man have built a house, the house is his."—*Wayland's Moral Science*, p. 286.

[FORMULE.—Not proper, because the verb *have built*, which extends the subjunctive mood into the perfect tense, has the appearance of disagreeing with its nominative *man*. But, according to Note 10th to Rule 14th, "Every such use or extension of the subjunctive mood, as the reader will be likely to mistake for a discord between the verb and its nominative, ought to be avoided as an impropriety." Therefore, *have built* should be *has built*; thus, "If a man *has built* a house, the house is his."]

"If God have required them of him, as is the fact, he has time."—*Ib.*, p. 351. "Unless a previous understanding to the contrary have been had with the Principal."—*Berrian's Circular*, p. 5. "O if thou have Hid them in some flowery cave."—*Milton's Comus*, l. 239. "O if Jove's will Have linked that amorous power to thy soft lay."—*Milton, Sonnet* 1. "SUBJUNCTIVE MOOD: If thou love, If thou loved, If thou have loved, If thou had loved, If thou shall or will love, If thou shall or will have loved."—*L. Murray's Gram.*, 2d Ed., p. 71; *Cooper's Murray*, 58; *D. Adams's Gram.*, 48; and others. "Till religion, the pilot of the soul, have lent thee her unfathomable coil."—*Tupper's Thoughts*, p. 170. "Whether nature or art contribute most to form an orator, is a trifling inquiry."—*Blair's Rhet.*, p. 338. "Year after year steals something from us; till the decaying fabric totter of itself, and crumble at length into dust."—*Murray's Key*, 8vo, p. 225. "If spiritual pride have not entirely vanquished humility."—*West's Letters*, p. 184. "Whether he have gored a son, or have gored a daughter."—*Exodus*, xxi, 31. "It is doubtful whether the object introduced by way of simile, relate to what goes before, or to what follows."—*Kames, El. of Crit.*, ii, 45.

> "And bridle in thy headlong wave,
> Till thou our summons answer'd have."—*Milt., Comus*, l. 887.

RULE XV.—FINITE VERBS.

When the nominative is a collective noun conveying the idea of plurality, the Verb must agree with it in the plural number: as, "The *council were divided*."—"The *college* of cardinals *are* the electors of the pope."—*Murray's Key*, p. 176. "Quintus Curtius relates, that a *number* of them *were drowned* in the river Lycus."—*Home's Art of Thinking*, p. 125.

> "Yon *host come* learn'd in academic rules."
> —*Rowe's Lucan*, vii, 401.

> "While heaven's high *host* on hallelujahs *live*."
> —*Young's N. Th.*, iv, 378.

OBSERVATIONS ON RULE XV.

OBS. 1.—To this rule there are *no exceptions*; because, the collective noun being a name which even in the singular number "signifies *many*," the verb which agrees with it, can never properly be singular, unless the collection be taken literally as one aggregate, and not as "conveying the idea of plurality." Thus, the collective noun singular being in general susceptible of two senses, and consequently admitting two modes of concord, the form of the verb, whether singular or plural, becomes the principal index to the particular sense in which the nominative is taken. After such a noun, we can use either a singular verb, agreeing with it literally, strictly, formally, according to Rule 14th; as, "The whole *number* WAS two thousand and six hundred;" or a plural one, agreeing with it figuratively, virtually, ideally, according to Rule 15th; as, "The whole *number* WERE two thousand and six hundred."—*2 Chron.*, xxvi, 12. So, when the collective noun is an antecedent, the relative having in itself no distinction of the numbers, its verb becomes the index to the sense of all three; as, "Wherefore lift up thy prayer for the *remnant that* IS *left.*"—*Isaiah*, xxxvii, 4. "Wherefore lift up thy prayer for the *remnant that* ARE *left.*"—*2 Kings*, xix, 4. Ordinarily the word *remnant* conveys no idea of plurality; but, it being here applied to persons, and having a meaning to which the mere singular neuter noun is not well adapted, the latter construction is preferable to the former. The Greek version varies more in the two places here cited; being plural in Isaiah, and singular in Kings. The Latin Vulgate, in both, is, "*pro reliquiis quæ repertæ sunt*:" i.e., "for the *remains*, or *remnants*, that are found."

OBS. 2.—Dr. Adam's rule is this: "A collective noun may be joined with a verb either of the singular or of the plural number; as, *Multitudo stat*, or *stant*; the multitude stands, or stand."—*Latin and English Gram.* To this doctrine, Lowth, Murray, and others, add: "Yet not without regard to the *import of the word*, as conveying *unity or plurality of idea.*"—*Lowth*, p. 74; *Murray*, 152. If these latter authors mean, that collective nouns are permanently divided in import, so that some are invariably determined to the idea of unity, and others to that of plurality, they are wrong in principle; for, as Dr. Adam remarks, "A collective noun, when joined with a verb singular, expresses many considered as one whole; but when joined with a verb plural, it signifies many separately, or as individuals."—*Adam's Gram.*, p. 154. And if this alone is what their addition means, it is entirely useless; and so, for all the purposes of parsing, is the singular half of the rule itself. Kirkham divides this rule into two, one for "unity of idea," and the other for "plurality of idea," shows how each is to be applied in parsing, according to his "*systematick order*;" and then, turning round with a gallant tilt at his own work, condemns both, as idle fabrications, which it were better to reject than to retain; alleging that, "The existence of such a thing as 'unity or plurality of idea,' as applicable to nouns of this class, is *doubtful*."—*Kirkham's Gram.*, p. 59.[394] How then shall a plural verb or pronoun, after a collective noun, be parsed, seeing it does not agree with the noun by the ordinary rule of agreement? Will any one say, that every such construction is *bad English*? If this cannot be maintained, rules eleventh and fifteenth of this series are necessary. But when the noun conveys the idea of unity or takes the plural form, the verb or pronoun has no other than a literal agreement by the common rule; as,

"A *priesthood*, such *as* Baal's *was* of old,
A *people*, such *as* never *was* till now."—*Cowper*.

OBS. 3.—Of the construction of the verb and collective noun, a late British author gives the following account: "Collective nouns are substantives *which* signify *many in the singular number*. Collective nouns are of two sorts: 1. Those which cannot become plural like other substantives; as, nobility, mankind, &c. 2. Those which can be made plural by the usual rules for a substantive; as, 'A multitude, multitudes; a crowd, crowds;' &c. Substantives which imply plurality in the singular number, and consequently have no other plural, generally require a plural verb. They are cattle, cavalry, clergy, commonalty, gentry, laity, mankind, nobility, peasantry people, populace, public, rabble, &c. [;] as, 'The public *are* informed.' Collective nouns which form a regular plural, such as, number, numbers; multitude, multitudes; have, like all other substantives, a singular verb, when they are in the singular number; and a plural verb, when they are in the plural number; as, 'A number of people *is* assembled; Numbers *are* assembled.'—'The fleet *was* dispersed; a *part* of it *was* injured; the several *parts are* now collected.'"— *Nixon's Parser*, p. 120. To this, his main text, the author appends a note, from which the following passages are extracted: "There are few persons acquainted with Grammar, who may not have noticed, in many authors as well as speakers, an irregularity in supposing collective nouns to have, at one time, a singular meaning, and consequently to require a singular verb; and, at an other time, to have a plural meaning, and therefore to require a plural verb. This irregularity appears to have arisen from the want of a clear idea of the nature of a collective noun. This defect the author has endeavoured to supply; and, upon his definition, he has founded the two rules above. It is allowed on all sides that, hitherto, no satisfactory rules have been produced to enable the pupil to ascertain, with any degree of certainty, when a collective noun should have a singular verb, and when a plural one. A rule that simply tells its examiner, that when a collective noun in the nominative case conveys the idea of unity, its verb should be singular; and when it implies plurality, its verb should be plural, is of very little value; for such a rule will prove the *pupil's being in the right*, whether he *should* put the verb in the singular or the plural."—*Ibid.*

OBS. 4.—The foregoing explanation has many faults; and whoever trusts to it, or to any thing like it, will certainly be very much misled. In the first place, it is remarkable that an author who could suspect in others "the *want of a clear idea* of the nature of a collective noun," should have hoped to supply the defect by a definition so ambiguous and ill-written as is the one above. Secondly, his subdivision of this class of nouns into two sorts, is both baseless and nugatory; for that plurality which has reference to the individuals of an assemblage, has no manner of connexion or affinity with that which refers to more than one such aggregate; nor is there any interference of the one with the other, or any ground at all for supposing that the absence of the latter is, has been, or ought to be, the occasion for adopting the former. Hence, thirdly, his two rules, (though, so far as they go, they seem not untrue in themselves,) by their limitation under this false division, exclude and deny the true construction of the verb with the greater part of our collective nouns. For, fourthly, the first of these rules rashly presumes that any collective noun which in the singular number implies a plurality of individuals, is consequently destitute of any other plural; and the second accordingly supposes that no such nouns as, council, committee, jury, meeting, society, assembly, court, college, company, army, host, band, retinue, train, multitude, number, part, half, portion, majority, minority, remainder, set, sort, kind, class, nation, tribe, family, race, and a hundred more, can ever be properly used with a plural verb, except when they assume the plural form. To prove the falsity of this supposition, is needless. And, finally, the objection which this author advances against the common rules, is very far from proving them useless, or not greatly preferable to his own. If they do not in every instance enable the student to ascertain with certainty which form of concord he ought to prefer, it is only because no rules can possibly tell a man precisely when he ought to entertain the idea of unity, and when that of plurality. In some instances, these ideas are unavoidably mixed or associated, so that it is of little or no consequence which form of the verb we prefer; as, "Behold, the *people* IS *one,* and *they have all* one language."—*Gen.*, xi, 6.

"Well, if a king's a lion, at the least
The *people* ARE a many-headed *beast*."—*Pope*, Epist. i, l. 120.

OBS. 5.—Lindley Murray says, "On many occasions, *where* a noun of multitude is used, it is very difficult to decide, whether the verb should be in the singular, or in the plural number; and this difficulty has induced some grammarians to cut the knot at once, and to assert that every noun of multitude must always be considered as conveying the idea of unity."—*Octavo Gram.*, p. 153. What these occasions, or who these grammarians, are, I know not; but it is certain that the difficulty here imagined does not concern the application of such rules as require the verb and pronoun to conform to the sense intended; and, where there is no apparent impropriety in adopting either number, there is no occasion to raise a scruple as to which is right. To cut knots by dogmatism, and to tie them by sophistry, are employments equally vain. It cannot be denied that there are in every multitude both a unity and a plurality, one or the other of which must be preferred as the principle of concord for the verb or the pronoun, or for both. Nor is the number of nouns small, or their use unfrequent, which, according to our best authors, admit of either construction: though Kirkham assails and repudiates *his own rules*, because, "Their application is quite limited."—*Grammar in Familiar Lectures*, p. 59.

OBS. 6.—Murray's doctrine seems to be, not that collective nouns are generally susceptible of two senses in respect to number, but that some naturally convey the idea of unity, others, that of plurality, and a few, either of these senses. The last, which are probably ten times more numerous than all the rest, he somehow merges or forgets, so as to speak of *two classes* only: saying, "Some nouns of multitude certainly convey to the mind an idea of plurality, others, that of a whole as one thing, and others again, sometimes that of unity, and sometimes that of plurality. On this ground, it is warrantable, and consistent with the nature of things, to apply a plural verb and pronoun *to the one class*, and a singular verb and pronoun *to the other*. We shall immediately perceive the *impropriety* of the following constructions: 'The clergy *has* withdrawn *itself* from the temporal courts;' 'The assembly *was* divided in *its* opinion;' &c."—*Octavo Gram.*, p. 153. The simple fact is, that *clergy, assembly*, and perhaps every other collective noun, may sometimes convey the idea of unity, and sometimes that of plurality; but an "*opinion*" or a voluntary "*withdrawing*" is a *personal* act or quality; *wherefore* it is here more consistent to adopt the plural sense and construction, in which alone we take the collection as individuals, or persons.

OBS. 7.—Although a uniformity of number is generally preferable to diversity, in the construction of words that refer to the same collective noun: and although many grammarians deny that any departure from such uniformity is allowable; yet, if the singular be put first, a plural pronoun may sometimes follow without obvious impropriety: as, "So Judah *was* carried away out of *their* land."—*2 Kings*, xxv, 21. "Israel is reproved and threatened for *their* impiety and idolatry."—*Friends' Bible, Hosea*, x. "There *is* the enemy *who wait* to give us battle."—*Murray's Introductory Reader*, p. 36. When the idea of plurality predominates in the author's mind, a plural verb is sometimes used *before* a collective noun that has the singular article *an* or *a*; as, "There *are a sort* of authors, *who seem* to take up with appearances."— *Addison*. "Here *are a number* of facts or incidents leading to the end in view."—*Kames, El. of Crit.*, ii, 296. "There *are a great number* of exceedingly good writers among the French."—*Maunder's Gram.*, p. 11.

"There in the forum *swarm a numerous train*,
The subject of debate a townsman slain."
—*Pope, Iliad*, B. xviii, l. 578.

OBS. 8.—Collective nouns, when they are merely *partitive* of the plural, like the words *sort* and *number* above, are usually connected with a plural verb, even though they have a singular definitive; as, "And *this sort of* adverbs commonly *admit* of Comparison."—*Buchanan's English Syntax*, p. 64. Here, perhaps, it would be better to say, "*Adverbs of this sort* commonly admit of comparison." "*A part* of the exports *consist* of raw silk."—*Webster's Improved Gram.*, p. 100. This construction is censured by Murray, in his octavo Gram., p. 148; where we are told, that the verb should agree with the first noun only. Dr. Webster alludes to this circumstance, in *improving* his grammar, and admits that, "A part of the exports *consists,* seems to be more correct."—*Improved Gram.*, p. 100. Yet he retains his original text, and obviously thinks it a light thing, that, "in some cases," his rules or examples "may not be vindicable." (See Obs. 14th, 15th, and 16th, on Rule 14th, of this code.) It would, I think, be better to say, "The exports consist *partly* of raw silk." Again: "*A multitude* of Latin words *have,* of late, been poured in upon us."—*Blair's Rhet.*, p. 94. Better, perhaps: "*Latin words, in great multitude*, have, of late, been poured in upon us." So: "For *the bulk* of *writers* are very apt to confound them with each other."—*Ib.*, p. 97. Better: "For *most writers* are very apt to confound them with each other." In the following example, (here cited as *Kames* has it, *El. of Crit.*, ii, 247,) either the verb *is,* or the phrase, "*There are some moveless men*" might as well have been used:

"There *are a sort* of men, whose visages
Do cream and mantle like a standing pond."—*Shak.*

OBS. 9.—Collections of *things* are much less frequently and less properly regarded as individuals, or under the idea of plurality, than collections of *persons.* This distinction may account for the difference of construction in the two clauses of the following example; though I rather doubt whether a plural verb ought to be used in the former: "The *number* of commissioned *officers* in the guards *are* to the marching regiments as one to eleven: the *number* of *regiments* given to the guards, compared with those given to the line, *is* about three to one."—*Junius*, p. 147. Whenever the multitude is spoken of with reference to a personal act or quality, the verb ought, as I before suggested, to be in the plural number; as, "The public *are informed*."—"The plaintiff's counsel *have assumed* a difficult task."—"The committee *were instructed* to prepare a remonstrance." "The English nation *declare* they are grossly injured by *their* representatives."—*Junius*, p. 147. "One particular class of men *are* permitted to call *themselves* the King's friends."—*Id.*, p. 176. "The Ministry *have* realized the compendious ideas of Caligula."—*Id.*, p. 177. It is in accordance with this principle, that the following sentences have plural verbs and pronouns, though their definitives are singular, and perhaps ought to be singular: "So depraved *were that people* whom in their history we so much admire."—HUME: *M'Ilvaine's Lect.*, p. 400. "Oh, *this people have sinned* a great sin, and have made them gods of gold."—*Exodus*, xxxii, 31. "*This people* thus gathered *have* not wanted those trials."—*Barclay's Works*, i, 460. The following examples, among others, are censured by Priestley, Murray, and the copyists of the latter, without sufficient discrimination, and for a reason which I think fallacious; namely, "because the ideas they represent seem not to be sufficiently divided in the mind:"—"The court of Rome *were* not without solicitude."—*Hume*. "The house of Lords *were* so much influenced by these reasons."—*Id.* See *Priestley's Gram.*, p. 188; *Murray's*, 152; *R. C. Smith's*, 129; *Ingersoll's*, 248; and others.

OBS. 10.—In general, a collective noun, unless it be made plural in form, no more admits a plural adjective before it, than any other singular noun. Hence the impropriety of putting *these* or *those* before *kind* or *sort*; as, "*These kind* of knaves I know."—*Shakspeare*. Hence, too, I infer that *cattle* is not a collective noun, as Nixon would have it to be, but an irregular plural which has no singular; because we can say *these cattle* or *those cattle*, but neither a bullock nor a herd is ever called *a cattle, this cattle*, or *that cattle*. And if "*cavalry, clergy, commonalty*," &c., were like this word, they would all be plurals also, and not "substantives which imply plurality in the singular number, and consequently have no other plural." Whence it appears, that the writer who most broadly charges others with not understanding the nature of a collective noun, has most of all misconceived it himself. If there are not *many clergies*, it is because *the clergy* is one body, with one Head, and not because it is in a particular sense many. And, since the forms of words are not necessarily confined to things that exist, who shall say that the plural word *clergies*, as I have just used it, is not good English?

OBS. 11.—If we say, "*these people*," "*these gentry*," "*these folk*," we make *people, gentry*, and *folk*, not only irregular plurals, but plurals to which there are no correspondent singulars; but by these phrases, we must mean certain individuals, and not more than one people, gentry, or folk. But these names are sometimes collective nouns singular; and, as such, they may have verbs of either number, according to the sense; and may also form regular plurals, as *peoples*, and *folks*; though we seldom, if ever, speak of *gentries*; and *folks* is now often irregularly applied to persons, as if one person were *a folk*. So *troops* is sometimes irregularly, if not improperly, put for *soldiers*, as if a soldier were *a troop*; as, "While those gallant *troops*, by *whom* every hazardous, every laborious service is performed, are left to perish."—*Junius*, p. 147. In Genesis, xxvii, 29th, we read, "Let *people* serve thee, and nations bow down to thee." But, according to the Vulgate, it ought to be, "Let *peoples* serve thee, and nations bow down to thee;" according to the Septuagint, "Let *nations* serve thee, and *rulers* bow down to thee." Among Murray's "instances of false syntax," we find the text, "This people draweth near to me with their mouth," &c.—*Octavo Gram.*, Vol. ii, p. 49. This is corrected in his Key, thus: "*These* people *draw* near to me with their mouth."—*Ib.*, ii, 185. The Bible has it: "This people *draw near me* with their mouth."—*Isaiah,* xxix, 13. And again: "This people *draweth nigh unto me* with their mouth.,"—*Matt.,* xv, 8. Dr. Priestley thought it ought to be, "This people *draws* nigh unto me with their *mouths.*"—*Priestley's Gram.,* p. 63. The second evangelist omits some words: "This people *honoureth* me with their lips, but *their heart* is far from me."—*Mark,* vii, 6. In my opinion, the plural verb is here to be preferred; because the pronoun *their* is plural, and the worship spoken of was a personal rather than a national act. Yet the adjective *this* must be retained, if the text specify the Jews as a people. As to the words *mouth* and *heart,* they are to be understood figuratively of *speech* and *love;* and I agree not with Priestley, that the plural number must necessarily be used. See Note 4th to Rule 4th.

OBS. 12.—In making an assertion concerning a number or quantity with some indefinite excess or allowance, we seem sometimes to take for the subject of the verb what is really the object of a preposition; as, "In a sermon, there *may be* from three to five, or six heads."—*Blair's Rhet.,* p. 313. "In those of Germany, there *are* from eight to twelve professors."—*Dwight, Lit. Convention,* p. 138. "About a million and a half *was subscribed* in a few days."—*N. Y. Daily Advertiser.* "About one hundred feet of the Muncy dam *has been swept off.*"—*N. Y. Observer.* "Upwards of one hundred thousand dollars *have been appropriated.*"—*Newspaper.* "But I fear there *are* between twenty and thirty of them."—*Tooke's Diversions,* ii, 441. "Besides which, there *are* upwards of fifty smaller islands."—*Balbi's Geog.,* p. 30. "On board of which *embarked* upwards of three hundred passengers."—*Robertson's Amer.,* ii, 419. The propriety of using *above* or *upwards of* for *more than,* is questionable, but the practice is not uncommon. When there is a preposition before what seems at first to be the subject of the verb, as in the foregoing instances, I imagine there is an ellipsis of the word *number, amount, sum* or *quantity*; the first of which words is a collective noun and may have a verb either singular or plural: as, "In a sermon, there may be *any number* from three to five or six heads."

This is awkward, to be sure; but what does the Doctor's sentence *mean*, unless it is, that there *may be an optional number* of heads, varying from three to six?

OBS. 13.—Dr. Webster says, "When an aggregate amount is expressed by the plural names of the particulars composing that amount, the verb may be in the singular number; as, 'There *was* more than a hundred and fifty thousand pounds sterling.' *Mavor's Voyages*." To this he adds, "However repugnant to the principles of grammar this may seem at first view, the practice is correct; for the affirmation is not made of the individual parts or divisions named, the *pounds*, but of the entire sum or amount."— *Philosophical Gram.*, p. 146; *Improved Gram.*, p. 100. The fact is, that the Doctor here, as in some other instances, deduces a false rule from a correct usage. It is plain that either the word *more*, taken substantively, or the noun to which it relates as an adjective, is the only nominative to the verb *was*. Mavor does not affirm that there *were* a hundred and fitly thousand pounds; but that there *was more*—i.e., more *money* than so many pounds *are*, or *amount to*. Oliver B. Peirce, too. falls into a multitude of strange errors respecting the nature of *more than*, and the construction of other words that accompany these. See his "Analytical Rules," and the manner in which he applies them, in "*The Grammar,*" p. 195 *et seq.*

OBS. 14.—Among certain educationists,—grammarians, arithmeticians, schoolmasters, and others,—there has been of late not a little dispute concerning the syntax of the phraseology which we use, or should use, in expressing *multiplication*, or in speaking of *abstract numbers*. For example: is it better to say, "Twice one *is* two," or, "Twice one *are* two?"—"Two times one *is* two," or, "Two times one *are* two?"—"Twice two *is* four," or, "Twice two *are* four?"—"Thrice one *is* or *are*, three?"—"Three times one *is*, or *are*, three?"—"Three times naught *is*, or *are*, naught?"—"Thrice three *is*, or *are*, nine?"—"Three times four *is*, or *are*, twelve?"—"Seven times three *make,* or *makes,* twenty-one?"—"Three times his age *do* not, or *does* not, equal mine?"—"Three times the quantity *is* not, or *are* not, sufficient?"—"Three quarters of the men were discharged; and three quarters of the money *was,* or *were,* sent back?"—"As 2 *is* to 4, so *is* 6 to 12;" or, "As two *are* to four, so *are* six to twelve?"

OBS. 15.—Most of the foregoing expressions, though all are perhaps intelligible enough in common practice, are, in some respect, difficult of analysis, or grammatical resolution. I think it possible, however, to frame an argument of some plausibility in favour of every one of them. Yet it is hardly to be supposed, that any *teacher* will judge them all to be alike justifiable, or feel no interest in the questions which have been raised about them. That the language of arithmetic is often defective or questionable in respect to grammar, may be seen not only in many an ill choice between the foregoing variant and contrasted modes of expression, but in sundry other examples, of a somewhat similar character, for which it may be less easy to find advocates and published arguments. What critic will not judge the following phraseology to be faulty? "4 times two units *is* 8 units, and 4 times 5 tens *is* twenty tens."—*Chase's Common School Arithmetic,* 1848, p. 42. Or this? "1 time 1 is l. 2 times 1 are 2; 1 time 4 is 4, 2 times 4 are 8."— *Ray's Arithmetic,* 1853. Or this? "8 and 7 *is* 15, 9's out leaves 6; 3 and 8 *is* 11, 9's out leaves 2."—*Babcock's Practical Arithmetic,* 1829, p. 22. Or this again? "3 times 3 *is* 9, and 2 we had to carry *is* 11."—*Ib.,* p. 20.

OBS. 16.—There are several different opinions as to what constitutes the grammatical subject of the verb in any ordinary English expression of multiplication. Besides this, we have some variety in the phraseology which precedes the verb; so that it is by no means certain, either that the multiplying terms are always of the same part of speech, or that the true nominative to the verb is not essentially different in different examples. Some absurdly teach, that an abstract number is necessarily expressed by "*a singular noun,*" with only a singular meaning; that such a number, when multiplied, is always, of itself the subject of the assertion; and, consequently, that the verb must be singular, as agreeing only with this "singular noun." Others, not knowing how to parse separately the multiplying word or words and the number multiplied, take them both or all together as "the grammatical subject" with which the verb must agree. But, among these latter expounders, there are two opposite opinions on the very essential point, whether this "*entire expression*" requires a singular verb or a plural one:—as, whether we ought to say, "Twice one *is* two," or, "Twice one *are* two;"—"Twice two *is* four," or, "Twice two *are* four;"—"Three times one *is* three," or, "Three times one *are* three;"—"Three times three *is* nine," or, "Three times three *are* nine." Others, again, according to Dr. Bullions, and possibly according to their own notion, find the grammatical subject, sometimes, if not generally, in the multiplying term only; as, perhaps, is the case with those who write or speak as follows: "If we say, 'Three times one *are* three,' we make '*times*' the subject of the verb."—*Bullions, Analyt. and Pract. Gram.*, 1849, p. 39. "Thus, 2 times 1 *are* 2; 2 times 2 *are* four; 2 times 3 *are* 6."—*Chase's C. S. Arith.*, p. 43. "Say, 2 times O *are* O; 2 times 1 *are* 2."—*Robinson's American Arith.*, 1825, p. 24.

OBS. 17.—Dr. Bullions, with a strange blunder of some sort in almost every sentence, propounds and defends his opinion on this subject thus: "Numeral *adjectives*, being *also names* of numbers, are often used as nouns, and so have the inflection and construction of nouns: thus, by *twos*, by *tens*, by *fifties*. *Two* is an even number. Twice *two* is four. Four *is* equal to twice two. In some arithmetics the language employed in the operation of multiplying—such as 'Twice two *are* four, twice three *are* six'—is incorrect. It should be, 'Twice two *is* four,' &c.; for the word *two* is used as a singular noun—the name of a number. The adverb '*twice*' is *not in construction with it*, and consequently does not make it plural. The meaning is, 'The number two taken twice is equal to four.' For the same reason we should say, 'Three times *two* is six,' because the meaning is, 'Two taken three times *is* six.' If we say, 'Three times one *are* three,' we make '*times*' the subject of the verb, whereas the subject of the verb really is '*one*,' and '*times*' is in the *objective of number* (§828). 2:4:: 6:12, should be read, 'As 2 *is* to 4, so *is* 6 to 12;' not 'As two *are* to four, so *are* six to twelve.' But when numerals denoting more than one, are used as adjectives, with a substantive expressed or understood, they must have a plural construction."—*Bullions, Analyt. and Pract. Gram.*, 1849, p. 39.

OBS. 18.—Since nouns and adjectives are different parts of speech, the suggestion, that, "Numeral *adjectives* are *also names*, or *nouns*," is, upon the very face of it, a flat absurdity; and the notion that "the name of a number" above unity, conveys only and always the idea of unity, like an ordinary "singular noun," is an other. A number in arithmetic is most commonly an *adjective* in grammar; and it is always, in form, an expression that tells *how many*, or—"denotes *how many things* are spoken of."—*Chase*, p. 11. But the *name* of a number is also a number, whenever it is *not made plural* in form. Thus *four* is a number, but *fours* is not; so *ten* is a number, but *tens* is not. Arithmetical numbers, which run on to infinity, severally *consist* of a *definite idea of how many*; each is a *precise count* by the unit; *one* being the beginning of the series, and the measure of every successive step. Grammatical numbers are only the verbal forms which distinguish one thing from more of the same sort. Thus the word *fours* or *tens*, unless some arithmetical number be prefixed to it, signifies nothing but a mere plurality which repeats indefinitely the collective idea of *four* or *ten*.

OBS. 19.—All actual *names* of numbers calculative, except *one*, (for *naught*, though it fills a place among numbers, is, in itself, a mere negation of number; and such terms as *oneness, unity, duality*, are not used in calculation,) are *collective nouns*—a circumstance which seems to make the discussion of the present topic appropriate to the location which is here given it under Rule 15th. Each of them denotes a particular aggregate *of units*. And if each, as signifying one whole, may convey the idea of unity, and take a singular verb; each, again, as denoting so many units, may quite as naturally take a plural verb, and be made to convey the idea of plurality. For the mere abstractness of numbers, or their separation from all "*particular objects*," by no means obliges us to limit them always to the construction with verbs singular. If it is right to say, "Two *is* an even number;" it is certainly no error to say, "Two *are* an even number." If it is allowable to say, "As 2 *is* to 4, so *is* 6 to 12;" it is as well, if not better, to say, "As two *are* to four, so *are* six to twelve." If it is correct to say, "Four *is* equal to twice two;" it is quite as grammatical to say, "Four *are* equal to twice two." Bullions bids say, "Twice two *is* four," and, "Three times two *is* six;" but I very much prefer to say, "Twice two *are* four," and, "Three times two *are* six." The Doctor's reasoning, whereby he condemns the latter phraseology, is founded only upon false assumptions. This I expect to show; and more—that the word which he prefers, is wrong.

OBS. 20.—As to what constitutes the subject of the verb in multiplication, I have already noticed *three different opinions*. There are yet three or four more, which must not be overlooked in a general examination of this grammatical dispute. Dr. Bullions's notion on this point, is stated with so little consistency, that one can hardly say what it is. At first, he seems to find his nominative in the multiplicand, "used as a singular noun;" but, when he ponders a little on the text, "*Twice two is four*," he finds the leading term not to be the word "*two*," but the word "*number*," understood. He resolves, indeed, that no one of the four words used, "is in construction with" any of the rest; for he thinks, "The meaning is, '*The number* two *taken* twice is *equal to* four.'" Here, then, is a *fourth opinion* in relation to the subject of the verb: it must be "*number*" understood. Again, it is conceded by the same hand, that, "When numerals denoting more than one, are used as adjectives, with a substantive expressed or understood, they must have a plural construction." Now who can show that this is not the case in general with the numerals of multiplication? To explain the syntax of "*Twice two are four*," what can be more rational than to say, "The sense is, 'Twice two *units*, or *things*, are four?'" Is it not plain, that twice two things, of any sort, are four things of that same sort, and only so? Twice two duads are how many? Answer: *Four duads*, or *eight units*. Here, then, is a *fifth opinion*,— and a very fair one too,—according to which we have for the subject of the verb, not "*two*" nor "*twice*" nor "*twice two*," nor "*number*," understood before "*two*," but the plural noun "*units*" or "*things*" implied in or after the multiplicand.

OBS. 21.—It is a doctrine taught by sundry grammarians, and to some extent true, that a neuter verb between two nominatives "may agree with either of them." (See Note 5th to Rule 14th, and the footnote.) When, therefore, a person who knows this, meets with such examples as, "Twice one *are* two;"—"Twice one unit *are* two units;"—"Thrice one *are* three;"— he will of course be apt to refer the verb to the nominative which follows it, rather than to that which precedes it; taking the meaning to be, "*Two are* twice one;"—"*Two units are* twice one unit;"—"*Three are* thrice one." Now, if such is the sense, the construction in each of these instances is right, because it accords with such sense; the interpretation is right also, because it is the only one adapted to such a construction; and we have, concerning the subject of the verb, a *sixth opinion*,—a very proper one too,—that it is found, not where it is most natural to look for it, in the expression of the *factors*, but in a noun which is either uttered or implied in the *product*. But, no doubt, it is better to avoid this construction, by using such a verb as may be said to agree with the number multiplied. Again, and lastly, there may be, touching all such cases as, "Twice *one are* two," a *seventh opinion*, that the subject of the verb is the product taken *substantively*, and not as a numeral *adjective*. This idea, or the more comprehensive one, that all abstract numbers are nouns substantive, settles nothing concerning the main question, What form of the verb is required by an abstract number above unity? If the number be supposed an adjective, referring to the implied term *units*, or *things*, the verb must of course be plural; but if it be called a *collective noun*, the verb only follows and fixes "the idea of plurality," or "the idea of unity," as the writer or speaker chooses to adopt the one or the other.

OBS. 22.—It is marvellous, that four or five monosyllables, uttered together in a common simple sentence, could give rise to all this diversity of opinion concerning the subject of the verb; but, after all, the chief difficulty presented by the phraseology of multiplication, is that of ascertaining, not "the grammatical subject of the verb," but the grammatical relation between the multiplier and the multiplicand—the true way of parsing the terms *once, twice, three times*, &c., but especially the word *times*. That there must be some such relation, is obvious; but what is it? and how is it to be known? To most persons, undoubtedly, "*Twice two*," and, "*Three times two*," seem to be *regular phrases*, in which the words cannot lack syntactical connexion; yet Dr. Bullions, who is great authority with some thinkers, denies all immediate or direct relation between the word "*two*," and the term before it, preferring to parse both "*twice*" and "*three times*" as adjuncts to the participle "*taken*," understood. He says, "The adverb '*twice*' is not in construction with '*two*,' and consequently does not make it plural." His first assertion here is, in my opinion, untrue; and the second implies the very erroneous doctrine, that the word *twice*, if it relate to a singular term, *will "make it plural*." From a misconception like this, it probably is, that some who ought to be very accurate in speech, are afraid to say, "Twice one *is* two," or, "Thrice one *is* three," judging the singular verb to be wrong; and some there are who think, that "*usage* will not permit" a careful scholar so to speak. Now, analysis favours the singular form here; and it is contrary to a plain principle of General Grammar, to suppose that a *plural* verb can be demanded by any phrase which is made *collectively* the subject of the assertion. (See Note 3d, and Obs. 13th, 14th, 15th, and 16th, under Rule 14th.) *Are* is, therefore, *not required here*; and, if allowable, it is so only on the supposition that the leading nominative is put after it.

OBS. 23.—In Blanchard's small Arithmetic, published in 1854, the following inculcations occur: "When we say, 3 times 4 trees are 12 trees, we have reference to the *objects* counted; but in saying 3 times 4 *is* twelve, we mean, that 3 times the *number* 4, *is the number* 12. Here we use 4 and 12, not as numeral *adjectives*, but as *nouns*, the *names* of particular *numbers*, and as such, each conveys the idea of *unity*, and *the entire expression* is the subject of *is*, and conveys the *idea of unity*."—P. iv. Here we have, with an additional error concerning "the entire expression," a repetition of Dr. Bullions's erroneous assumption, that the name of a particular number, as being "a singular noun," must "convey the idea of unity," though the number itself be a distinct plurality. These men talk as if there were an absurdity in affirming that "the number 4" is *plural*! But, if *four* be taken as only one thing, how can *three* multiply this one thing into *twelve*? It is by no means proper to affirm, that, "*Every* four, taken three times, *is*, or *are*, twelve;" for three instances, or "*times*," of the *figure* 4, or of the *word four*, are only three 4's, or three verbal *fours*. And is it not *because* "*the number* 4" *is plural—is in itself four units*—and because the word *four*, or the figure 4, conveys explicitly the *idea of this plurality*, that the multiplication table is true, where it says, "3 times 4 *are* 12?" It is not right to say, "Three times one quaternion is twelve;" nor is it quite unobjectionable to say, with Blanchard "3 *times the number* 4, *is the number* 12." Besides, this pretended interpretation explains nothing. The syntax of the shorter text, "3 times 4 *is* 12," is in no way justified or illustrated by it. Who does not perceive that *the four* here spoken of must be four *units*, or four *things* of some sort; and that no *such* "four," multiplied by 3, or *till* "3 *times*," can "convey the idea of unity," or match a singular verb? Dr. Webster did not so conceive of this "abstract number," or of "the entire expression" in which it is multiplied; for he says, "Four times four *amount* to sixteen."—*American Dict., w. Time.*

OBS. 24.—In fact no phrase of multiplication is of such a nature that it can, with any plausibility be reckoned a composite subject of the verb. *Once, twice,* and *thrice,* are adverbs; and each of them may, in general, be parsed as relating directly to the multiplicand. Their construction, as well as that of the plural verb, is agreeable to the Latin norm; as, when Cicero says of somebody, "Si, *bis bina* quot *essent,* didicisset,"—"If he had learned how many *twice two are.*"—See *Ainsworth's Dict., w. Binus.* The phrases, "*one time,*" for *once,* and "*two times*" for *twice,* seem puerile expressions: they are not often used by competent teachers. *Thrice* is a good word, but more elegant than popular. Above *twice,* we use the phrases, *three times, four times,* and the like, which are severally composed of a numeral adjective and the noun *times.* If these words were united, as some think they ought to be, the compounds would be *adverbs* of *time repeated*; as, *threetimes, fourtimes,* &c., analogous to *sometimes.* Each word would answer, as each phrase now does, to the question, *How often?* These expressions are taken by some as having a direct adverbial relation to the terms which they qualify; but they are perhaps most commonly explained as being dependent on some preposition understood. See Obs. 1st on Rule 5th, and Obs. 6th on Rule 7th.

OBS. 25.—In multiplying one only, it is evidently best to use a singular verb: as, "Twice *naught* is naught;"—"Three times *one is* three." And, in multiplying any number above *one,* I judge a plural verb to be necessary: as, "Twice *two are* four;"—"Three times *two are six*;" because this number must be just *so many* in order to give the product. Dr. Bullions says, "We should say, 'Three times two *is* six,' because the meaning is, 'Two *taken* three times *is* six.'" This is neither reasoning, nor explanation, nor good grammar. The relation between "*two*" and "*three,*" or the syntax of the word "*times*," or the propriety of the *singular verb*, is no more apparent in the latter expression than in the former. It would be better logic to affirm, "We should say, 'Three times two *are* six;' because the meaning is, 'Two (*units*), taken *for, to,* or *till* three times, are six.'" The preposition *till,* or *until,* is sometimes found in use before an expression of *times numbered*; as, "How oft shall I forgive? *till* seven times? I say not unto thee, *Until* seven times; but, *Until* seventy times seven."—*Matt.,* xviii, 21. But here is still a difficulty with repect to the *multiplying* term, or the word "*times.*" For, unless, by an unallowable ellipsis, "*seventy times seven,*" is presumed to mean, "seventy times *of* seven," the preposition *Until* must govern, not this noun "*times.*" expressed, but an other, understood after "*seven;*" and the meaning must be, "Thou shalt forgive him until *seventy-times* seven times;" or—"until seven *times taken for, to,* or *till,* seventy times."

OBS. 26.—With too little regard to consistency. Dr. Bullions suggests that when "we make '*times*' the subject of the verb," it is not "really" such, but "is in *the objective of number*." He is, doubtless, right in preferring to parse this word as an objective case, rather than as a nominative, in the construction to which he alludes; but to call it an "objective of *number,*" is an uncouth error, a very strange mistake for so great a grammarian to utter: there being in grammar no such thing as "*the objective of number:*" nothing of the sort, even under his own "Special Rule," to which he refers us for it! And, if such a thing there were, so that a *number* could be "*put in the objective case without a governing word,*" (see his §828,) the plural word *times,* since it denotes no particular aggregate of units, could never be an example of it. It is true that *times,* like *days, weeks,* and other nouns of *time,* may be, and often is, in the objective case without a governing word *expressed*; and, in such instances, it may be called the objective of *repetition,* or of *time repeated.* But the construction of the word appears to be such as is common to many nouns of time, of value, or of measure; which, in their relation to other words, seem to resemble adverbs, but which are usually said to be governed by prepositions understood: as, "Three *days* later;" i.e., "Later *by* three days."—"Three *shillings* cheaper;" i.e., "Cheaper *by* three shillings."—"Seven *times* hotter;" i.e., "Hotter *by* seven times."—"Four *feet* high;" i.e., "High *to* four feet."—"Ten *years* old;" i.e., "Old *to* ten years."—"Five *times* ten;" i.e., "Ten *by* five times;" or, perhaps, "Ten *taken till* five times."

NOTE TO RULE XV.

A collective noun conveying the idea of unity, requires a verb in the third person, singular; and generally admits also the regular plural construction: as, "His *army was* defeated."—"His *armies were* defeated."

IMPROPRIETIES FOR CORRECTION.

FALSE SYNTAX UNDER RULE XV.

UNDER THE RULE ITSELF.—THE IDEA OF PLURALITY.

"The gentry is punctilious in their etiquette."

[FORMULE.—Not proper, because the verb *is* is of the singular number, and does not correctly agree with its nominative *gentry*, which is a collective noun conveying rather the idea of plurality. But, according to Rule 15th, "When the nominative is a collective noun conveying the idea of plurality, the verb must agree with it in the plural number." Therefore, *is* should be *are*; thus, "The gentry *are* punctilious in their etiquette."]

"In France the peasantry goes barefoot, and the middle sort makes use of wooden shoes."—HARVEY: *Priestley's Gram.*, p. 188. "The people rejoices in that which should cause sorrow."—See *Murray's Exercises*, p. 49. "My people is foolish, they have not known me."—*Jer.*, iv, 22; *Lowth's*

Gram., p. 75. "For the people speaks, but does not write."—*Philological Museum*, i, 646. "So that all the people that was in the camp, trembled."—*Exodus*, xix, 16. "No company likes to confess that they are ignorant."—*Student's Manual*, p. 217. "Far the greater part of their captives was anciently sacrificed."—*Robertson's America*, i, 339. "Above one half of them was cut off before the return of spring."—*Ib.*, ii, 419. "The other class, termed Figures of Thought, supposes the words to be used in their proper and literal meaning."—*Blair's Rhet.*, p. 133; *Murray's Gram.*, 337. "A multitude of words in their dialect approaches to the Teutonic form, and therefore afford excellent assistance."—*Dr. Murray's Hist of Lang.*, i, 148. "A great majority of our authors is defective in manner."—*James Brown's Crit.* "The greater part of these new-coined words has been rejected."—*Tooke's Diversions*, ii, 445. "The greater part of the words it contains is subject to certain modifications and inflections."—*The Friend*, ii, 123. "While all our youth prefers her to the rest."—*Waller's Poems*, p. 17. "Mankind is appointed to live in a future state."—*Butler's Analogy*, p. 57. "The greater part of human kind speaks and acts wholly by imitation."—*Wright's Gram.*, p. 169. "The greatest part of human gratifications approaches so nearly to vice."—*Ibid.*

"While still the busy world is treading o'er
The paths they trod five thousand years before."—*Young.*

UNDER THE NOTE.—THE IDEA OF UNITY.

"In old English this species of words were numerous."—*Dr. Murray's Hist. of Lang.*, ii, 6. "And a series of exercises in false grammar are introduced towards the end."—*Frost's El. of E. Gram.*, p. iv. "And a jury, in conformity with the same idea, were anciently called *homagium*, the homage, or manhood."—*Webster's Essays*, p. 296. "With respect to the former, there are indeed plenty of means."—*Kames, El. of Crit.*, ii, 319. "The number of school districts have increased since the last year."—*Governor Throop*, 1832. "The Yearly Meeting have purchased with its funds these publications."—*Foster's Reports*, i, 76. "Have the legislature power to prohibit assemblies?"—*Wm. Sullivan*. "So that the whole number of the streets were fifty."—*Rollin's Ancient Hist.*, ii, 8. "The number of inhabitants were not more than four millions."—SMOLLETT: see *Priestley's Gram.*, p. 193. "The House of Commons were of small weight."—HUME: *Ib.*, p. 188. "The assembly of the wicked have enclosed me."—*Psal.* xxii, 16; *Lowth's Gram.*, p. 75. "Every kind of convenience and comfort are provided."—*Com. School Journal*, i, 24. "Amidst the great decrease of the inhabitants of Spain, the body of the clergy have suffered no diminution; but has rather been gradually increasing."—*Payne's Geog.*, ii, 418. "Small as the number of inhabitants are, yet their poverty is extreme."—*Ib.*, ii, 417. "The number of the names were about one hundred and twenty."—*Ware's Gram.*, p. 12; see *Acts*, i, 15.

RULE XVI.—FINITE VERBS.

When a Verb has two or more nominatives connected by *and*, it must agree with them jointly in the plural, because they are taken together: as, "True rhetoric *and* sound logic *are* very nearly allied."—*Blair's Rhet.*, p. 11. "Aggression and injury in no case *justify* retaliation."—*Wayland's Moral Science*, p. 406.

"Judges and senates *have been bought* for gold,
Esteem *and* love *were* never to be sold."—*Pope*.

EXCEPTION FIRST.

When two nominatives connected by *and* serve merely to describe one person or thing, they are either in apposition or equivalent to one name, and do not require a plural verb; as, "Immediately *comes a hue and cry* after a gang of thieves."—*L'Estrange*. "The *hue and cry* of the country *pursues* him."—*Junius*, Letter xxiii. "Flesh and blood [i. e. man, or man's nature,] *hath not revealed* it unto thee."—*Matt.*, xvi, 17." Descent and fall to us *is* adverse."—*Milton, P. L.*, ii, 76. "This *philosopher* and *poet was banished* from his country."—"Such a *Saviour* and *Redeemer is* actually *provided* for us."—*Gurney's Essays*, p. 386. "Let us then declare what great things our *God and Saviour has done* for us."—*Dr. Scott*, on Luke viii. "*Toll, tribute, and custom, was paid* unto them."—*Ezra*, iv, 20.

"Whose icy *current* and compulsive *course*
Ne'er *feels* retiring ebb, but *keeps* due on."—*Shakspeare.*

EXCEPTION SECOND.

When two nominatives connected by *and*, are emphatically distinguished, they belong to different propositions, and, if singular, do not require a plural verb; as, "*Ambition*, and not the *safety* of the state, *was concerned*."—*Goldsmith*. "*Consanguinity*, and not *affinity, is* the ground of the prohibition."—*Webster's Essays*, p. 324. "But a *modification*, and oftentimes a total *change, takes* place."—*Maunder*. "*Somewhat*, and, in many circumstances, a great *deal* too, *is put* upon us."—*Butler's Analogy*, p. 108. "*Disgrace*, and perhaps *ruin, was* the certain consequence of attempting the latter."—*Robertson's America*, i, 434.

"*Ay*, and *no* too, *was* no good divinity."—_Shakespeare.

"Love_, and *love only*, is the loan for love."—*Young.*

EXCEPTION THIRD.

When two or more nominatives connected by *and* are preceded by the adjective *each, every, or no,* they are taken separately, and do not require a plural verb; as, "When *no part* of their substance, and *no one* of their properties, *is* the same."—*Bp. Butler.* "Every limb and feature *appears* with its respective grace."—*Steele.* "Every person, and every occurrence, *is beheld* in the most favourable light."—*Murray's Key,* p. 190. "Each worm, and each insect, *is* a marvel of creative power."

"Whose every look and gesture *was* a joke
To clapping theatres and shouting crowds."—*Young.*

EXCEPTION FOURTH.

When the verb separates its nominatives, it agrees with that which precedes it, and is understood to the rest; as, "The *earth is* the Lord's, and the *fullness* thereof."—*Murray's Exercises,* p. 36.

"*Disdain forbids* me, and my *dread* of shame."—*Milton.*

"————Forth in the pleasing spring,
Thy *beauty walks,* thy *tenderness,* and *love.*"—*Thomson.*

OBSERVATIONS ON RULE XVI.

OBS. 1.—According to Lindley Murray, (who, in all his compilation, from whatever learned authorities, refers us to *no places* in any book but his own.) "Dr. Blair observes, that 'two or more substantives, joined by a copulative, *must always require* the verb or pronoun to which they refer, to be *placed* in the plural number:' and this," continues the great Compiler, "is the *general sentiment* of English grammarians."—*Murray's Gram.,* Vol. i, p. 150. The same thing is stated in many other grammars: thus, *Ingersoll* has the very same words, on the 238th page of his book; and *R. C. Smith* says,

"Dr. Blair *very justly* observes," &c.—*Productive Gram.*, p. 126. I therefore doubt not, the learned rhetorician has somewhere made some such remark: though I can neither supply the reference which these gentlemen omit, nor vouch for the accuracy of their quotation. But I trust to make it very clear, that so many grammarians as hold this sentiment, are no great readers, to say the least of them. Murray himself acknowledges *one* exception to this principle, and unconsciously furnishes examples of one or two more; but, in stead of placing the former in his Grammar, and under the rule, where the learner would be likely to notice it, he makes it an obscure and almost unintelligible note, in the *margin of his Key*, referring by an asterisk to the following correction: "Every man and every woman *was* numbered."—*Murray's Gram.*, 8vo, Vol. ii. p. 190. To justify this phraseology, he talks thus: "*Whatever number* of nouns may be connected *by a conjunction with the pronoun* EVERY, this *pronoun* is as applicable to *the whole mass* of them, as to any *one of the nouns*; and *therefore* the verb is correctly put in the singular number, and *refers to the whole* separately and individually considered."—*Ib.* So much, then, for "*the pronoun* EVERY!" But, without other exceptions, what shall be done with the following texts from Murray himself? "The flock, *and* not the fleece, *is*, or *ought* to be the object of the shepherd's care."—*Ib.*, ii, 184. "This prodigy of learning, this scholar, critic, *and* antiquary, *was* entirely destitute of breeding and civility."—*Ib.*, ii, 217. And, in the following line, what conjunction appears, or what is the difference between "horror" and "black despair." that the verb should be made plural?

"What black despair, what horror, *fill* his *mind*!"—*Ib.*, ii, 183.

"What black despair, what horror *fills* his *heart*!"—*Thomson.*[395]

OBS. 2.—Besides the many examples which may justly come under the four exceptions above specified, there are several questionable but customary expressions, which have some appearance of being deviations from this rule, but which may perhaps be reasonably explained on the principle of ellipsis: as, "All work and no play, *makes* Jack a dull boy."—"Slow and steady often *outtravels* haste."—*Dillwyn's Reflections*, p. 23. "Little and often *fills* the purse."—*Treasury of Knowledge*, Part i, p. 446. "Fair and softly *goes* far." These maxims, by universal custom, lay claim to a singular verb; and, for my part, I know not how they can well be considered either real exceptions to the foregoing rule, or real inaccuracies under it; for, in most of them, the words connected are not *nouns*; and those which are so, may not be nominatives. And it is clear, that every exception must have some specific character by which it may be distinguished; else it destroys the rule, in stead of confirming it, as known exceptions are said to do. Murray appears to have thought the singular verb *wrong*; for, among his examples for parsing, he has, "Fair and softly *go* far," which instance is no more entitled to a plural verb than the rest. See his *Octavo Gram.*, Vol. ii, p. 5. Why not suppose them all to be elliptical? Their meaning may be as follows: "*To have* all work and no play, *makes* Jack a dull boy."—"*What is* slow and steady, often *outtravels* haste."—"To *put in* little and often, *fills* the purse."—"*What proceeds* fair and softly, *goes* far." The following line from Shakspeare appears to be still more elliptical:

"Poor and content *is* rich, and rich enough."—*Othello.*

This may be supposed to mean, "*He who is* poor and content," &c. In the following sentence again, we may suppose an ellipsis of the phrase *To have*, at the beginning; though here, perhaps, to have pluralized the verb, would have been as well:

"One eye on death and one full fix'd on heaven, *Becomes* a mortal and immortal man."—*Young.*

OBS. 3.—The names of two persons are not unfrequently used jointly as the name of their story; in which sense, they must have a singular verb, if they have any; as, "Prior's *Henry and Emma contains* an other beautiful example."—*Jamieson's Rhetoric*, p. 179. I somewhat hesitate to call this an exception to the foregoing rule, because here too the phraseology may be supposed elliptical. The meaning is, "Prior's *little poem, entitled,* 'Henry and Emma,' contains," &c.;—or, "Prior's *story of* Henry and Emma contains," &c. And, if the first expression is only an abbreviation of one of these, the construction of the verb *contains* may be referred to Rule 14th. See Exception 1st to Rule 12th, and Obs. 2d on Rule 14th.

OBS. 4.—The conjunction *and,* by which alone we can with propriety connect different words to make them joint nominatives or joint antecedents, is sometimes suppressed and *understood*; but then its effect is the same, as if it were inserted; though a singular verb might sometimes be quite as proper in the same sentences, because it would merely imply a disjunctive conjunction or none at all: as, "The high breach of trust, the notorious corruption, *are stated* in the strongest terms."—*Junius*, Let. xx. "Envy, self-will, jealousy, pride, often *reign* there."—*Abbott's Corner Stone*, p. 111. (See Obs. 4th on Rule 12th.)

"Art, empire, earth itself, to change *are* doomed."—*Beattie.*

"Her heart, her mind, her love, *is* his alone."—*Cowley.*

In all the foregoing examples, a singular verb might have been used without impropriety; or the last, which is singular, might have been plural. But the following couplet evidently requires a plural verb, and is therefore correct as the poet wrote it; both because the latter noun is plural, and because the conjunction *and* is understood between the two. Yet a late grammarian, perceiving no difference between the joys of sense and the pleasure of reason, not only changes "*lie*" to "*lies,*" but uses the perversion for a *proof text,* under a rule which refers the verb to the first noun only, and requires it to be singular. See *Oliver B. Peirce's Gram.,* p. 250.

> "Reason's whole pleasure, all the joys of sense.
> *Lie* in three words—health, peace, and competence."
> —*Pope's Ess.,* Ep. iv, l. 80.

OBS. 5.—When the speaker changes his nominative to take a stronger expression, he commonly uses no conjunction; but, putting the verb in agreement with the noun which is next to it, he leaves the other to an implied concord with its proper form of the same verb: as, "The man whose *designs,* whose *whole conduct, tends* to reduce me to subjection, that man is at war with me, though not a blow has yet been given, nor a sword drawn."—*Blair's Rhet.,* p. 265. "All *Greece,* all the barbarian *world, is* too narrow for this man's ambition."—*Ibid.* "This *self-command,* this *exertion* of reason in the midst of passion, *has* a wonderful effect both to please and to persuade."—*Ib.,* p. 260. "In the mutual influence of body and soul, there *is a wisdom,* a *wonderful wisdom,* which we cannot fathom."—*Murray's Gram.,* Vol. i, p. 150. If the principle here stated is just, Murray has written the following models erroneously: "Virtue, honour, nay, even self-interest, *conspire* to recommend the measure."—*Ib.,* p. 150. "Patriotism, morality, every public and private consideration, *demand* our submission to just and lawful government."—*Ibid.* In this latter instance, I should prefer the singular verb *demands*; and in the former, the expression ought to be otherwise altered, thus. "Virtue, honour, *and* interest, all *conspire* to recommend the measure." Or thus: "Virtue, honour—nay, even self-interest, *recommends* the measure." On this principle, too, Thomson was right, and this critic wrong, in the example cited at the close of the first observation above. This construction is again recurred to by Murray, in the second chapter of his Exercises; where he explicitly condemns the following sentence because the verb is singular: "Prudence, policy, nay, his own true interest, strongly *recommends* the line of conduct proposed to him."—*Octavo Gram.*, Vol. ii, p. 22.

OBS. 6.—When two or more nominatives are in apposition with a preceding one which they explain, the verb must agree with the first word only, because the others are adjuncts to this, and not joint subjects to the verb; as, "Loudd, the ancient Lydda and Diospolis, *appears* like a place lately ravaged by fire and sword."—*Keith's Evidences*, p. 93. "Beattie, James,—a philosopher and poet,—*was born* in Scotland, in the year 1735."—*Murray's Sequel*, p. 306. "For, the quantity, the length, and shortness of our syllables, *is* not, by any means, so fixed."—*Blair's Rhet.*, p. 124. This principle, like the preceding one, persuades me again to dissent from Murray, who corrects or *perverts* the following sentence, by changing *originates* to *originate*: "All that makes a figure on the great theatre of the world; the employments of the busy, the enterprises of the ambitious, and the exploits of the warlike; the virtues which form the happiness, and the crimes which occasion the misery of mankind; *originates* in that silent and secret recess of thought, which is hidden from every human eye."—See *Murray's Octavo Gram.*, Vol. ii, p. 181; or his *Duodecimo Key*, p. 21. The true subject of this proposition is the noun *all*, which is singular; and the other nominatives are subordinate to this, and merely explanatory of it.

OBS. 7.—Dr. Webster says, "*Enumeration* and addition of numbers are *usually* expressed in the singular *number*; [as,] two and two *is* four; seven and nine *is* sixteen; that is, *the sum of* seven and nine *is* sixteen. But modern usage inclines to reject the use of the verb in the singular number, in these and similar phrases."—*Improved Gram.*, p. 106. Among its many faults, this passage exhibits a virtual contradiction. For what "*modern usage* inclines to reject," can hardly be the fashion in which any ideas "*are usually expressed*." Besides, I may safely aver, that this is a kind of phraseology which all correct usage always did reject. It is not only a gross vulgarism, but a plain and palpable violation of the foregoing rule of syntax; and, as such it must be reputed, if the rule has any propriety at all. What "*enumeration*" has to do with it, is more than I can tell. But Dr. Webster once admired and commended this mode of speech, as one of the "wonderful proofs of ingenuity in the *framers* of language;" and laboured to defend it as being "correct upon principle;" that is, upon the principle that "*the sum of*" is understood to be the subject of the affirmation, when one says, "Two *and* two *is* four," in stead of, "Two and two *are* four."—See *Webster's Philosophical Gram.*, p. 153. This seems to me a "wonderful proof" of *ignorance* in a very learned man. OBS. 8.—In Greek and Latin, the verb frequently agrees with the nearest nominative, and is understood to the rest; and this construction is sometimes imitated in English, especially if the nouns follow the verb: as, "[Greek: Nuni do MENEI pistis, elpis agape, ta tria tanta]."—"Nunc vero *manet* fides, spes, charitas; tria hæc."—"Now *abideth* faith, hope, charity; these three."—*1 Cor.*, xiii, 13. "And now *abideth* confession, prayer, and praise, these three; but the greatest of these is praise."—ATTERBURY: *Blair's Rhet.*, p. 300. The propriety of this usage, so far as our language is concerned, I doubt. It seems to open a door for numerous deviations from the foregoing rule, and deviations of such a sort, that if they are to be considered exceptions, one can hardly tell why. The practice, however, is not uncommon, especially if there are more nouns than two, and each is emphatic; as, "Wonderful *was* the patience, fortitude, self-denial, *and* bravery of our ancestors."—*Webster's Hist. of U. S.*, p. 118. "It is the very thing I would have you make out: for therein *consists* the form, and use, and nature of language."—*Berkley's Alciphron*, p. 161. "There *is* the proper noun, and the common noun. There *is* the singular noun, and the plural noun."—*Emmons's Gram.*, p. 11. "From him *proceeds* power, sanctification, truth, grace, and every other blessing we can conceive."—*Calvin's Institutes*, B. i, Ch. 13. "To what purpose *cometh* there to me incense from Sheba, *and* the sweet cane from a far country?"—*Jer.*, vi, 20. "For thine *is* the kingdom, *and* the power, *and* the glory, forever."—*Matt.*, vi, 13. In all these instances, the plural verb might have been used; and yet perhaps the singular may be justified on the ground that there is a distinct and emphatic enumeration of the nouns. Thus, it would be proper to say, "Thine *are* the kingdom, the power, and the glory;" but this construction seems less emphatic than the preceding, which means, "For thine is the kingdom, *thine is* the power, and *thine is* the glory, forever;" and this repetition is still more emphatic, and perhaps more proper, than the elliptical form. The repetition of the conjunction "*and*," in the original text as above, adds time and emphasis to the reading, and makes the singular verb more proper than it would otherwise be; for which reason, the following form, in which the Rev. Dr. Bullions has set the sentence down for bad English, is in some sort a *perversion* of the Scripture: "Thine is the kingdom, the power, and the glory."—*Bullions's E. Gram.*, p. 141.

OBS. 9.—When the nominatives are of different *persons*, the verb agrees with the first person in preference to the second, and with the second in preference to the third; for *thou* and *I*, or *he, thou,* and *I*, are equivalent to *we*; and *thou* and *he* are equivalent to you: as, "Why speakest thou any more of thy matters? I have said, *thou and Ziba divide* the land."—*2 Sam.*, xix. 29. That is, "divide *ye* the land." "And *live thou* and thy *children* of the rest."—*2 Kings*, iv, 7. "That *I* and thy *people have found* grace in thy sight."—*Exodus*, xxxiii, 16. "*I* and my *kingdom are* guiltless."—*2 Sam.*, iii, 28. "*I*, and *you*, and *Piso* perhaps too, *are* in a state of dissatisfaction."—*Zenobia*, i, 114.

"Then *I*, and *you*, and *all* of us, *fell* down,
Whilst bloody treason flourish'd over *us*."—*Shak., J. Cæsar.*

OBS. 10.—When two or more nominatives connected by *and* are of the same form but distinguished by adjectives or possessives, one or more of them may be omitted by ellipsis, but the verb must be plural, and agree with them all; as, "A literary, a scientific, a wealthy, and a poor man, *were assembled* in one room."—*Peirce's Gram.*, p. 263. Here four different men are clearly spoken of. "Else the rising and the falling emphasis *are* the same."—*Knowles's Elocutionist*, p. 33. Here the noun *emphasis* is understood after *rising*. "The singular and [the] plural form *seem* to be confounded."—*Lowth's Gram.*, p. 22. Here the noun *form* is presented to the mind twice; and therefore the article should have been repeated. See Obs. 15th on Rule 1st. "My farm and William's *are* adjacent to each other."—*Peirce's Gram.*, p. 220. Here the noun *farm* is understood after the possessive *William's*, though the author of the sentence foolishly attempts to explain it otherwise. "Seth's, Richard's and Edmund's *farms* are those which their fathers left them."—*Ib.*, p. 257. Here the noun *farms* is understood after *Seth's*, and again after *Richard's*; so that the sentence is written wrong, unless each man has more than one farm. "*Was* not Demosthenes's style, and his master Plato's, perfectly Attic; and yet none more lofty?"—*Milnes's Greek Gram.*, p. 241. Here *style* is understood after *Plato's*; wherefore *was* should rather be *were*, or else *and* should be changed to *as well as*. But the text, as it stands, is not much unlike some of the exceptions noticed above. "The character of a fop, and of a rough warrior, *are* no where more successfully contrasted."—*Kames, El. of Crit.*, Vol. i, p. 236. Here the ellipsis is not very proper. Say, "the character of a fop, and *that* of a rough warrior," &c. Again: "We may observe, that the eloquence of the bar, of the legislature, and of public assemblies, *are* seldom *or ever* found united *to high perfection in* the same person."—*J. Q. Adams's Rhet.*, Vol. i, p. 256. Here the ellipsis cannot so well be avoided by means of the pronominal adjective *that*, and therefore it may be thought more excusable; but I should prefer a repetition of the nominative: as, "We may observe, that the eloquence of the bar, *the eloquence* of the legislature, and *the eloquence* of public assemblies, are seldom *if ever* found united, *in any high degree*, in the same person."

OBS. 11.—The conjunction *as*, when it connects nominatives that are in *apposition*, or significant of the same person or thing, is commonly placed at the beginning of a sentence, so that the verb agrees with its proper nominative following the explanatory word: thus, "As *a poet, he holds* a high rank."—*Murray's Sequel*, p. 355. "As *a poet, Addison claims* a high praise."—*Ib.*, p. 304. "As *a model* of English prose, his *writings merit* the greatest praise."—*Ib.*, p. 305. But when this conjunction denotes a *comparison* between different persons or things signified by two nominatives, there must be two verbs expressed or understood, each agreeing with its own subject; as, "Such *writers* as *he [is,] have* no reputation worth any man's envy." [396]

"Such *men* as *he [is] be* never at heart's ease
Whiles they behold a greater than themselves."—*Shakspeare.*

OBS. 12.—When two nominatives are connected by *as well as, but,* or *save,* they must in fact have two verbs, though in most instances only one is expressed; as, "Such is the mutual dependence of words in sentences, that several *others,* as well as [is] the *adjective, are* not to be used alone."—*Dr. Wilson's Essay*, p. 99. "The Constitution was to be the one fundamental law of the land, to which *all,* as well *States* as *people,* should submit."—W. I. BOWDITCH: *Liberator,* No. 984. "As well those which history, as those which experience *offers* to our reflection."— *Bolingbroke, on History,* p. 85. Here the words "*offers to our reflection*" are understood after "*history.*" "*None* but *He* who discerns futurity, *could have foretold* and described all these things."—*Keith's Evidences*, p. 62. "That there *was* in those times no other *writer,* of any degree of eminence, save *he* himself."—*Pope's Works,* Vol. iii, p. 43.

"I do entreat you not a man depart,
Save *I* alone, till Antony have spoke."—*Shak., J. Cæsar.*

OBS. 13.—Some grammarians say, that *but* and *save*, when they denote exception, should govern the objective case as *prepositions*. But this idea is, without doubt, contrary to the current usage of the best authors, either ancient or modern. Wherefore I think it evident that these grammarians err. The objective case of *nouns* being like the nominative, the point can be proved only by the *pronouns*; as, "There is none *but he* alone."—*Perkins's Theology*, 1608. "There is none other *but he*."—*Mark*, xii, 32. (This text is good authority as regards the *case*, though it is incorrect in an other respect: it should have been, "There is *none but* he," or else, "There is *no other than he*.") "No man hath ascended up to heaven, *but he* that came down from heaven."—*John*, iii, 13. "Not that any man hath seen the father, *save he* which is of God."—*John*, vi, 46. "Few can, *save he* and *I*."—*Byron's Werner*. "There is none justified, *but he* that is in measure sanctified."—*Isaac Penington. Save*, as a conjunction, is nearly obsolete.

OBS. 14.—In Rev., ii, 17th, we read, "Which no man knoweth, *saving he* that receiveth it;" and again, xiii, 17th, "That no man might buy or sell, *save he* that had the mark." The following text is inaccurate, but not in the construction of the nominative *they*: "All men cannot receive this saying, *save they* to whom it is given."—*Matt.*, xix, 11. The version ought to have been, "*Not all* men can receive this saying, *but they only* to whom it is given:" i.e., "they only *can receive it*, to whom *there is given power to receive it*." Of *but* with a nominative, examples may be multiplied indefinitely. The following are as good as any: "There is no God *but He*."—*Sale's Koran*, p. 27. "The former none *but He* could execute."—*Maturin's Sermons*, p. 317. "There was nobody at home *but I*."—*Walker's Particles*, p. 95. "A fact, of which as none *but he* could be conscious, [so] none *but he* could be the publisher of it."—*Pope's Works*, Vol. iii, p. 117. "Few *but they*

who are involved in the vices, are involved in the irreligion of the times."—
Brown's Estimate, i, 101.

> "I claim my right. No Grecian prince but *I*
> Has power this bow to grant, or to deny."
> —*Pope, Odys.*, B. xxi, l. 272.

> "Thus she, and none *but she*, the insulting rage
> Of heretics oppos'd from age to age."
> —*Dryden's Poems*, p. 98.

In opposition to all these authorities, and many more that might be added, we have, with now and then a text of false syntax, the absurd opinion of perhaps *a score or two* of our grammarians; one of whom imagines he has found in the following couplet from Swift, an example to the purpose; but he forgets that the verb *let* governs the *objective* case:

> "Let *none but him* who rules the thunder,
> Attempt to part these twain asunder."
> —*Perley's Gram.*, p. 62.

OBS. 15.—It is truly a wonder, that so many professed critics should not see the absurdity of taking *but* and *save* for "*prepositions*," when this can be done only by condemning the current usage of nearly all good authors, as well as the common opinion of most grammarians; and the greater is the wonder, because they seem to do it innocently, or to teach it childishly, as not knowing that they cannot justify both sides, when the question lies between opposite and contradictory principles. By this sort of simplicity, which approves of errors, if much practised, and of opposites, or essential contraries, when authorities may be found for them, no work, perhaps, is more strikingly characterized, than the popular School Grammar of W. H. Wells. This author says, "The use of *but* as a preposition is *approved* by J.

E. Worcester, John Walker, R. C. Smith, Picket, Hiley, Angus, Lynde, Hull, Powers, Spear, Farnum, Fowle, Goldsbury, Perley, Cobb, Badgley, Cooper, Jones, Davis, Beall, Hendrick, Hazen, and Goodenow."—*School Gram.*, 1850, p. 178. But what if all these authors do prefer, "*but him*," and "*save him*," where ten times as many would say, "*but he*," "*save he*?" Is it therefore difficult to determine which party is right? Or is it proper for a grammarian to name sundry authorities on both sides, excite doubt in the mind of his reader, and leave the matter *unsettled*? "The use of *but* as a preposition," he also states, "is *discountenanced* by G. Brown, Sanborn, Murray, S. Oliver, and several other grammarians. (See also an able article in the Mass. Common School Journal, Vol. ii, p. 19.)"—*School Gram.*, p. 178.

OBS. 16.—Wells passes no censure on the use of nominatives after *but* and *save*; does not intimate which case is fittest to follow these words; gives no false syntax under his rule for the regimen of prepositions; but inserts there the following brief remarks and examples:

"REM. 3.—The word *save* is frequently used to perform the office of a preposition; as, 'And all desisted, all *save him* alone.'—*Wordsworth*."

"REM. 4.—*But* is sometimes employed as a preposition, in the sense of *except*; as, 'The boy stood on the burning deck, Whence all *but him* had fled.'—*Hemans*."—*Ib.*, p. 167.

Now, "BUT," says Worcester, as well as Tooke and others, was "originally *bot*, contracted from *be out*;" and, if this notion of its etymology is just, it must certainly be followed by the nominative case, rather than by the objective; for the imperative *be* or *be out* governs no case, admits no additional term but a nominative—an obvious and important fact, quite overlooked by those who call *but* a preposition. According to Allen H. Weld, *but* and *save* "are *commonly* considered *prepositions*," but "are *more commonly* termed *conjunctions*!" This author repeats Wells's examples of "*save him*," and "*but him*," as being *right*; and mixes them with opposite examples of "*save he*," "*but he*," "*save I*," which he thinks to be *more right*! —*Weld's Gram.*, p. 187.

OBS. 17.—Professor Fowler, too, an other author remarkable for a facility of embracing incompatibles, contraries, or dubieties, not only condemns as "false syntax" the use of *save* for an exceptive conjunction. (§587. ¶28,) but cites approvingly from Latham the following very strange absurdity: "One and the same word, in one and the same sentence, may be a Conjunction or [a] Preposition, as the case may be: [as] All fled *but* John."—*Fowler's E. Gram.*, 8vo, 1850, § 555. This is equivalent to saying, that "one and the same sentence" *may be two different sentences*; may, without error, be understood in two different senses; may be rightly taken, resolved, and parsed in two different ways! Nay, it is equivalent to a denial of the old logical position, that "It is impossible for a thing *to be* and *not be* at the same time;" for it supposes "*but*," in the instance given, to be at once both a conjunction and *not* a conjunction, both a preposition and *not* a preposition, "*as the case may be*!" It is true, that "one and the same word" may sometimes be differently parsed *by different grammarians*, and possibly even an adept may doubt who or what is right. But what ambiguity of construction, or what diversity of interpretation, proceeding from the same hand, can these admissions be supposed to warrant? The foregoing citation is a boyish attempt to justify different modes of parsing the same expression, on the ground that the expression itself is equivocal. "All fled *but John*," is thought to mean equally well, "All fled *but he*," and, "All fled *but him*;" while these latter expressions are erroneously presumed to be alike good English, and to have a difference of meaning corresponding to their difference of construction. Now, what is equivocal, or ambiguous, being therefore erroneous, is to be *corrected*, rather than parsed in any way. But I deny both the ambiguity and the difference of meaning which these critics profess to find among the said phrases. "*John fled not, but all the rest fled*," is virtually what is told us in each of them; but, in the form, "All fled but *him*," it is told ungrammatically; in the other two, correctly.

OBS. 18.—In Latin, *cum* with an ablative, sometimes has, or is supposed to have, the force of the conjunction *et* with a nominative; as, "Dux *cum* aliquot principibus capiuntur."—LIVY: *W. Allen's Gram.*, p. 131. In imitation of this construction, some English writers have substituted *with* for *and*, and varied the verb accordingly; as, "A long course of time, *with* a variety of accidents and circumstances, *are* requisite to produce those revolutions."—HUME: *Allen's Gram.*, p. 131; *Ware's*, 12; *Priestley's*, 186. This phraseology, though censured by Allen, was expressly approved by Priestley, who introduced the present example, as his proof text under the following observation: "It is not necessary that the two *subjects of an affirmation* should stand in the very same construction, to require the verb to be in the plural number. If one of them be made to depend upon the other *by a connecting particle*, it may, *in some cases*, have the same force, as if it were independent of it."—*Priestley's Gram.*, p. 186. Lindley Murray, on the contrary, condemns this doctrine, and after citing the same example with others, says: "It is however, proper to observe that these modes of expression do not appear to be warranted by *the just principles* of construction."— *Octavo Gram.*, p. 150. He then proceeds to prove his point, by alleging that the preposition governs the objective case in English, and the ablative in Latin, and that what is so governed, cannot be the nominative, or any part of it. All this is true enough, but still some men who know it perfectly well, will now and then write as if they did not believe it. And so it was with the writers of Latin and Greek. They sometimes wrote bad syntax; and the grammarians have not always seen and censured their errors as they ought. Since the preposition makes its object only an adjunct of the preceding noun, or of something else, I imagine that any construction which thus assumes two different cases as joint nominatives or joint antecedents, must needs be inherently faulty.

OBS. 19.—Dr. Adam simply remarks, "The plural is sometimes used after the preposition *cum* put for *et*; as, *Remo cum fratre Quirinus jura dabunt*. Virg."—*Latin and English Gram.*, p. 207; *Gould's Adam's Latin Gram.*, p. 204; *W. Allen's English Gram.*, 131. This example is not fairly cited; though many have adopted the perversion, as if they knew no better. Alexander has it in a worse form still: "Quirinus, cum fratre, jura dabunt."—*Latin Gram.*, p. 47. Virgil's words are, "*Cana* FIDES, *et* VESTA, *Remo cum fratre Quirinus, Jura dabunt*."—*Æneid*, B. i, l. 296. Nor is *cum* here "put for *et*," unless we suppose also an antiptosis of *Remo fratre* for *Remus frater*; and then what shall the literal meaning be, and how shall the rules of syntax be accommodated to such changes? Fair examples, that bear upon the point, may, however, be adduced from good authors, and in various languages; but the question is, are they *correct* in syntax? Thus Dr. Robertson: "The palace of Pizarro, *together with* the houses of several of his adherents, *were* pillaged by the soldiers."— *Hist. of Amer.*, Vol. ii, p. 133. To me, this appears plainly ungrammatical; and, certainly, there are ways enough in which it may be corrected. First, with the present connective retained, "*were*" ought to be *was*. Secondly, if *were* be retained, "*together with*" ought to be changed to *and*, or *and also*. Thirdly, we may well change both, and say, "The palace of Pizarro, *as well as* the houses of several of his adherents, *was* pillaged by the soldiers." Again, in Mark, ix, 4th, we read: "And there appeared *unto them* Elias, *with* Moses; and *they* were talking with Jesus." If this text meant that *the three disciples* were talking with Jesus, it would be right as it stands; but St. Matthew has it, "And, behold, there appeared unto them *Moses and Elias, talking* with him;" and our version in Luke is, "And, behold, there talked with him two men, which were Moses and Elias."—Chap. ix, 30. By these corresponding texts, then, we learn, that the pronoun *they*, which our translators inserted, was meant for "*Elias with Moses*;" but the Greek verb for "*appeared*," as used by Mark, is *singular*, and agrees only with Elias. "[Greek: *Kai ophthœ autois Aelias sun Mosei, kai hæsan syllalountes to Iæsoy.*]"—"Et *apparuit* illis Elias cum Mose, et erant colloquentes Jesu."—*Montanus.* "Et *visus est* eis Elias cum Mose, qui colloquebantur cum Jesu."—*Beza.* This is as discrepant as our version, though not so ambiguous. The French Bible avoids the incongruity: "Et iis virent paroître *Moyse et Elie*, qui s'entretenoient avec Jésus." That is, "And there appeared to them *Moses and Elias*, who were talking with Jesus." Perhaps the closest and best version of the Greek would be, "And there appeared to them Elias, with Moses;[397] and *these two* were talking with Jesus." There is, in our Bible, an other instance of the construction now in question; but it has no support from the Septuagint, the Vulgate, or the French: to wit, "The second [lot came forth] to Gedaliah, *who with* his brethren and sons *were* twelve."—*1 Chron.*, xxv, 9. Better: "*and he*, his brethren, and *his* sons, were twelve."

OBS. 20.—Cobbett, who, though he wrote several grammars, was but a very superficial grammarian, seems never to have doubted the propriety of putting *with* for *and*; and yet he was confessedly not a little puzzled to find out when to use a singular, and when a plural verb, after a nominative with such "a sort of addition made to it." The 246th paragraph of his English Grammar is a long and fruitless attempt to fix a rule for the guidance of the learner in this matter. After dashing off a culpable example, "Sidmouth, *with* Oliver the *spye*, have brought Brandreth to the block;" or, as his late editions have it, "The *Tyrant, with* the *Spy, have* brought *Peter* to the block." He adds: "We hesitate which to employ, the singular or the plural verb; that is to say, *has* or *have*. The meaning must be our guide. If we mean, that the act has been done by the Tyrant himself, and that the spy has been a mere involuntary agent, then we ought to use the singular; but if we believe that the spy has been a co-operator, an associate, an accomplice, then we must use the plural verb." Ay, truly; but must we not also, in the latter case, use *and*, and not *with*? After some further illustrations, he says: "When *with* means *along with, together with, in Company with*, and the like, it is nearly the same as *and*; and then the plural verb must be used: [as,] 'He, with his brothers, *are* able to do much.' Not, '*is* able to do much.' If the pronoun be used instead of *brothers*, it will be in the objective case: 'He, *with* them, *are* able to do much.' But this is *no impediment* to the including of the noun (represented by *them*) in the nominative." I wonder what would be an impediment to the absurdities of such a dogmatist! The following is his last example: "'Zeal, with discretion, *do* much;' and not '*does* much;' for we mean, on the contrary, that it *does nothing*. It is the meaning that must determine which of the numbers we ought to employ." This author's examples are all fictions of his own, and such of them as here have a plural verb, are wrong. His rule is also wrong, and contrary to the best authority. St. Paul says to Timothy, "Godliness *with* contentment *is* great gain:"—*1 Tim.*, vi, 6. This text is right; but Cobbett's principle would go to prove it erroneous. Is he the only man who has ever had a right notion of its *meaning*? or is he not rather at fault in his interpretations?

OBS. 21.—There is one other apparent exception to Rule 16th, (or perhaps a real one,) in which there is either an ellipsis of the preposition *with*, or else the verb is made singular because the first noun only is its true subject, and the others are explanatory nominatives to which the same verb must be understood in the plural number; as, "A *torch*, snuff and all, *goes out* in a moment, when dipped in the vapour."—ADDISON: *in Johnson's Dict.*, *w. All.* "Down *comes* the *tree*, nest, eagles, and all."—See *All, ibidem.* Here *goes* and *comes* are necessarily made singular, the former agreeing with *torch* and the latter with *tree*; and, if the other nouns, which are like an explanatory parenthesis, are nominatives, as they appear to me to be, they must be subjects of *go* and *come* understood. Cobbett teaches us to say, "The bag, *with* the guineas and dollars in it, *were* stolen," and not, *was* stolen. "For," says he, "if we say *was* stolen, it is possible for us to mean, that the *bag only* was stolen,"—*English Gram.*, ¶ 246. And I suppose he would say, "The bag, guineas, dollars, and all, *were* stolen," and not, "*was* stolen;" for here a rule of syntax might be urged, in addition to his false argument from the sense. But the meaning of the former sentence is, "The bag was stolen, with the guineas and dollars in it;" and the meaning of the latter is, "The bag was stolen, guineas, dollars, and all." Nor can there be any doubt about the meaning, place the words which way you will; and whatever, in either case, may be the true construction of the words in the parenthetical or explanatory phrase, they should not, I think, prevent the verb from agreeing with the first noun only. But if the other nouns intervene without affecting this concord, and without a preposition to govern them, it may be well to distinguish them in the punctuation; as, "The bag, (guineas, dollars, and all,) was stolen."

NOTES TO RULE XVI.

NOTE I.—When the conjunction *and* between two nominatives appears to require a plural verb, but such form of the verb is not agreeable, it is better to reject or change the connective, that the verb may stand correctly in the singular number; as, "There *is* a peculiar force *and* beauty in this figure."—*Kames, El. of Crit.*, ii, 224. Better: "There is a peculiar force, *as well as a peculiar* beauty, in this figure." "What *means* this restless stir and commotion of mind?"—*Murray's Key*, 8vo, p. 242. Better: "What means this restless stir, *this* commotion of mind?"

NOTE II.—When two subjects or antecedents are connected, one of which is taken affirmatively, and the other negatively, they belong to different propositions; and the verb or pronoun must agree with the affirmative subject, and be understood to the other: as "Diligent *industry*, and not mean savings, *produces* honourable competence."—"Not a loud *voice* but strong *proofs bring* conviction."—"My *poverty*, but not my will, consents."—*Shakespeare.*

NOTE III.—When two subjects or antecedents are connected by *as well as, but,* or *save,* they belong to different propositions; and, (unless one of them is preceded by the adverb *not,*) the verb and pronoun must agree with the former and be understood to the latter: as, "*Veracity,* as well as justice, *is* to be our rule of life."—*Butler's Analogy,* p. 283. "The lowest *mechanic,* as well as the richest citizen, *may boast* that thousands of *his* fellow-creatures are employed for *him.*"—*Percival's Tales,* ii, 177. "These *principles,* as well as every just rule of criticism, *are founded* upon the sensitive part of our nature."—*Kames, El. of Crit.,* Vol. i, p. xxvi. "*Nothing* but wailings *was* heard."—"*None* but thou *can aid* us."—"No mortal *man,* save he," &c., "*had e'er survived* to say *he* saw."—*Sir W. Scott.*

NOTE IV.—When two or more subjects or antecedents are preceded by the adjective *each, every,* or *no,* they are taken separately; and, (except *no* be followed by a plural noun,) they require the verb and pronoun to be in the singular number: as, "No rank, no honour, no fortune, no condition in life, *makes* the guilty mind happy."—"Every phrase and every figure *which* he uses, *tends* to render the picture more lively and complete."—*Blair's Rhet.,* p. 179.

"And every sense, and every heart, *is* joy."—*Thomson.*

"Each beast, each insect, happy in *its* own."—*Pope.*

NOTE V.—When any words or terms are to be taken conjointly as subjects or antecedents, the conjunction *and,* (in preference to *with, or, nor,* or any thing else,) must connect them. The following sentence is therefore inaccurate; *with* should be *and;* or else *were* should be *was:* "One of them, [the] wife of Thomas Cole, *with* her husband, *were* shot down, the others escaped."—*Hutchinson's Hist.,* Vol. ii, p. 86. So, in the following couplet, *or* should be *and,* or else *engines* should be *engine:*

"What if the head, the eye, *or* ear repined,
   To serve mere *engines* to the ruling mind?"—*Pope.*

NOTE VI.—Improper omissions must be supplied; but when there occurs a true ellipsis in the construction of joint nominatives or joint antecedents, the verb or pronoun must agree with them in the plural, just as if all the words were expressed: as, "The *second* and the *third Epistle* of John *are* each but one short chapter."—"The metaphorical and the literal meaning *are* improperly mixed."—*Murray's Gram.*, p. 339. "The Doctrine of Words, separately consider'd, and in a Sentence, *are* Things distinct enough."—*Brightland's Gram.*, Pref., p. iv. Better perhaps: "The doctrine of words separately considered, and *that of words* in a sentence, *are* things distinct enough."

"The *Curii's* and the *Camilli's* little *field*,
   To vast extended territories *yield*."—*Rowe's Lucan*, B. i, l. 320.

NOTE VII.—Two or more distinct subject phrases connected by *and*, require a plural verb, and generally a plural noun too, if a nominative follow the verb; as, "*To be wise in our own eyes, to be wise in the opinion of the world,* and *to be wise in the sight of our Creator,* are three things so very different, as rarely to coincide."—*Blair.* "'*This picture of my friend,*' and '*This picture of my friend's,*' suggest very different ideas."—*Priestley's Gram.*, p. 71; *Murray's*, i, 178.

"Read of this burgess—on the stone *appear,*
   How worthy he! how virtuous! and how dear!"—*Crabbe.*

IMPROPRIETIES FOR CORRECTION.

FALSE SYNTAX UNDER RULE XVI.

"So much ability and merit is seldom found."—*Murray's Key*, 12mo, p. 18; *Merchant's School Gram.*, p. 190.

[FORMULE.—Not proper, because the verb *is* is in the singular number, and does not correctly agree with its two nominatives, *ability* and *merit,* which are connected by *and,* and taken conjointly. But, according to Rule 16th, "When a verb has two or more nominatives connected by *and,* it must agree with them jointly in the plural, because they are taken together." Therefore, *is* should be *are*; thus, "So much ability and merit *are* seldom found." Or: "So much ability and *so much* merit *are* seldom found."]

"The syntax and etymology of the language is thus spread before the learner."—*Bullions's English Gram.*, 2d Edition, Rec., p. iii. "Dr. Johnson tells us, that in English poetry the accent and the quantity of syllables is the same thing."—*J. Q. Adams's Rhet.*, ii, 213. "Their general scope and tendency, having never been clearly apprehended, is not remembered at all."—*Murray's Gram.*, i, p. 126. "The soil and sovereignty was not purchased of the natives."—*Knapp's Lect. on Amer. Lit.*, p. 55. "The boldness, freedom, and variety of our blank verse, is infinitely more favourable than rhyme, to all kinds of sublime poetry."—*Blair's Rhet.*, p. 40. "The vivacity and sensibility of the Greeks seems to have been much greater than ours."—*Ib.*, p. 253. "For sometimes the Mood and Tense is signified by the Verb, sometimes they are signified of the Verb by something else.'"—*Johnson's Gram. Com.*, p. 254. "The Verb and the Noun making a complete Sense, which the Participle and the Noun does not."—*Ib.*, p. 255. "The growth and decay of passions and emotions, traced through all their mazes, is a subject too extensive for an undertaking like the present."—*Kames El. of Crit.*, i, 108. "The true meaning and etymology of some of his words was lost."—*Knight, on the Greek Alph.*, p. 37. "When the force and direction of personal satire is no longer understood."—*Junius*, p. 5. "The frame and condition of man admits of no other principle."—*Brown's Estimate*, ii, 54. "Some considerable time and care was necessary."—*Ib.*, ii 150. "In consequence of this idea, much ridicule and censure has been thrown upon Milton."—*Blair's Rhet.*, p. 428. "With rational beings, nature and reason is the same thing."—*Collier's Antoninus*, p. 111. "And the flax and the barley was smitten."—*Exod.*, ix, 31. "The colon, and semicolon, divides a period, this with, and that without a connective."—*J. Ware's Gram.*, p. 27. "Consequently wherever space and time is found, there God must also be."—*Sir Isaac Newton.* "As the past tense and perfect participle of *love* ends in *ed*, it is regular."—*Chandler's Gram.*, p. 40; New Edition, p. 66. "But the usual arrangement and nomenclature prevents this from being readily seen."—*Butler's Practical Gram.*, p. 3. "*Do* and *did* simply implies opposition or emphasis."—*Alex. Murray's Gram.*, p. 41. "*I* and *another* make *we*, plural: *Thou* and *another* is as much as *ye*: *He, she*, or *it* and *another* make *they*"—*Ib.*, p. 124. "I and another, is as much as (we) the first Person Plural; Thou and another, is as much as (ye) the second Person Plural; He, she, or it, and another, is as much as (they) the third Person Plural."—*British Gram.*, p. 193; *Buchanan's Syntax*, p. 76. "God and thou art two, and thou and thy neighbour are two."—*The Love Conquest*, p. 25. "Just as *an* and *a* has arisen out of the numeral *one*."—*Fowler's E. Gram.*, 8vo. 1850, §200. "The tone and style of each of them, particularly the first and the last, is very different."—*Blair's Rhet.*, p. 246. "Even as the roebuck and the hart is eaten."—*Deut.*, xiii, 22. "Then I may conclude that two and three makes not five."—*Barclay's Works*, iii, 354. "Which at sundry times thou and thy brethren hast received from us."—*Ib.*, i, 165. "Two and two is four, and one is five."—POPE: *Lives of the Poets*, p. 490. "Humility and knowledge with poor apparel, excels pride and ignorance under costly array."—*Day's Gram., Parsing Lesson*, p. 100. "A page and a half has been added to the section on composition."—*Bullions's E. Gram.*, 5th Ed., Pref., p. vii. "Accuracy and expertness in this exercise is an important acquisition."—*Ib.*, p. 71.

"Woods and groves are of thy dressing,
 Hill and dale doth boast thy blessing."—*Milton's Poems*, p. 139.

UNDER THE RULE ITSELF.—THE VERB BEFORE JOINT NOMINATIVES.

"There is a good and a bad, a right and a wrong in taste, as in other things."—*Blair's Rhet.*, p. 21. "Whence has arisen much stiffness and affectation."—*Ib.*, p. 133. "To this error is owing, in a great measure, that intricacy and harshness, in his figurative language, which I before remarked."—*Ib.*, p. 150; *Jamieson's Rhet.*, 157. "Hence, in his Night Thoughts, there prevails an obscurity and hardness in his style."—*Blair's Rhet.*, p. 150. "There is, however, in that work much good sense, and excellent criticism."—*Ib.*, p. 401. "There is too much low wit and scurrility in Plautus."—*Ib.*, p. 481. "There is too much reasoning and refinement; too much pomp and studied beauty in them."—*Ib.*, p. 468. "Hence arises the structure and characteristic expression of exclamation."—*Rush on the Voice*, p. 229. "And such pilots is he and his brethren, according to their own confession."—*Barclay's Works*, iii, 314. "Of whom is Hymeneus and Philetus: who concerning the truth have erred."—*2 Tim.*, ii, 17. "Of whom is Hymeneus and Alexander; whom I have delivered unto Satan."—*1 Tim.*, i, 20. "And so was James and John, the sons of Zebedee."—*Luke*, v, 10. "Out of the same mouth proceedeth blessing and cursing."—*James*, iii, 10. "Out of the mouth of the Most High proceedeth not evil and good."—*Lam.*, iii, 38. "In which there is most plainly a right and a wrong."—*Butler's Analogy*, p. 215. "In this sentence there is both an actor and an object."—*Smith's Inductive Gram.*, p. 14. "In the breast-plate was placed the mysterious Urim and Thummim."—*Milman's Jews*, i, 88. "What is the gender, number, and person of those in the first?"—*Smith's Productive Gram.*, p. 19. "There seems to be a familiarity and want of dignity in it."—*Priestley's Gram.*, p. 150. "It has been often asked, what is Latin and Greek?"—*Literary Convention*, p. 209. "For where does beauty and high wit But in your constellation meet?"—*Hudibras*, p. 134. "Thence to the land where flows Ganges and Indus."—*Paradise Lost*, B. ix, l. 81. "On these foundations seems to rest the midnight riot and dissipation of modern assemblies."—*Brown's Estimate*, ii, 46. "But what has disease, deformity, and filth, upon which the thoughts can be allured to dwell?"—*Johnson's Life of Swift*, p. 492. "How is the gender and number of the relative known?"—*Bullions, Practical Lessons*, p. 32.

"High rides the sun, thick rolls the dust,
And feebler speeds the blow and thrust."—*Sir W. Scott.*

UNDER NOTE I.—CHANGE THE CONNECTIVE.

"In every language there prevails a certain structure and analogy of parts, which is understood to give foundation to the most reputable usage."—*Blair's Rhet.*, p. 90. "There runs through his whole manner, a stiffness and affectation, which renders him very unfit to be considered a general model."—*Ib.*, p. 102. "But where declamation and improvement in speech is the sole aim"—*Ib.*, p. 257. "For it is by these chiefly, that the train of thought, the course of reasoning, and the whole progress of the mind, in continued discourse of all kinds, is laid open."—*Lowth's Gram.*, p. 103. "In all writing and discourse, the proper composition and structure of sentnences is of the highest importance."—*Blair's Rhet.*, p. 101. "Here the wishful look and expectation of the beggar naturally leads to a vivid conception of that which was the object of his thoughts."—*Campbell's*

Rhet., p. 386. "Who say, that the outward naming of Christ, and signing of the cross, puts away devils."—*Barclay's Works*, i, 146. "By which an oath and penalty was to be imposed upon the members."—*Junius*, p. 6. "Light and knowledge, in what manner soever afforded us, is equally from God."—*Butler's Analogy*, p. 264. "For instance, sickness and untimely death is the consequence of intemperance."—*Ib.*, p. 78. "When grief, and blood ill-tempered vexeth him."—*Beauties of Shakspeare*, p. 256. "Does continuity and connexion create sympathy and relation in the parts of the body?"—*Collier's Antoninus*, p. 111. "His greatest concern, and highest enjoyment, was to be approved in the sight of his Creator."—*Murray's Key*, p. 224. "Know ye not that there is a prince and a great man fallen this day in Israel?"—*2 Sam*, iii, 38. "What is vice and wickedness? No rarity, you may depend on it."—*Collier's Antoninus*, p. 107. "There is also the fear and apprehension of it."—*Butler's Analogy*, p. 87. "The apostrophe and *s*, ('s,) is an abbreviation for *is*, the termination of the old English genitive."—*Bullions, E. Gram.*, p. 17. "*Ti*, *ce*, and *ci*, when followed by a vowel, usually has the sound of *sh*; as in *partial, special, ocean*."—*Weld's Gram.*, p. 15.

> "Bitter constraint and sad occasion dear
> Compels me to disturb your season due."—*Milton's Lycidas.*

> "Debauches and excess, though with less noise,
> As great a portion of mankind destroys."—*Waller*, p. 55.

UNDER NOTE II.—AFFIRMATION WITH NEGATION.

"Wisdom, and not wealth, procure esteem."—*Brown's Inst.*, p. 156. "Prudence, and not pomp, are the basis of his fame."—*Ib.* "Not fear, but labour have overcome him."—*Ib.* "The decency, and not the abstinence, make the difference."—*Ib.* "Not her beauty, but her talents attracts attention."—*Ib.* "It is her talents, and not her beauty, that attracts attention."—*Ib.* "It is her beauty, and not her talents that attract attention."—*Ib.*

"His belly, not his brains, this impulse give:
He'll grow immortal; for he cannot live."—*Young, to Pope.*

UNDER NOTE III.—AS WELL AS, BUT, OR SAVE.

"Common sense as well as piety tell us these are proper."—*Family Commentary*, p. 64. "For without it the critic, as well as the undertaker, ignorant of any rule, have nothing left but to abandon themselves to chance."—*Kames, El. of Crit.*, i, 42. "And accordingly hatred as well as love are extinguished by long absence."—*Ib.*, i, 113. "But at every turn the richest melody as well as the sublimest sentiments are conspicuous."—*Ib.*, ii, 121. "But it, as well as the lines immediately subsequent, defy all translation."—*Coleridge's Introduction*, p. 96. "But their religion, as well as their customs, and manners, were strangely misrepresented."— BOLINGBROKE, ON HISTORY, p. 123; *Priestley's Gram.*, p. 192; *Murray's Exercises*, p. 47. "But his jealous policy, as well as the fatal antipathy of Fonseca, were conspicuous."—*Robertson's America*, i, 191. "When their extent as well as their value were unknown."—*Ib.*, ii, 138. "The Etymology, as well as the Syntax, of the more difficult parts of speech are reserved for his attention [at a later period]."—*Parker and Fox's E. Gram.*, Part i, p. 3. "What I myself owe to him, no one but myself know."— See *Wright's Athens*, p. 96. "None, but thou, O mighty prince! canst avert the blow."—*Inst.*, p. 156. "Nothing, but frivolous amusements, please the indolent."—*Ib.*

"Nought, save the gurglings of the rill, were heard."—*G. B.*

"All songsters, save the hooting owl, was mute."—*G. B.*

UNDER NOTE IV.—EACH, EVERY, OR NO.

"Give every word, and every member, their due weight and force."—*Blair's Rhet.*, p. 110. "And to one of these belong every noun, and every third person of every verb."—*Wilson's Essay on Gram.*, p. 74. "No law, no restraint, no regulation, are required to keep him in bounds."—*Literary Convention*, p. 260. "By that time, every window and every door in the street were full of heads."—*N. Y. Observer*, No. 503. "Every system of religion, and every school of philosophy, stand back from this field, and leave Jesus Christ alone, the solitary example"—*The Corner Stone*, p. 17. "Each day, and each hour, bring their portion of duty."—*Inst.*, p. 156. "And every one that was in distress, and every one that was in debt, and every one that was discontented, gathered themselves unto him."—*1 Sam.*, xxii, 2. "Every private Christian and member of the church ought to read and peruse the Scriptures, that they may know their faith and belief founded upon them."—*Barclay's Works*, i, 340. "And every mountain and island were moved out of their places."—*Rev.*, vi, 14.

"No bandit fierce, no tyrant mad with pride,
No cavern'd hermit rest self-satisfied."

UNDER NOTE V.—WITH, OR, &c. FOR AND.

"The side A, with the sides B and C, compose the triangle."—*Tobitt's Gram.*, p. 48; *Felch's*, 69; *Ware's*, 12. "The stream, the rock, or the tree, must each of them stand forth, so as to make a figure in the imagination."—*Blair's Rhet.*, p. 390. "While this, with euphony, constitute, finally, the whole."—*O. B. Peirce's Gram.*, p. 293. "The bag, with the guineas and dollars in it, were stolen."—*Cobbett's E. Gram.*, ¶246. "Sobriety, with great industry and talent, enable a man to perform great deeds."—*Ib.*, ¶245. "The *it*, together with the verb *to be*, express states of being."—*Ib.*, ¶190. "Where

Leonidas the Spartan king, with his chosen band, fighting for their country, were cut off to the last man."—*Kames, El. of Crit.*, Vol. i, p. 203. "And Leah also, with her children, came near and bowed themselves."—*Gen.*, xxxiii, 7. "The First or Second will, either of them, by themselves coalesce with the Third, but not with each other."—*Harris's Hermes*, p. 74. "The whole must centre in the query, whether Tragedy or Comedy are hurtful and dangerous representations?"—*Formey's Belles-Lettres*, p. 215. "Grief as well as joy are infectious: the emotions they raise in the spectator resemble them perfectly."—*Kames, El. of Crit.*, i, 157. "But in all other words the *Qu* are both sounded."—*Ensell's Gram.*, p. 16. "*Qu* (which are always together) have the sound of *ku* or *k*, as in *queen, opaque*."— *Goodenow's Gram.*, p. 45. "In this selection the *ai* form distinct syllables."—*Walker's Key*, p. 290. "And a considerable village, with gardens, fields, &c., extend around on each side of the square."— *Liberator*, Vol. ix, p. 140. "Affection, or interest, guide our notions and behaviour in the affairs of life; imagination and passion affect the sentiments that we entertain in matters of taste."— *Jamieson's Rhet.*, p. 171. "She heard none of those intimations of her defects, which envy, petulance, or anger, produce among children."— *Rambler*, No. 189. "The King, with the Lords and Commons, constitute an excellent form of government."—*Crombie's Treatise*, p. 242. "If we say, 'I am the man, who commands you,' the relative clause, with the antecedent *man*, form the predicate."—*Ib.*, p. 266.

"The spacious firmament on high,
With all the blue ethereal sky,
And spangled heav'ns, a shining frame,
Their great Original proclaim."
    —ADDISON. *Murray's Key*, p. 174; *Day's Gram.*, p. 92;
        Farnum's, 106.

UNDER NOTE VI.—ELLIPTICAL CONSTRUCTIONS.

"There is a reputable and a disreputable practice."—*Adams's Rhet.*, Vol. i, p. 350. "This and this man was born in her."—*Milton's Psalms*, lxxxvii. "This and that man was born in her."—*Psal.* lxxxvii, 5. "This and that man was born there."—*Hendrick's Gram.*, p. 94. "Thus *le* in *l~ego* and *l~egi* seem to be sounded equally long."—*Adam's Gram.*, p. 253; *Gould's*, 243. "A distinct and an accurate articulation forms the groundwork of good delivery."—*Kirkham's Elocution*, p. 25. "How is vocal and written language understood?"—*C. W. Sanders, Spelling-Book*, p. 7. "The good, the wise, and the learned man is an ornament to human society."—*Bartlett's Reader.* "On some points, the expression of song and speech is identical."—*Rush, on the Voice*, p. 425. "To every room there was an open and secret passage."—*Johnson's Rasselas*, p. 13. "There iz such a thing az tru and false taste, and the latter az often directs fashion, az the former."—*Webster's Essays*, p. 401. "There is such a thing as a prudent and imprudent institution of life, with regard to our health and our affairs"—*Butler's Analogy*, p. 210. "The lot of the outcasts of Israel and the dispersed of Judah, however different in one respect, have in another corresponded with wonderful exactness."—*Hope of Israel*, p. 301. "On these final syllables the radical and vanishing movement is performed."—*Rush, on the Voice*, p. 64. "To be young or old, good, just, or the contrary, are physical or moral events."—SPURZHEIM: *Felch's Comp. Gram.*, p. 29. "The eloquence of George Whitfield and of John Wesley was of a very different character each from the other."—*Dr. Sharp.* "The affinity of *m* for the series *b*, and of *n* for the series *t*, give occasion for other Euphonic changes."—*Fowler's E. Gram.*, §77.

"Pylades' soul and mad Orestes', was
In these, if we believe Pythagoras"—*Cowley's Poems*, p. 3.

UNDER NOTE VII.—DISTINCT SUBJECT PHRASES.

"To be moderate in our views, and to proceed temperately in the pursuit of them, is the best way to ensure success."—*Murray's Key*, 8vo, p. 206. "To be of any species, and to have a right to the name of that species, is all one."—*Locke's Essay*, p. 300. "With whom to will and to do is the same."—*Jamieson's Sacred History*, Vol. ii, p. 22. "To profess, and to possess, is very different things."—*Inst.*, p. 156. "To do justly, to love mercy, and to walk humbly with God, is duties of universal obligation."—*Ib.* "To be round or square, to be solid or fluid, to be large or small, and to be moved swiftly or slowly, is all equally alien from the nature of thought."—*Ib.* "The resolving of a sentence into its elements or parts of speech and stating the Accidents which belong to these, is called PARSING."—*Bullion's Pract. Lessons*, p. 9. "To spin and to weave, to knit and to sew, was once a girl's employment; but now to dress and catch a beau, is all she calls enjoyment."—*Lynn News*, Vol. 8, No. 1.

RULE XVII.—FINITE VERBS.

When a Verb has two or more nominatives connected by *or* or *nor*, it must agree with them singly, and not as if taken together: as, "Fear *or* jealousy *affects* him."—*W. Allen's Gram.*, p. 133. "Nor eye, *nor* listening ear, an object *finds*: creation sleeps."—*Young.* "Neither character *nor* dialogue *was* yet understood."—*L. Murray's Gram.*, p. 151.

"The wife, where danger *or* dishonour *lurks*,
Safest and seemliest by her husband stays."—*Milton, P. L.*, ix, 267.

OBSERVATIONS ON RULE XVII.

OBS. 1.—To this rule, so far as its application is practicable, there are properly no exceptions; for, *or* and *nor* being disjunctive conjunctions, the nominatives are of course to assume the verb separately, and as agreeing with each. Such agreement seems to be positively required by the alternativeness of the expression. Yet the ancient grammarians seldom, if at all, insisted on it. In Latin and Greek, a plural verb is often employed with singular nominatives thus connected; as,

"Tunc nec mens mini, nec color
Certa sede *manent*."—HORACE. See *W. Allen's Gram.*, p. 133.

[Greek: "Ean de adelphos æ adelphæ lumnoi huparchosi, kai leipomenoi osi tæs ephæmerou trophæs."]—*James*, ii. 15. And the best scholars have sometimes *improperly* imitated this construction in English; as, "Neither Virgil nor Homer *were* deficient in any of the former beauties."—DRYDEN'S PREFACE: *Brit. Poets*, Vol. iii, p. 168. "Neither Saxon nor Roman *have availed* to add any idea to his [Plato's] categories."—R. W. EMERSON: *Liberator*, No. 996.

"He comes—nor want *nor* cold his course *delay*:
Hide, blushing Glory! hide Pultowa's day."—*Dr. Johnson.*

"No monstrous height, *or* breadth, *or* length, *appear*;
The whole at once is bold and regular."—*Pope, on Crit.*, l. 250.

OBS. 2.—When two collective nouns of the singular form are connected by *or* or *nor,* the verb may agree with them in the plural number, because such agreement is adapted to each of them, according to Rule 15th; as, "Why *mankind*, or such a *part* of mankind, are placed in this condition."—*Butler's Analogy*, p. 213. "But neither the *Board* of Control nor the *Court* of Directors *have* any scruples about sanctioning the abuses of which I have spoken."—*Glory and Shame of England*, Vol. ii, p. 70.

OBS. 3.—When a verb has nominatives of different persons or numbers, connected by *or* or *nor*, an explicit concord with each is impossible; because the verb cannot be of different persons or numbers at the same time; nor is it so, even when its form is made the same in all the persons and numbers: thus, "I, thou, [or] he, *may affirm*; we, ye, or they, *may affirm*."—*Beattie's Moral Science*, p. 36. Respecting the proper management of the verb when its nominatives thus disagree, the views of our grammarians are not exactly coincident. Few however are ignorant enough, or rash enough, to deny that there may be an implicit or implied concord in such cases,—a *zeugma* of the verb in English, as well as of the verb or of the adjective in Latin or Greek. Of this, the following is a brief example: "But *he nor I feel* more."—*Dr. Young*, Night iii, p. 35. And I shall by-and-by add others—enough, I hope, to confute those false critics who condemn all such phraseology.

OBS. 4.—W. Allen's rule is this: "If the nominatives are of different numbers or persons, the verb agrees with *the last*; as, he *or* his *brothers were* there; neither *you nor I am* concerned."—*English Gram.*, p. 133. Lindley Murray, and others, say: (1.) "When singular pronouns, or a noun and pronoun, of different *persons*, are disjunctively connected, the verb must agree with that person which is placed *nearest to it*: as, 'I or thou *art* to blame;' 'Thou or I *am* in fault;' 'I, or thou, or he, *is* the author of it;' 'George or I *am* the person.' But it would be better to say; 'Either I am to blame, or thou art,' &c. (2.) When a disjunctive occurs between a singular noun, *or* pronoun, and a plural one, the verb is made to agree with the *plural* noun *and* pronoun: as, 'Neither poverty nor riches *were* injurious to him;' 'I or they *were* offended by it.' But in this case, the plural noun *or* pronoun, when *it* can conveniently be *done*, should be placed next to the verb."—*Murray's Gram.*, 8vo, p. 151; *Smith's New Gram.*, 128; *Alger's Gram.*, 54; *Comly's*, 78 and 79; *Merchant's*, 86; *Picket's*, 175; and many more. There are other grammarians who teach, that the verb must agree with the nominative which is placed next to it, whether this be singular or plural; as, "Neither the servants nor the master *is* respected;"—"Neither the master nor the servants *are* respected."—*Alexander Murray's Gram.*, p. 65. "But if neither the writings nor the author *is* in existence, the Imperfect should be used."—*Sanborn's Gram.*, p. 107.

OBS. 5.—On this point, a new author has just given us the following precept and criticism: "Never connect by *or,* or *nor,* two or more names or substitutes that have the same *asserter* [i.e. *verb*] depending on them for sense, if when taken separately, they require different forms of the *asserters*. Examples. 'Neither you nor I *am concerned.* Either he *or* thou *wast* there. Either they *or* he is faulty.' These examples are as erroneous as it would be to say, 'Neither *you am* concerned, nor am I.' 'Either he *wast* there, or thou wast.' 'Either *they is* faulty, or he is.' The sentences should stand thus—'Neither of us *is* concerned,' or, 'neither *are you* concerned, nor *am I.*' 'Either *he was* there, or *thou wast.*' 'Either *they are* faulty, or *he is.* They are, however, in all their impropriety, writen [sic—KTH] according to the principles of Goold Brown's *grammar!* and the theories of most of the former writers."—*Oliver B. Peirce's Gram.*, p. 252. We shall see by-and-by who is right.

OBS. 6.—Cobbett also—while he approves of such English as, "*He, with them, are* able to do much," for, "*He and they are* able to do much"— condemns expressly every possible example in which the verb has not a full and explicit concord with each of its nominatives, if they are connected by *or* or *nor*. His doctrine is this: "If nominatives of different *numbers* present themselves, we must not give them a verb which *disagrees* with either the one or the other. We must not say: 'Neither the halter *nor* the bayonets *are* sufficient to prevent us from obtaining our rights.' We must avoid this bad grammar by using a different form of words: as, 'We are to be prevented from obtaining our rights by neither the halter nor the bayonets.' And, why should we *wish* to write bad grammar, if we can express our meaning in good grammar?"—*Cobbett's E. Gram.*, ¶ 242. This question would have more force, if the correction here offered did not convey a meaning *widely different* from that of the sentence corrected. But he goes on: "We cannot say, 'They or I *am* in fault; I, or they, or he, *is* the author of it; George or I *am* the person.' Mr. Lindley Murray says, that we *may* use these phrases; and that we have only to take care that the verb agree with that person which is *placed nearest* to it; but, he says also, that it would be *better* to avoid such phrases by giving a different turn to our words. I do not like to leave any thing to chance or to discretion, when we have a *clear principle* for our guide."—*Ib.*, ¶ 243. This author's "clear principle" is merely his own confident assumption, that every form of figurative or implied agreement, every thing which the old grammarians denominated *zeugma*, is at once to be condemned as a solecism. He is however supported by an other late writer of much greater merit. See *Churchill's New Gram.*, pp. 142 and 312.

OBS. 7.—If, in lieu of their fictitious examples, our grammarians would give us actual quotations from reputable authors, their instructions would doubtless gain something in accuracy, and still more in authority. "*I or they were offended by it*," and, "*I, or thou, or he, is the author of it*," are expressions that I shall not defend. They imply an *egotistical* speaker, who either does not know, or will not tell, whether he is *offended* or not,— whether he *is the author* or not! Again, there are expressions that are unobjectionable, and yet not conformable to any of the rules just quoted. That nominatives may be correctly connected by *or* or *nor* without an express agreement of the verb with each of them, is a point which can be proved to as full certainty as almost any other in grammar; Churchill, Cobbett, and Peirce to the contrary notwithstanding. But with which of the nominatives the verb shall expressly agree, or to which of them it may most properly be understood, is a matter not easy to be settled by any *sure* general rule. Nor is the lack of such a rule a very important defect, though the inculcation of a false or imperfect one may be. So judged at least the ancient grammarians, who noticed and named almost every possible form of the zeugma, without censuring any as being ungrammatical. In the Institutes of English Grammar, I noted first the usual form of this concord, and then the allowable exceptions; but a few late writers, we see, denounce every form of it, exceptions and all: and, standing alone in their notions of the figure, value their own authority more than that of all other critics together.

OBS. 8.—In English, as in other languages, when a verb has discordant nominatives connected disjunctively, it most commonly agrees expressly with that which is nearest, and only by implication, with the more remote; as, "When some word or words *are* dependent on the attribute."—*Webster's Philos. Gram.*, p. 153. "To the first of these qualities, dulness or refinements *are* dangerous enemies."—*Brown's Estimate*, Vol. ii, p. 15. "He hazards his own life with that of his enemy, and one or both *are* very *honorably* murdered."—*Webster's Essays*, p. 235. "The consequence is, that they frown upon everyone whose faults or negligence *interrupts* or *retards* their lessons."—*W. C. Woodbridge: Lit. Conv.*, p. 114. "Good intentions, or at least sincerity of purpose, *was* never denied her."—*West's Letters*, p. 43. "Yet this proves not that either he or we *judge* them to be the rule."—*Barclay's Works*, i, 157. "First clear yourselves of popery before you or thou *dost throw* it upon us."—*Ib.*, i, 169. "*Is* the gospel or glad tidings of this salvation brought nigh unto all?"—*Ib.*, i, 362. "Being persuaded, that either they, or their cause, *is* naught."—*Ib.*, i, 504. "And the reader may judge whether he or I *do* most fully acknowledge man's fall."—*Ib.*, iii, 332. "To do justice to the Ministry, they have not yet pretended that any one, or any two, of the three Estates, *have* power to make a new law, without the concurrence of the third."—*Junius*, Letter xvii. "The forest, or hunting-grounds, *are* deemed the property of the tribe."—*Robertson's America*, i, 313. "Birth or titles *confer* no preëminence."—*Ib.*, ii, 184. "Neither tobacco nor hides *were* imported from Caraccas into Spain."—*Ib.*, ii, 507. "The keys or seed-vessel of the maple *has* two large side-wings."—*The Friend*, vii, 97. "An example or two *are* sufficient to illustrate the general observation."—*Dr. Murray's Hist. of Lang.*, i, 58.

> "Not thou, nor those thy factious arts engage, *Shall* reap that harvest of rebellious rage."—*Dryden*, p. 60.

OBS. 9.—But when the remoter nominative is the principal word, and the nearer one is expressed parenthetically, the verb agrees literally with the former, and only by implication, with the latter; as, "One example, (or ten,) *says* nothing against it."—*Leigh Hunt*. "And we, (or future ages,) *may* possibly *have* a proof of it."—*Bp. Butler*. So, when the alternative is merely in the *words*, not in the *thought*, the former term is sometimes considered the principal one, and is therefore allowed to control the verb; but there is always a harshness in this mixture of different numbers, and, to render such a construction tolerable, it is necessary to read the latter term like a parenthesis, and make the former emphatic: as, "A *parenthesis*, or brackets, *consists* of two angular strokes, or hooks, enclosing one or more words."—*Whiting's Reader*, p. 28. "To show us that our own *schemes*, or prudence, *have* no share in our advancements."—*Addison*. "The Mexican *figures*, or picture-writing, *represent* things, not words; *they* exhibit images to the eye, not ideas to the understanding."—*Murray's Gram.*, p. 243; *English Reader*, p. xiii. "At Travancore, *Koprah*, or dried cocoa-nut kernels, *is* monopolized by government."—*Maunder's Gram.*, p. 12. "The *Scriptures*, or Bible, *are* the only authentic source."—*Bp. Tomline's Evidences*.

> "Nor foes nor fortune *take* this power away;
> And is my Abelard less kind than *they*?"—*Pope*, p. 334.

OBS. 10.—The English adjective being indeclinable, we have no examples of some of the forms of zeugma which occur in Latin and Greek.

But adjectives differing in *number,* are sometimes connected without a repetition of the noun; and, in the agreement of the verb, the noun which is understood, is less apt to be regarded than that which is expressed, though the latter be more remote; as, "There *are one or two* small *irregularities* to be noted."—*Lowth's Gram.,* p. 63. "There *are one or two persons,* and but one or two."—*Hazlitt's Lectures.* "There *are one or two* others."—*Crombie's Treatise,* p. 206. "There *are one or two.*"—*Blair's Rhet.,* p. 319. "There *are one or more* seminaries in every province."—*H. E. Dwight: Lit. Conv.,* p. 133. "Whether *one or more* of the clauses *are* to be considered the nominative case."—*Murray's Gram.,* Vol. i, p. 150. "So that, I believe, there *is* not *more* than *one* genuine example extant."—*Knight, on the Greek Alphabet,* p. 10. "There *is,* properly, no *more* than *one* pause or rest in the sentence."—*Murray's Gram.,* Vol. i, p. 329; *Blair's Rhet.,* p. 125. "Sometimes a small *letter or two is* added to the capital."—*Adam's Lat. Gram.,* p. 223; *Gould's,* 283. Among the examples in the seventh paragraph above, there is one like this last, but with a plural verb; and if either is objectionable, *is* should here be *are.* The preceding example, too, is such as I would not imitate. To L. Murray, the following sentence seemed false syntax, because *one* does not agree with *persons*: "He saw *one or more persons* enter the garden."—*Murray's Exercises,* Rule 8th, p. 54. In his Key, he has it thus: "He saw one *person,* or *more than one,* enter the garden."—*Oct. Gram.,* Vol. ii, p. 189. To me, this stiff *correction,* which many later grammarians have copied, seems worse than none. And the effect of the principle may be noticed in Murray's style elsewhere; as, "When a *semicolon, or more than one,* have preceded."—*Octavo Gram.,* i, p. 277; *Ingersoll's Gram.,* p. 288. Here a ready writer would be very apt to prefer one of the following phrases: "When a semicolon *or two* have preceded,"—"When *one or two semicolons* have preceded,"—"When *one or more semicolons* have preceded." It is better to write by guess, than to become systematically awkward in expression.

OBS. 11.—In Greek and Latin, the pronoun of the first person, according to our critics, is *generally*[398] placed first; as, "[Greek: Ego kai su ta dikaia poiæsomen]. Xen."—*Milnes's Gr. Gram.*, p. 120. That is, "*Ego et tu justa faciemus.*" Again: "*Ego et Cicero valemus. Cic.*"—*Buchanan's Pref.*, p. x; *Adam's Gram.*, 206; *Gould's*, 203. "I and Cicero are well."—*Ib.* But, in English, a modest speaker usually gives to others the precedence, and mentions himself last; as, "He, or thou, or I, must go."—"Thou and I will do what is right."—"Cicero and I are well."—*Dr. Adam.*[399] Yet, in speaking of himself and his *dependants*, a person most commonly takes rank before them; as, "Your inestimable letters supported *myself, my wife*, and *children*, in adversity."—*Lucien Bonaparte, Charlemagne*, p. v. "And I shall be destroyed, *I* and *my house.*"—*Gen.*, xxxiv, 30. And in acknowledging a fault, misfortune, or censure, any speaker may assume the first place; as, "Both *I and thou* are in the fault."—*Adam's Gram.*, p. 207. "Both *I and you* are in fault."—*Buchanan's Syntax*, p. ix. "Trusty did not do it; *I and Robert* did it."—*Edgeworth's Stories.*

"With critic scales, weighs out the partial wit,
What *I*, or *you*, or *he*, or *no one* writ."
    —*Lloyd's Poems*, p. 162.

OBS. 12.—According to the theory of this work, verbs themselves are not unfrequently connected, one to an other, by *and, or,* or *nor*; so that two or more of them, being properly in the same construction, may be parsed as agreeing with the same nominative: as, "So that the blind and dumb [*man*] both *spake* and *saw.*"—*Matt.*, xii, 22. "That no one *might buy* or *sell.*"—*Rev.*, xiii, 17. "Which *see* not, nor *hear*, nor *know.*"—*Dan.*, v, 23. We have certainly very many examples like these, in which it is neither convenient nor necessary to suppose an ellipsis of the nominative before the latter verb, or before all but the first, as most of our grammarians do, whenever they find two or more finite verbs connected in this manner. It is true, the nominative may, in most instances, be repeated without injury to the sense; but this fact is no proof of such an ellipsis; because many a sentence which is not incomplete, may possibly take additional words without change of meaning. But these authors, (as I have already suggested under the head of conjunctions,) have not been very careful of their own consistency. If they teach, that, "Every finite verb has its own separate nominative, either expressed or implied," which idea Murray and others seem to have gathered from Lowth; or if they say, that, "Conjunctions really unite sentences, when they appear to unite only words," which notion they may have acquired from Harris; what room is there for that common assertion, that, "Conjunctions connect the same moods and tenses of verbs," which is a part of Murray's eighteenth rule, and found in most of our grammars? For no agreement is usually required between verbs that have separate nominatives; and if we supply a nominative wherever we do not find one for each verb, then in fact no two verbs will ever be connected by any conjunction.

OBS. 13.—What agreement there must be, between verbs that are in the same construction, it is not easy to determine with certainty. Some of the Latin grammarians tell us, that certain conjunctions connect "sometimes similar moods and tenses, and sometimes similar moods but different tenses." See *Prat's Grammatica Latina, Octavo*, Part ii, p. 95. Ruddiman, Adam, and Grant, omit the concord of tenses, and enumerate certain conjunctions which "couple like cases and moods." But all of them acknowledge some exceptions to their rules. The instructions of Lindley Murray and others, on this point, may be summed up in the following canon: "When verbs are connected by a conjunction, they must either agree in mood, tense, and form, or have separate nominatives expressed." This rule, (with a considerable exception to it, which other authors had not noticed,) was adopted by myself in the Institutes of English Grammar, and also retained in the Brief Abstract of that work, entitled, The First Lines of

English Grammar. It there stands as the thirteenth in the series of principal rules; but, as there is no occasion to refer to it in the exercise of parsing, I now think, a less prominent place may suit it as well or better. The principle may be considered as being less certain and less important than most of the usual rules of syntax: I shall therefore both modify the expression of it, and place it among the notes of the present code. See Notes 5th and 6th below.

OBS. 14.—By the agreement of verbs with each other in *form*, it is meant, that the simple form and the compound, the familiar form and the solemn, the affirmative form and the negative, or the active form and the passive, are not to be connected without a repetition of the nominative. With respect to *our* language, this part of the rule is doubtless as important, and as true, as any other. A thorough agreement, then, in mood, tense, and form, is *generally* required, when verbs are connected by *and, or,* or *nor*; and, under each part of this concord, there may be cited certain errors which ought to be avoided, as will by-and-by be shown. But, at the same time, there seem to be many allowable violations of the rule, some or other of which may perhaps form exceptions to every part of it. For example, the *tense* may be varied, as it often is in Latin; thus, "As the general state of religion *has been, is,* or *shall be,* affected by them."—*Butlers Analogy,* p. 241. "Thou art righteous, O Lord, which *art,* and *wast,* and *shall be,* because thou hast judged thus."—*Rev.,* xvi, 5. In the former of these examples, a repetition of the nominative would not be agreeable; in the latter, it would perhaps be an improvement: as, "*who* art, and *who* wast, and *who* shalt be." (I here change the pronoun, because the relative *which* is not now applied as above.) "This dedication may serve for almost any book, that *has been,* or *shall be* published."—*Campbell's Rhet.* p. 207; *Murray's Gram.,* p. 222. "It ought to be, '*has been, is,* or *shall be,* published.'"—*Crombie's Treatise,* p. 383. "Truth and good sense *are* firm, and *will* establish themselves."—*Blair's Rhet.* p. 286. "Whereas Milton *followed* a different plan, and *has given* a tragic conclusion to a poem otherwise epic in its form."—*Ib.*, p. 428. "I am certain, that such *are not*, nor ever *were*, the tenets of the church of England."—*West's Letters*, p. 148. "They *deserve*, and *will meet with*, no regard."—*Blair's Rhet.*, p. 109.

"Whoever thinks a faultless piece to see,
Thinks what ne'er *was*, nor *is*, nor e'er *shall be*."
    —*Pope, on Crit.*

OBS. 15.—So verbs differing in *mood* or *form* may sometimes agree with the same nominative, if the simplest verb be placed first—rarely, I think, if the words stand in any other order: as, "One *may be* free from affectation and *not have* merit"—*Blair's Rhet.*, p. 189. "There *is*, and *can be*, no other person."—*Murray's Key.* 8vo. p. 224. "To see what *is*, and *is allowed* to be, the plain natural rule."—*Butler's Analogy*, p. 284. "This great experiment *has worked*, and *is working*, well, every way well"—BRADBURN: *Liberator*, ix. 162. "This edition of Mr. Murray's works on English Grammar, *deserves* a place in Libraries, and *will not fail* to obtain it."—BRITISH CRITIC: *Murray's Gram.*, 8vo, ii, 299.

"What nothing earthly *gives*, or *can destroy*."—*Pope.*

"Some *are*, and *must be*, greater than the rest."—*Id.*

OBS. 16.—Since most of the tenses of an English verb are composed of two or more words, to prevent a needless or disagreeable repetition of auxiliaries, participles, and principal verbs, those parts which are common to two or more verbs in the same sentence, are generally expressed to the first, and understood to the rest; or reserved, and put last, as the common supplement of each; as, "To which they *do* or *can extend*."—*Butler's Analogy*, p. 77. "He *may*, as any one *may*, if he *will*, *incur* an infamous execution from the hands of civil justice."—*Ib.*, p. 82. "All that has usurped the name of virtue, and [*has*] deceived us by its semblance, must be a mockery and a delusion."—*Dr. Chalmers.* "Human praise, and human eloquence, may acknowledge it, but the Discerner of the heart never will" [*acknowledge it*].—*Id.* "We use thee not so hardly, as prouder livers do" [*use thee*].—*Shak.* "Which they might have foreseen and [*might have*] avoided."—*Butler.* "Every sincere endeavour to amend, shall be assisted, [*shall be*] accepted, and [*shall be*] rewarded."—*Carter.* "Behold, I thought, He will surely come out to me, and [*will*] stand and [*will*] call on the name of the Lord his God, and [*will*] strike his hand over the place, and [*will*] recover the leper."—*2 Kings*, v, 11. "They mean to, and will, hear patiently."—*Salem Register.* That is, "They mean to *hear patiently*, and *they will hear patiently.*" "He can create, and he destroy."—*Bible.* That is,—"and he *can* destroy."

"Virtue *may be assail'd*, but never *hurt*,
Surpris'd by unjust force, but not *inthrall'd*."—*Milton.*

"Mortals whose pleasures are their only care,
First wish to be *imposed on*, and then *are*."—*Cowper.*

OBS. 17.—From the foregoing examples, it may be seen, that the complex and divisible structure of the English moods and tenses, produces, when verbs are connected together, a striking peculiarity of construction in our language, as compared with the nearest corresponding construction in Latin or Greek. For we can connect different auxiliaries, participles, or principal verbs, without repeating, and apparently without connecting, the other parts of the mood or tense. And although it is commonly supposed that these parts are necessarily understood wherever they are not repeated, there are sentences, and those not a few, in which we cannot express them, without inserting also an additional nominative, and producing distinct clauses; as, "*Should* it not *be taken* up and *pursued?*"—*Dr. Chalmers.* "Where thieves *do* not *break* through nor *steal.*"—*Matt.*, vi, 20. "None present *could* either *read* or *explain* the writing-."—*Wood's Dict.*, Vol. i, p. 159. Thus we sometimes make a single auxiliary an index to the mood and tense of more than one verb.

OBS. 18.—The verb *do*, which is sometimes an auxiliary and sometimes a principal verb, is thought by some grammarians to be also fitly made a *substitute* for other verbs, as a pronoun is for nouns; but this doctrine has not been taught with accuracy, and the practice under it will in many instances be found to involve a solecism. In this kind of substitution, there must either be a true ellipsis of the principal verb, so that *do* is only an auxiliary; or else the verb *do*, with its *object* or *adverb*, if it need one, must exactly correspond to an action described before; so that to speak of *doing this* or *thus*, is merely the shortest way of repeating the idea: as, "He *loves* not plays, as thou *dost*. Antony."—*Shak.* That is, "as thou *dost love plays.*" "This fellow is wise enough *to play the fool*; and, *to do that* well, craves a kind of wit."—*Id.* Here, "*to do that*," is, "*to play the fool.*" "I will not *do it*, if I find thirty there."—*Gen.*, xviii, 30. Do what? Destroy the city, as had been threatened. Where *do* is an auxiliary, there is no real substitution; and, in the other instances, it is not properly the verb *do*, that is the substitute, but rather the word that follows it—or perhaps, both. For, since every action consists in *doing something* or in *doing somehow*, this general verb *do*, with *this, that, it, thus*, or *so*, to identify the action, may assume the import of many a longer phrase. But care must be taken not to substitute this verb for any term to which it is not equivalent; as, "The *a* is certainly to be sounded as the English *do*."—*Walker's Dict., w. A.* Say, "as the English *sound it*;" for *do* is here absurd, and grossly solecistical. "The duke had not behaved with that loyalty with which he ought to have *done*."—*Lowth's Gram.*, p. 111; *Murray's*, i, 212; *Churchill's*, 355; *Fisk's*, 137; *Ingersoll's*, 269. Say, "with which he ought to have *behaved*;" for, to have *done* with loyalty is not what was meant—far from it. Clarendon wrote the text thus: "The Duke had not behaved with that loyalty, *as* he ought to have done." This should have been corrected, not by changing *"as"* to *"with which"*, but by saying—"with that loyalty *which* he ought to have *observed;"* or, *"which would have become him"*.

OBS. 19.—It is little to the credit of our grammarians, to find so many of them thus concurring in the same obvious error, and even making bad English worse. The very examples which have hitherto been given to prove that *do* may be a substitute for other verbs, are *none of them in point*, and all of them have been constantly and shamefully *misinterpreted.* Thus: "They [*do* and *did*] sometimes also supply the place of *another verb*, and make the repetition of it, in the same or a subsequent sentence, unnecessary: as, 'You attend not to your studies as he *does*;' (i. e. as he *attends*, &c.) 'I shall come if I can; but if I *do not*, please to excuse me;' (i. e. if I *come* not.)"—*L. Murray's Gram.*, Vol. i, p. 88; *R. C. Smith's*, 88; *Ingersoll's*, 135; *Fisk's*, 78; *A. Flint's*, 41; *Hiley's*, 30. This remark, but not the examples, was taken from *Lowths Gram.*, p. 41. Churchill varies it thus, and retains Lowth's example: "It [i. e., *do*] is used also, to supply the *place of another verb*, in order to avoid the repetition of it: as, 'He *loves* not plays, As thou *dost*, Antony.' SHAKS."—*New Gram.*, p. 96. Greenleaf says, "To prevent the repetition of *one or more verbs*, in the same, or [a] following sentence, we frequently make use of *do* AND *did*; as, 'Jack learns the English language as fast as Henry *does*;' that is, 'as fast as Henry *learns*.' 'I shall come if I can; but if I *do* not, please to excuse me;' that is, 'if I *come* not.'"—*Gram. Simplified*, p. 27. Sanborn says, "*Do* is also used *instead of another verb*, and not unfrequently instead of both *the verb and its object*; as, 'he *loves* work as well as you *do*;' that is, as well as you *love work*."—*Analyt. Gram.*, p. 112. Now all these interpretations are wrong; the word *do, dost*, or *does*, being simply an auxiliary, after which the principal verb (with its object where it has one) is *understood.* But the first example is *bad English*, and its explanation is still worse. For, *"As he attends, &c.,"* means, "As *he* attends *to your studies!"* And what good sense is there in this? The sentence ought to have been, "You do not attend to your studies, as he does *to his*." That is—"as he does *attend* to his *studies*." This plainly shows that there is, in the text, no real substitution of *does* for *attends*. So of all other examples exhibited in our grammars, under this head: there is nothing to the purpose, in any of them; the common principle of *ellipsis* resolves them all. Yet, strange to say, in the latest and most learned of this sort of text-books, we find the same sham example, fictitious and solecistical as it is, still blindly repeated, to show that "*does*" is not in its own place, as an auxiliary, but "supplies the place of another verb."—*Fowler's E. Gram.*, 8vo. 1850. p. 265.

NOTES TO RULE XVII.

NOTE I.—When a verb has nominatives of different persons or numbers, [400] connected by *or* or *nor*, it must agree with the nearest, (unless an other be the principal term,) and must be understood to the rest, in the person and number required; as, "Neither you nor I *am* concerned."—*W. Allen.* "That neither they nor ye also *die*."—*Numb.*, xviii, 3.

> "But neither god, nor shrine, nor mystic rite,
> Their city, nor her walls, his soul *delight*."
> —*Rowe's Lucan*, B. x, l. 26.

NOTE II.—But, since all nominatives that require different forms of the verb, virtually produce separate clauses or propositions, it is better to complete the concord whenever we conveniently can, by expressing the verb or its auxiliary in connexion with each of them; as, "Either thou *art* to blame, or I *am*."—*Comly's Gram.*, p. 78. "Neither *were* their numbers, nor *was* their destination, known."—*W. Allen's Gram.*, p. 134. So in clauses connected by *and*: as, "But declamation *is* idle, and *murmurs* fruitless."—*Webster's Essays*, p. 82. Say,—"and murmurs *are* fruitless."

NOTE III.—In English, the speaker should always mention himself last; unless his own superior dignity, or the confessional nature of the expression, warrant him in taking the precedence: as, "*Thou or I* must go."—"He then addressed his discourse to *my father and me*."—"*Ellen and I* will seek, apart, the refuge of some forest cell."—*Scott.* See Obs. 11th above.

NOTE IV.—Two or more distinct subject phrases connected by *or* or *nor*, require a singular verb; and, if a nominative come after the verb, that must be singular also: as, "That a drunkard should be poor, *or* that a fop should be ignorant, *is* not strange."—"To give an affront, or to take one tamely, *is* no *mark* of a great mind." So, when the phrases are unconnected: as, "To spread suspicion, to invent calumnies, to propagate scandal, *requires* neither labour nor courage."—*Rambler*, No. 183.

NOTE V.—In general, when *verbs* are connected by *and, or,* or *nor*, they must either agree in mood, tense, and form, or the simplest in form must be placed first; as, "So Sennacherib king of Assyria *departed*, and *went* and *returned*, and *dwelt* at Nineveh."—*Isaiah*, xxxvii, 37. "For if I *be* an offender, or *have committed* any thing worthy of death, I refuse not to die."—*Acts*, xxv, 11.

NOTE VI.—In stead of conjoining discordant verbs, it is in general better to repeat the nominative or insert a new one; as, "He was greatly heated, and [*he] drank* with avidity."—*Murray's Key*, 8vo, p. 201. "A person may be great or rich by chance; but *cannot be* wise or good, without taking pains for it."—*Ib.*, p. 200. Say,—"but *no one can be* wise or good, without taking pains for it."

NOTE VII.—A mixture of the forms of the solemn style and the familiar, is inelegant, whether the verbs refer to the same nominative or have different ones expressed; as, "What *appears* tottering and in hazard of tumbling, *produceth* in the spectator the painful emotion of fear."—*Kames, El. of Crit.*, ii, 356. "And the milkmaid *singeth* blithe, And the mower *whets* his sithe."—*Milton's Allegro*, l. 65 and 66.

NOTE VIII.—To use different moods under precisely the same circumstances, is improper, even if the verbs have separate nominatives; as, "Bating that one *speak* and an other *answers*, it is quite the same."—*Blair's Rhet.*, p. 368. Say,—"that one *speaks*;" for both the speaking and the answering are assumed as facts.

NOTE IX.—When two terms are connected, which involve different forms of the same verb, such parts of the compound tenses as are not common to both forms, should be inserted in full: except sometimes after the auxiliary *do*; as, "And then he *falls*, as I *do*."—*Shak.* That is, "as I *do fall*." The following sentences are therefore faulty: "I think myself highly obliged *to make* his fortune, as he *has* mine."—*Spect.*, No. 474. Say,—"as he *has made* mine." "Every attempt to remove them, *has*, and likely *will prove* unsuccessful."—*Gay's Prosodical Gram.*, p. 4. Say,—"*has proved*, and likely *will prove*, unsuccessful."

NOTE X.—The verb *do* must never be substituted for any term to which its own meaning is not adapted; nor is there any use in putting it for a preceding verb that is equally short: as, "When we see how confidently men rest on groundless surmises in reference to their own souls, we cannot wonder that they *do it* in reference to others."—*Simeon.* Better:—"that they *so rest* in reference to *the souls of* others;" for this repeats the idea with more exactness. NOTE XI.—The preterit should not be employed to form the compound tenses of the verb; nor should the perfect participle be used for the preterit or confounded with the present. Thus: say, "To have *gone*," not, "To have *went*;" and, "I *did* so," not, "I *done* so;" or, "He *saw* them," not, "He *seen* them." Again: say not, "It was *lift* or *hoist* up;" but, "It was *lifted* or *hoisted* up."

NOTE XII.—Care should be taken, to give every verb or participle its appropriate form, and not to confound those which resemble each other; as, *to flee* and *to fly, to lay* and *to lie, to sit* and *to set, to fall* and *to fell,* &c. Thus: say, "He *lay* by the fire;" not, "He *laid* by the fire;"—"He *has become* rich;" not, "He *is become* rich;"—"I *would* rather *stay*;" not, "I *had* rather *stay*."

NOTE XIII.—In the syntax of words that express time, whether they be verbs, adverbs, or nouns, the order and fitness of time should be observed, that the tenses may be used according to their import. Thus: in stead of, "I *have seen* him *last week*;" say, "I *saw* him *last week*;"—and, in stead of, "I *saw* him *this week*;" say, "I *have seen* him *this week*." So, in stead of, "I *told* you *already*;" or, "I *have told* you *before*;" say, "I *have told* you *already*;"—"I *told* you *before*."

NOTE XIV.—Verbs of commanding, desiring, expecting, hoping, intending, permitting, and some others, in all their tenses, refer to actions or events, relatively present or future: one should therefore say, "I hoped you *would come*;" not, "I hoped you *would have come*;"—and, "I intended *to do* it;" not, "I intended *to have done* it;"—&c.

NOTE XV.—Propositions that are as true now as they ever were or will be, should generally be expressed in the present tense: as, "He seemed hardly to know, that two and two *make* four;" not, "*made*."—*Blair's Gram.*, p. 65. "He will tell you, that whatever *is, is* right." Sometimes the present tense is improper with the conjunction *that*, though it would be quite proper without it; as, "Others said, *That* it *is* Elias. And others said, *That* it *is* a prophet."—*Mark*, vi, 15. Here *That* should be omitted, or else *is* should be *was*. The capital *T* is also improper.

IMPROPRIETIES FOR CORRECTION.

FALSE SYNTAX UNDER RULE XVII.

UNDER THE RULE ITSELF.—NOMINATIVES CONNECTED BY OR.

"We do not know in what either reason or instinct consist."—*Rambler*, No. 41.

[FORMULE.—Not proper, because the verb *consist* is of the plural number, and does not correctly agree with its two nominatives, *reason* and *instinct*, which are connected by *or*, and taken disjunctively. But, according to Rule 17th, "When a verb has two or more nominatives connected by *or* or *nor*, it must agree with them singly, and not as if taken together." Therefore, *consist* should be *consists*; thus, "We do not know in what either reason or instinct *consists*."]

"A noun or a pronoun joined with a participle, constitute a nominative case absolute."—*Bicknell's Gram.*, Part ii, p. 50. "The relative will be of that case, which the verb or noun following, or the preposition going before, use to govern."—*Dr. Adam's Gram.*, p. 203. "Which the verb or noun following, or the preposition going before, usually govern."—*Gould's Adam's Gram.*, p. 200.[401] "In the different modes of pronunciation which habit or caprice give rise to."—*Knight, on the Greek Alphabet*, p. 14. "By which he, or his deputy, were authorized to cut down any trees in Whittlebury forest."—*Junius*, p. 251. "Wherever objects were to be named, in which sound, noise, or motion were concerned, the imitation by words was abundantly obvious."—*Blair's Rhet.*, p. 55. "The pleasure or pain resulting from a train of perceptions in different circumstances, are a beautiful contrivance of nature for valuable purposes."—*Kames, El. of Crit.*, i, 262. "Because their foolish vanity or their criminal ambition represent the principles by which they are influenced, as absolutely perfect."—*Life of Madame De Stael*, p. 2. "Hence naturally arise indifference or aversion between the parties."—*Brown's Estimate*, ii, 37. "A penitent unbeliever, or an impenitent believer, are characters no where to be found."—*Tract*, No. 183. "Copying whatever is peculiar in the talk of all those whose birth or fortune entitle them to imitation."—*Rambler*, No. 194. "Where love, hatred, fear, or contempt, are often of decisive influence."—*Duncan's Cicero*, p. 119. "A lucky anecdote, or an enlivening tale relieve the folio page."—*D'Israeli's Curiosities*, Vol. i, p. 15. "For outward matter or event, fashion not the character within."—*Book of Thoughts*, p. 37. "Yet sometimes we have seen that wine, or chance, have warmed cold brains."—*Dryden's Poems*, p. 76. "Motion is a Genus; Flight, a Species; this Flight or that Flight are Individuals."—*Harris's Hermes*, p. 38. "When *et, aut, vel, sine*, or *nec*, are joined to different members of the same sentence."—*Adam's Lat. and Eng. Gram.*, p. 206; *Gould's Lat. Gram.*, 203; *Grant's*, 266. "Wisdom or folly govern us."—*Fisk's English Gram.*, 84. "*A* or *an* are styled indefinite articles."—*Folker's Gram.*, p. 4. "A rusty nail, or a crooked pin, shoot up into prodigies."—*Spectator*, No. 7. "Are either the subject or the predicate in the second sentence modified?"—*Fowler's E. Gram.*, 8vo, 1850, p. 578, §589.

"Praise from a friend, or censure from a foe,
Are lost on hearers that our merits know."
—*Pope, Iliad*, B. x, l. 293.

UNDER THE RULE ITSELF.—NOMINATIVES CONNECTED BY NOR.

"Neither he nor she have spoken to him."—*Perrin's Gram.*, p. 237. "For want of a process of events, neither knowledge nor elegance preserve the reader from weariness."—JOHNSON: *in Crabb's Syn.*, p. 511. "Neither history nor tradition furnish such information."—*Robertson's Amer.*, Vol. i, p. 2. "Neither the form nor power of the liquids have varied materially."—*Knight, on the Greek Alph.*, p. 16. "Where neither noise nor motion are concerned."—*Blair's Rhet.*, p. 55. "Neither Charles nor his brother were qualified to support such a system."—*Junius*, p. 250. "When, therefore, neither the liveliness of representation, nor the warmth of passion, serve, as it were, to cover the trespass, it is not safe to leave the beaten track."—*Campbell's Rhet.*, p. 381. "In many countries called Christian, neither Christianity, nor its evidence, are fairly laid before men."—*Butler's Analogy*, p. 269. "Neither the intellect nor the heart are capable of being driven."—*Abbott's Teacher*, p. 20. "Throughout this hymn, neither Apollo nor Diana are in any way connected with the Sun or Moon."—*Coleridge's Introd.*, p. 199. "Of which, neither he, nor this Grammar, take any notice."—*Johnson's Gram. Com.*, p. 346. "Neither their solicitude nor their foresight extend so far."—*Robertson's Amer.*, Vol. i, p. 287. "Neither Gomara, nor Oviedo, nor Herrera, consider Ojeda, or his companion

Vespucci, as the first discoverers of the continent of America."—*Ib.*, Vol. i, p. 471. "Neither the general situation of our colonies, nor that particular distress which forced the inhabitants of Boston to take up arms, have been thought worthy of a moment's consideration."—*Junius*, p. 174.

"Nor War nor Wisdom yield our Jews delight,
They will not study, and they dare not fight."
—*Crabbe's Borough*, p. 50.

"Nor time nor chance breed such confusions yet,
Nor are the mean so rais'd, nor sunk the great."
—*Rowe's Lucan*, B. iii, l. 213.

UNDER NOTE I.—NOMINATIVES THAT DISAGREE.

"The definite article *the*, designates what particular thing or things is meant."—*Merchant's School Gram.*, p. 23 and p. 33. "Sometimes a word or words necessary to complete the grammatical construction of a sentence, is not expressed, but omitted by ellipsis."—*Burr's Gram.*, p. 26. "Ellipsis, or abbreviations, is the wheels of language."—*Maunder's Gram.*, p. 12. "The conditions or tenor of none of them appear at this day."—*Hutchinson's Hist. of Mass.*, Vol. i, p. 16. "Neither men nor money were wanting for the service."—*Ib.*, Vol. i, p. 279. "Either our own feelings, or the representation of those of others, require frequent emphatic distinction."—*Barber's Exercises*, p. 13. "Either Atoms and Chance, or Nature are uppermost: now I am for the latter part of the disjunction,"—*Collier's Antoninus*, p. 181. "Their riches or poverty are generally proportioned to their activity or indolence."—*Ross Cox's Narrative.* "Concerning the other part of him, neither you nor he seem to have entertained an idea."—*Bp. Horne.* "Whose earnings or income are so small."—*N. E. Discipline*, p. 130. "Neither riches nor fame render a man happy."—*Day's Gram.*, p. 71. "The references to the pages, always point to the first volume, unless the Exercises or Key are mentioned."—*Murray's Gram.*, Vol. ii, p. 283.

UNDER NOTE II.—COMPLETE THE CONCORD.

"My lord, you wrong my father; nor he nor I are capable of harbouring a thought against your peace."—*Walpole*. "There was no division of acts; no pauses or interval between them; but the stage was continually full; occupied either by the actors, or the chorus."—*Blair's Rhet.*, p. 463. "Every word ending in B, P, F, as also many in V, are of this order."—*Dr. Murray's Hist. of Lang.*, i, 73. "As proud as we are of human reason, nothing can be more absurd than the general system of human life and human knowledge."—*Bolingbroke, on Hist.*, p. 347. "By which the body of sin and death is done away, and we cleansed."—*Barclay's Works*, i, 165. "And those were already converted, and regeneration begun in them."—*Ib.*, iii, 433. "For I am an old man, and my wife well stricken in years."—*Luke*, i, 18. "Who is my mother, or my brethren?"—*Mark*, iii, 33. "Lebanon is not sufficient to burn, nor the beasts thereof sufficient for a burnt-offering."—*Isaiah*, xl, 16. "Information has been obtained, and some trials made."—*Society in America*, i, 308. "It is as obvious, and its causes more easily understood."—*Webster's Essays*, p. 84. "All languages furnish examples of this kind, and the English as many as any other."—*Priestley's Gram.*, p. 157. "The winters are long, and the cold intense."—*Morse's Geog.*, p. 39. "How have I hated instruction, and my heart despised reproof!"—*Prov.*, v, 12. "The vestals were abolished by Theodosius the Great, and the fire of Vesta extinguished."—*Lempriere, w. Vestales*. "Riches beget pride; pride, impatience."—*Bullions's Practical Lessons*, p. 89. "Grammar is not reasoning, any more than organization is thought, or letters sounds."—*Enclytica*, p. 90. "Words are implements, and grammar a machine."—*Ib.*, p. 91.

UNDER NOTE III.—PLACE OF THE FIRST PERSON.

"I or thou art the person who must undertake the business proposed."—*Murray's Key*, 8vo, p. 184. "I and he were there."—*Dr. Ash's Gram.*, p. 51. "And we dreamed a dream in one night, I and he."—*Gen.*, xli, 11. "If my views remain the same as mine and his were in 1833."—GOODELL: *Liberator*, ix, 148. "I and my father were riding out."—*Inst.*, p. 158. "The premiums were given to me and George."—*Ib.* "I and Jane are invited."—*Ib.* "They ought to invite me and my sister."—*Ib.* "I and you intend going."—*Guy's Gram.*, p. 55. "I and John are going to Town."—*British Gram.*, p. 193. "I, and he are sick. I, and thou are well."—*James Brown's American Gram.*, Boston Edition of 1841, p. 123. "I, and he is. I, and thou art. I, and he writes."—*Ib.*, p. 126. "I, and they are well. I, thou, and she were walking."—*Ib.*, p. 127.

UNDER NOTE IV.—DISTINCT SUBJECT PHRASES.

"To practise tale-bearing, or even to countenance it, are great injustice."—*Brown's Inst.*, p. 159. "To reveal secrets, or to betray one's friends, are contemptible perfidy."—*Ib.* "To write all substantives with capital letters, or to exclude them from adjectives derived from proper names, may perhaps be thought offences too small for animadversion; but the evil of innovation is always something."—*Dr. Barrow's Essays*, p. 88. "To live in such families, or to have such servants, are blessings from God."—*Family Commentary*, p. 64. "How they portioned out the country, what revolutions they experienced, or what wars they maintained, are utterly unknown."—*Goldsmith's Greece*, Vol. i, p. 4. "To speak or to write perspicuously and agreeably, are attainments of the utmost consequence to all who purpose, either by speech or writing, to address the public."—*Blair's Rhet.*, p. 11.

UNDER NOTE V.—MAKE THE VERBS AGREE.

"Doth he not leave the ninety and nine, and goeth into the mountains, and seeketh that which is gone astray?"—*Matt.*, xviii, 12. "Did he not fear the Lord, and besought the Lord, and the Lord repented him of the evil which he had pronounced?"—*Jer.*, xxvi, 19. "And dost thou open thine eyes upon such an one, and bringest me into judgement with thee?"—*Job*, xiv, 3. "If any man among you seem to be religious, and bridleth not his tongue, but deceiveth his own heart, this man's religion is vain."—*James*, i, 26. "If thou sell aught unto thy neighbour, or buyest aught of thy neighbour's hand, ye shall not oppress one an other."—*Leviticus*, xxv, 14. "And if thy brother that dwelleth by thee, shall have become poor, and be sold to thee, thou shalt not compel him to serve as a bond servant."—WEBSTER'S BIBLE: *Lev.*, xxv, 39. "If thou bring thy gift to the altar, and there rememberest that thy brother hath aught against thee," &c.—*Matt.*, v, 23. "Anthea was content to call a coach, and crossed the brook."—*Rambler*, No. 34. "It is either totally suppressed, or appears in its lowest and most imperfect form."—*Blair's Rhet.*, p. 23. "But if any man be a worshiper of God, and doeth his will, him he heareth."—*John*, ix, 31. "Whereby his righteousness and obedience, death and sufferings without, become profitable unto us, and is made ours."—*Barclay's Works*, i, 164. "Who ought to have been here before thee, and object, if they had aught against me."—*Acts*, xxiv, 19.

"Yes! thy proud lords, unpitied land, shall see
That man hath yet a soul, and dare be free."—*Campbell.*

UNDER NOTE VI.—USE SEPARATE NOMINATIVES.

"*H* is only an aspiration or breathing; and sometimes at the beginning of a word is not sounded at all."—*Lowth's Gram.*, p. 4. "Man was made for society, and ought to extend his good will to all men."—*Ib.*, p. 12;

Murray's, i, 170. "There is, and must be, a supreme being, of infinite goodness, power, and wisdom, who created and supports them."—*Beattie's Moral Science*, p. 201. "Were you not affrighted, and mistook a spirit for a body?"—*Watson's Apology*, p. 122. "The latter noun or pronoun is not governed by the conjunction *than* or *as*, but agrees with the verb, or is governed by the verb or the preposition, expressed or understood."—*Murray's Gram.*, p. 214; *Russell's*, 103; *Bacon's*, 51; *Alger's*, 71; *R. C. Smith's*, 179. "He had mistaken his true interests, and found himself forsaken."—*Murray's Key*, 8vo, p. 201. "The amputation was exceedingly well performed, and saved the patient's life."—*Ib.*, p. 191. "The intentions of some of these philosophers, nay, of many [,] might have been, and probably were good."—*Ib.*, p. 216. "This may be true, and yet will not justify the practice."—*Webster's Essays*, p. 33. "From the practice of those who have had a liberal education, and are therefore presumed to be best acquainted with men and things."—*Campbell's Rhet.*, p. 161. "For those energies and bounties which created and preserve the universe."—*J. Q. Adams's Rhet.*, i, 327. "I shall make it once for all and hope it will be afterwards remembered."—*Blair's Lect.*, p. 45. "This consequence is drawn too abruptly, and needed more explanation."—*Ib.*, p. 229. "They must be used with more caution, and require more preparation."— *Ib.*, p. 153. "The apostrophe denotes the omission of an *i*, which was formerly inserted, and made an addition of a syllable to the word."— *Priestley's Gram.*, p. 67. "The succession may be rendered more various or more uniform, but in one shape or an other is unavoidable."—*Kames, El. of Crit.*, i. 253. "It excites neither terror nor compassion, nor is agreeable in any respect."—*Ib.*, ii, 277.

"Cheap vulgar arts, whose narrowness affords
No flight for thoughts, but poorly stick at words."—*Denham*.

UNDER NOTE VII.—MIXTURE OF DIFFERENT STYLES.

"Let us read the living page, whose every character delighteth and instructs us."—*Maunder's Gram.*, p. 5. "For if it be in any degree obscure, it puzzles, and doth not please."—*Kames, El. of Crit.*, ii, 357. "When a speaker addresseth himself to the understanding, he proposes the instruction of his hearers."—*Campbell's Rhet.*, p. 13. "As the wine which strengthens and refresheth the heart."—*H. Adams's View*, p. 221. "This truth he wrappeth in an allegory, and feigns that one of the goddesses had taken up her abode with the other."—*Pope's Works*, iii, 46. "God searcheth and understands the heart."—*Thomas à Kempis*. "The grace of God, that brings salvation hath appeared to all men."—*Barclays Works*, i, 366. "Also we speak not in the words, which man's wisdom teaches; but which the Holy Ghost teacheth."—*Ib.*, i, 388. "But he hath an objection, which he urgeth, and by which he thinks to overturn all."—*Ib.*, iii, 327. "In that it gives them not that comfort and joy which it giveth unto them who love it."—*Ib.*, i, 142. "Thou here misunderstood the place and misappliedst it."—*Ib.*, iii, 38. "Like the barren heath in the desert, which knoweth not when good comes."—*Friends' Extracts*, p. 128; *N. E. Discip.*, p. 75. "It speaketh of the time past, but shews that something was then doing, but not quite finished."—*E. Devis's Gram.*, p. 42. "It subsists in spite of them; it advanceth unobserved."—PASCAL: *Addison's Evidences*, p. 17.

"But where is he, the Pilgrim of my song?—
Methinks he cometh late and tarries long."—*Byron*, Cant. iv, St. 164.

UNDER NOTE VII.—CONFUSION OF MOODS.

"If a man have a hundred sheep, and one of them is gone astray, &c."—*Kirkham's Gram.*, p. 227 with 197. "As a speaker advances in his discourse, especially if it be somewhat impassioned, and increases in energy and earnestness, a higher and louder tone will naturally steal upon him."—

Kirkham's Elocution, p. 68. "If one man esteem a day above another, and another esteemeth every day alike; let every man be fully persuaded in his own mind."—*Barclay's Works*, i, 439. "If there be but one body of legislators, it is no better than a tyranny; if there are only two, there will want a casting voice."—*Addison, Spect.*, No. 287. "Should you come up this way, and I am still here, you need not be assured how glad I shall be to see you."—*Ld. Byron.* "If he repent and becomes holy, let him enjoy God and heaven."—*Brownson's Elwood*, p. 248. "If thy fellow approach thee, naked and destitute, and thou shouldst say unto him, 'Depart in peace; be you warmed and filled;' and yet shouldst give him not those things that are needful to him, what benevolence is there in thy conduct?"—*Kirkham's Elocution*, p. 108.

"Get on your nightgown, lost occasion calls us.
And show us to be watchers."
  —*Beauties of Shakspeare*, p. 278.

"But if it climb, with your assisting hands,
The Trojan walls, and in the city stands."
  —*Dryden's Virgil*, ii, 145.

_____"Though Heaven's king
Ride on thy wings, and thou with thy compeers,
Us'd to the yoke, draw'st his triumphant wheels."
  —*Milton, P. L.*, iv, l. 973.

"Us'd to the yoke, *draw'dst* his triumphant wheels."
  —*Lowth's Gram.*, p. 106.

UNDER NOTE IX.—IMPROPER ELLIPSES.

"Indeed we have seriously wondered that Murray should leave some things as he has."—*Education Reporter*. "Which they neither have nor can do."—*Barclay's Works*, iii, 73. "The Lord hath, and doth, and will reveal his will to his people, and hath and doth raise up members of his body," &c.—*Ib.*, i, 484. "We see then, that the Lord hath, and doth give such."—*Ib.*, i, 484. "Towards those that have or do declare themselves members."—*Ib.*, i, 494. "For which we can, and have given our sufficient reasons."—*Ib.*, i, 507. "When we mention the several properties of the different words in sentences, in the same manner as we have those of *William's*, above, what is the exercise called?"—*Smith's New Gram.*, p. 12. "It is, however to be doubted whether this peculiarity of the Greek idiom, ever has or will obtain extensively in the English."—*Nutting's Gram.*, p. 47. "Why did not the Greeks and Romans abound in auxiliary words as much as we?"—*Murray's Gram.*, Vol. i, p. 111. "Who delivers his sentiments in earnest, as they ought to be in order to move and persuade."—*Kirkham's Elocution*, p. 151.

UNDER NOTE X.—DO, USED AS A SUBSTITUTE.

"And I would avoid it altogether, if it could be done."—*Kames, El. of Crit.*, i, 36. "Such a sentiment from a man expiring of his wounds, is truly heroic, and must elevate the mind to the greatest height that can be done by a single expression."—*Ib.*, i, 204. "Successive images making thus deeper and deeper impressions, must elevate more than any single image can do."—*Ib.*, i, 205. "Besides making a deeper impression than can be done by cool reasoning."—*Ib.*, ii, 273. "Yet a poet, by the force of genius alone, can rise higher than a public speaker can do."—*Blair's Rhet.*, p. 338. "And the very same reason that has induced several grammarians to go so far as they have done, should have induced them to go farther."—*Priestley's Gram., Pref.*, p. vii. "The pupil should commit the first section perfectly, before he does the second part of grammar."— *Bradley's Gram.*, p. 77. "The Greek *ch* was pronounced hard, as we now do in *chord*."—*Booth's Introd. to Dict.*, p. 61. "They pronounce the syllables in a different manner from what they do at other times."— *Murray's Eng. Reader*, p. xi. "And give him the formal cool reception that Simon had done."—*Dr. Scott, on Luke*, vii. "I do not say, as some have done."—*Bolingbroke, on Hist.*, p. 271. "If he suppose the first, he may do the last."—*Barclay's Works*, ii, 406. "Who are now despising Christ in his inward appearance, as the Jews of old did him in his outward."—*Ib.*, i, 506. "That text of Revelations must not be understood, as he doth it."— *Ib.*, iii, 309. "Till the mode of parsing the noun is so familiar to him, that he can do it readily."—*Smith's New Gram.*, p. 13. "Perhaps it is running the same course which Rome had done before."—*Middleton's Life of Cicero*. "It ought even on this ground to be avoided; which may easily be done by a different construction."—*Churchill's Gram.*, p. 312. "These two languages are now pronounced in England as no other nation in Europe does besides."—*Creighton's Dict.*, p. xi. "Germany ran the same risk that Italy had done."—*Murray's Key*, 8vo, p. 211: see *Priestley's Gram.*, p. 196.

UNDER NOTE XI.—PRETERITS AND PARTICIPLES.

"The Beggars themselves will be broke in a trice."—*Swift's Poems*, p. 347. "The hoop is hoist above his nose."—*Ib.*, p. 404. "My heart was lift up in the ways of the Lord. 2 CHRON."—*Joh. Dict., w. Lift*. "Who sin so oft have mourned, Yet to temptation ran."—*Burns*. "Who would not have let them appeared."—*Steele*. "He would have had you sought for ease at the hands of Mr. Legality."—*Pilgrim's Progress*, p. 31. "From me his madding mind is start, And wooes the widow's daughter of the glen."—SPENSER: *Joh. Dict., w. Glen*. "The man has spoke, and still speaks."—*Ash's Gram.*, p. 54. "For you have but mistook me all this while."—*Beauties of Shak.*, p. 114. "And will you rent our ancient love asunder."—*Ib.*, p. 52. "Mr. Birney has plead the inexpediency of passing such resolutions."— *Liberator*, Vol. xiii,

p. 194. "Who have wore out their years in such most painful Labours."—*Littleton's Dict., Pref.* "And in the conclusion you were chose probationer."—*Spectator,* No. 32.

"How she was lost, took captive, made a slave;
And how against him set that should her save."—*Bunyan.*

UNDER NOTE XII.—VERBS CONFOUNDED.

"But Moses preferred to wile away his time."—*Parker's English Composition,* p. 15. "His face shown with the rays of the sun."—*Calvin's Inst.,* 4to, p. 76. "Whom they had sat at defiance so lately."— *Bolingbroke, on Hist.,* p. 320. "And when he was set, his disciples came unto him."—*Matt.,* v, 1. "When he was set down on the judgement-seat."— *Ib.,* xxvii, 19. "And when they had kindled a fire in the midst of the hall, and were set down together, Peter sat down among them."—*Luke,* xxii, 55. "So after he had washed their feet, and had taken his garments, and was set down again, he said unto them, Know ye what I have done to you?"—*John,* xiii, 12. "Even as I also overcame, and am set down with my Father in his throne."—*Rev.,* iii, 21. "We have such an high priest, who is set on the right hand of the throne of the Majesty in the heavens."— *Heb.,* viii, 1. "And is set down at the right hand of the throne of God."—*Ib.,* xii, 2.[402] "He sat on foot a furious persecution."— *Payne's Geog.,* ii, 418. "There layeth an obligation upon the saints, to help such."—*Barclay's Works,* i, 389. "There let him lay."—*Byron's Pilgrimage,* C. iv, st. 180. "Nothing but moss, and shrubs, and stinted trees, can grow upon it."—*Morse's Geog.,* p. 43. "Who had lain out considerable sums purely to distinguish themselves."—*Goldsmith's Greece,* i, 132. "Whereunto the righteous fly and are safe."—*Barclay's Works,* i, 146. "He raiseth from supper, and laid aside his garments."—*Ib.,* i, 438. "Whither—Oh! whither shall I fly?"—*Murray's*

English Reader, p. 123. "Flying from an adopted murderer."—*Ib.*, p. 122. "To you I fly for refuge."—*Ib.*, p. 124. "The sign that should warn his disciples to fly from approaching ruin."—*Keith's Evidences*, p. 62. "In one she sets as a prototype for exact imitation."—*Rush, on the Voice*, p. xxiii. "In which some only bleat, bark, mew, winnow, and bray, a little better than others."—*Ib.*, p. 90. "Who represented to him the unreasonableness of being effected with such unmanly fears."—*Rollin's Hist.*, ii, 106. "Thou sawedst every action."—*Guy's School Gram.*, p. 46. "I taught, thou taughtedst, he or she taught."—*Coar's Gram.*, p. 79. "Valerian is taken by Sapor and flead alive, A. D. 260."—*Lempriere's Chron. Table, Dict.*, p. xix. "What a fine vehicle is it now become for all conceptions of the mind!"—*Blair's Rhet.*, p. 139. "What are become of so many productions?" —*Volney's Ruins*, p. 8. "What are become of those ages of abundance and of life?"—*Keith's Evidences*, p. 107. "The Spartan admiral was sailed to the Hellespont."—*Goldsmiths Greece*, i, 150. "As soon as he was landed, the multitude thronged about him."—*Ib.*, i, 160. "Cyrus was arrived at Sardis."—*Ib.*, i, 161. "Whose year was expired."—*Ib.*, i, 162. "It had better have been, 'that faction which.'"—*Priestley's Gram.*, p. 97. "This people is become a great nation."—*Murray's Gram.*, p. 153; *Ingersoll's*, 249. "And here we are got into the region of ornament."—*Blair's Rhet.*, p. 181. "The ungraceful parenthesis which follows, had far better have been avoided."—*Ib.*, p. 215. "Who forced him under water, and there held him until drounded."—*Indian Wars*, p. 55.

"I had much rather be myself the slave,
And wear the bonds, than fasten them on him."—*Cowper*.

UNDER NOTE XIII.—WORDS THAT EXPRESS TIME.

"I had finished my letter before my brother arrived."—*Kirkham's Gram.*, p. 139. "I had written before I received his letter."—*Blair's Rhet.*, p. 82. "From what has been formerly delivered."—*Ib.*, p. 182. "Arts were of late introduced among them."—*Ib.*, p. 245. "I am not of opinion that such rules can be of much use, unless persons saw them exemplified."—*Ib.*, p. 336. "If we use the noun itself, we should say, 'This composition is John's.' "—*Murray's Gram.*, p. 174. "But if the assertion referred to something, that is not always the same, or supposed to be so, the past tense must be applied."—*Ib.*, p. 191. "They told him, that Jesus of Nazareth passeth by."—*Luke*, xviii, 37. "There is no particular intimation but that I continued to work, even to the present moment."—*R. W. Green's Gram.*, p. 39. "Generally, as was observed already, it is but hinted in a single word or phrase."—*Campbell's Rhet.*, p. 36. "The wittiness of the passage was already illustrated."—*Ib.*, p. 36. "As was observed already."—*Ib.*, p. 56. "It was said already in general."—*Ib.*, p. 95. "As I hinted already."—*Ib.*, p. 134. "What I believe was hinted once already."—*Ib.*, p. 148. "It is obvious, as hath been hinted formerly, that this is but an artificial and arbitrary connexion."—*Ib.*, p. 282. "They have done anciently a great deal of hurt."—*Bolingbroke, on Hist.*, p. 109. "Then said Paul, I knew not, brethren, that he is the High Priest."—*Dr. Webster's Bible*: Acts, xxiii, 5. "Most prepositions originally denote the relation of place, and have been thence transferred to denote by similitude other relations."—*Lowth's Gram.*, p. 65; *Churchill's*, 116. "His gift was but a poor offering, when we consider his estate."—*Murray's Key*, 8vo, p. 194. "If he should succeed, and should obtain his end, he will not be the happier for it."—*Murray's Gram.*, i, p. 207. "These are torrents that swell to-day, and have spent themselves by to-morrow."—*Blair's Rhet.*, p. 286. "Who have called that wheat to-day, which they have called tares to-morrow."—*Barclay's Works*, iii. 168. "He thought it had been one of his tenants."—*Ib.*, i, 11. "But if one went unto them from the dead, they will repent."—*Luke*, xvi, 30. "Neither will they be persuaded, though one rose from the dead."—*Ib.*, *verse* 31. "But it is while men slept that the archenemy has always sown his tares."—*The Friend*, x, 351. "Crescens would not fail to have exposed him."—*Addison's Evidences*, p. 30.

"Bent was his bow, the Grecian hearts to wound;
Fierce as he mov'd, his silver shafts resound."
   —*Pope, Iliad*, B. i, l. 64.

UNDER NOTE XIV.—VERBS OF COMMANDING, &c.

"Had I commanded you to have done this, you would have thought hard of it."—*G. B.* "I found him better than I expected to have found him."—*Priestley's Gram.*, p. 126. "There are several smaller faults, which I at first intended to have enumerated."—*Webster's Essays*, p. 246. "Antithesis, therefore, may, on many occasions, be employed to advantage, in order to strengthen the impression which we intend that any object should make."—*Blair's Rhet.*, p. 168. "The girl said, if her master would but have let her had money, she might have been well long ago."—See *Priestley's Gram.*, p. 127. "Nor is there the least ground to fear, that we should be cramped here within too narrow limits."—*Campbell's Rhet.*, p. 163; *Murray's Gram.*, i, 360. "The Romans, flushed with success, expected to have retaken it."—*Hooke's Hist.*, p. 37. "I would not have let fallen an unseasonable pleasantry in the venerable presence of Misery, to be entitled to all the wit that ever Rabelais scattered."—STERNE: *Enfield's Speaker*, p. 54. "We expected that he would have arrived last night."—*Inst.* p. 192. "Our friends intended to have met us."—*Ib.* "We hoped to have seen you."—*Ib.* "He would not have been allowed to have entered."—*Ib.*

UNDER NOTE XV.—PERMANENT PROPOSITIONS.

"Cicero maintained that whatsoever was useful was good."—"I observed that love constituted the whole moral character of God."—*Dwight.* "Thinking that one gained nothing by being a good man."—*Voltaire.* "I have already told you that I was a gentleman."—*Fontaine.* "If I should ask, whether ice and water were two distinct species of things."—*Locke.* "A stranger to the poem would not easily discover that this was verse."—*Murray's Gram.*, 12mo, p. 260. "The doctor affirmed, that fever always produced thirst."—*Inst.*, p. 192. "The ancients asserted, that virtue was its own reward."—*Ib.* "They should not have repeated the error, of insisting that the infinitive was a mere noun."—*Diversions of Purley*, Vol. i, p. 288. "It was observed in Chap. III. that the distinctive *or* had a double use."—*Churchill's Gram.*, p. 154. "Two young gentlemen, who have made a discovery that there was no God."—*Swift.*

RULE XVIII.—INFINITIVES.

The Infinitive Mood is governed in general by the preposition TO, which commonly connects it to a finite verb: as, "I desire TO *learn.*"—*Dr. Adam.* "Of me the Roman people have many pledges, which I must strive, with my utmost endeavours, TO *preserve*, TO *defend*, TO *confirm*, and TO *redeem.*"—*Duncan's Cicero*, p. 41.

> "What if the foot, ordain'd the dust TO *tread*,
> Or hand TO *toil*, aspir'd TO *be* the head?"—*Pope.*

OBSERVATIONS ON RULE XVIII.

OBS. 1.—No word is more variously explained by grammarians, than this word TO, which is put before the verb in the infinitive mood. Johnson, Walker, Scott, Todd, and some other lexicographers, call it an *adverb*; but, in explaining its use, they say it denotes certain *relations*, which it is not the office of an adverb to express. (See the word in *Johnson's Quarto Dictionary*.) D. St. Quentin, in his Rudiments of General Grammar, says, "*To*, before a verb, is an *adverb*;" and yet his "Adverbs are words that are joined to verbs or adjectives, and express some *circumstance* or *quality*." See pp. 33 and 39. Lowth, Priestley, Fisher, L. Murray, Webster, Wilson, S. W. Clark, Coar, Comly, Blair, Felch, Fisk, Greenleaf, Hart, Weld, Webber, and others, call it a *preposition*; and some of these ascribe to it the government of the verb, while others do not. Lowth says, "The *preposition* TO, placed before the verb, *makes* the infinitive mood."—*Short Gram.*, p. 42. "Now this," says Horne Tooke, "is manifestly not so: for TO placed before the verb *loveth*, will not make the infinitive mood. He would have said more truly, that TO placed before some *nouns*, makes *verbs*."—*Diversions of Purley*, Vol. i, p. 287.

OBS. 2.—Skinner, in his *Canones Etymologici*, calls this TO "an *equivocal article*,"—*Tooke*, ib., i, 288. Nutting, a late American grammarian, says: "The *sign* TO is no other than the Greek article *to*; as, *to agapan* [, to love]; or, as some say, it is the Saxon *do*"—*Practical Gram.*, p. 66. Thus, by suggesting two false and inconsistent derivations, though he uses not the name *equivocal article*, he first makes the word an *article*, and then *equivocal*—equivocal in etymology, and of course in meaning.[403] Nixon, in his English Parser, supposes it to be, *unequivocally*, the Greek article [Greek: to], *the*. See the work, p. 83. D. Booth says, "*To* is, by us, applied to Verbs; but it was the neuter Article (*the*) among the Greeks."—*Introd. to Analyt. Dict.*, p. 60. According to Horne Tooke, "Minshew also distinguishes between the preposition TO, and the *sign* of the infinitive TO. Of the former he is silent, and of the latter he says: 'To, as *to* make, *to* walk, *to* do, a Græco articulo [Greek: to].' But Dr. Gregory Sharpe is persuaded, that our language has taken it from the *Hebrew*. And Vossius derives the correspondent Latin preposition AD from the same source."—*Diversions of Purley*, Vol. i, p. 293.

OBS. 3.—Tooke also says, "I observe, that Junius and Skinner and Johnson, have not chosen to give the slightest hint concerning the derivation of TO."—*Ibid.* But, certainly, of his *adverb* TO, Johnson gives this hint: "TO, Saxon; *te*, Dutch." And Webster, who calls it not an adverb, but a preposition, gives the same hint of the source from which it comes to us. This is as much as to say, it is etymologically the old Saxon preposition *to*—which, truly, it is—the very same word that, for a thousand years or more, has been used before nouns and pronouns to govern the objective case. Tooke himself does not deny this; but, conceiving that almost all particles, whether English or any other, can be traced back to ancient verbs or nouns, he hunts for the root of this, in a remoter region, where he pretends to find that *to* has the same origin as *do*; and though he detects the former in a *Gothic noun*, he scruples not to identify it with an *auxiliary verb*! Yet he elsewhere expressly denies, "that *any* words change their nature by use, so as to belong sometimes to one part of speech, and sometimes to another."—*Div. of Pur.*, Vol. i, p. 68.

OBS 4.—From this, the fair inference is, that he will have both *to* and *do* to be "*nouns substantive*" still! "Do (the *auxiliary* verb, as it has been called) is derived from the same root, and is indeed the same word as TO."—*Ib.*, Vol. i, p. 290. "Since FROM means *commencement* or *beginning*, TO must mean *end* or *termination*."—*Ib.*, i, 283. "The preposition TO (in Dutch written TOE and TOT, a little nearer to the original) is the Gothic substantive [Gothic: taui] or [Gothic: tauhts], i. e. *act, effect, result, consummation.* Which Gothic substantive is indeed itself no other than the past participle of the verb [Gothic: taujan], *agere.* And what is *done*, is *terminated, ended, finished.*"—*Ib.*, i, 285. No wonder that Johnson, Skinner, and Junius, gave no hint of *this* derivation: it is not worth the ink it takes, if it cannot be made more sure. But in showing its bearing on the verb, the author not unjustly complains of our grammarians, that: "Of all the points which they endeavour to *shuffle over*, there is none in which they do it more grossly than in this of the infinitive."—*Ib.*, i, 287.

OBS. 5.—Many are content to call the word TO a *prefix*, a *particle*, a *little word*, a *sign of the infinitive*, a *part of the infinitive*, a *part of the verb*, and the like, without telling us whence it comes, how it differs from the preposition *to*, or to what part of speech it belongs. It certainly is not what we usually call a *prefix*, because we never *join it to* the verb; yet there are three instances in which it becomes such, before a noun: viz., *to-day, to-night, to-morrow*. If it is a "*particle*," so is any other preposition, as well as every small and invariable word. If it is a "*little word*," the whole bigness of a preposition is unquestionably found in it; and no "*word*" is so small but that it must belong to some one of the ten classes called parts of speech. If it is a "*sign of the infinitive*," because it is used before no other mood; so is it a *sign of the objective case*, or of what in Latin is called the dative, because it precedes no other case. If we suppose it to be a "*part of the infinitive*," or a "*part of the verb*," it is certainly no *necessary* part of either; because there is no verb which may not, in several different ways, be properly used in the infinitive without it. But if it be a part of the infinitive, it must be a *verb*, and ought to be classed with the *auxiliaries*. Dr. Ash accordingly placed it among the auxiliaries; but he says, (inaccurately, however,) "The auxiliary *sign seems* to have the nature of *adverbs*."—*Grammatical Institutes*, p. 33. "The auxiliary [signs] *are, to, do, did, have, had, shall, will, may, can, must, might*," &c.—*Ib.*, p. 31.

OBS. 6.—It is clear, as I have already shown, that the word *to* may be a *sign* of the infinitive, and yet not be a *part* of it. Dr. Ash supposes, it may even be a part of the *mood*, and yet not be a part of the *verb*. How this can be, I see not, unless the mood consists in something else than either the form or the parts of the verb. This grammarian says, "In parsing, every word should be considered as a *distinct part of speech*: for though two or more words may be united to form a mode, a tense, or a comparison; yet it seems quite improper to unite two or more words to make a noun, a verb, an adjective, &c."—*Gram. Inst.*, p. 28. All the auxiliaries, therefore, and the particle *to* among them, he parses separately; but he follows not his own advice, to make them distinct parts of speech; for he calls them all *signs* only, and signs are not one of his ten parts of speech. And the participle too, which is one of the ten, and which he declares to be "no part of the verb," he parses separately; calling it a verb, and not a participle, as often as it accompanies any of his auxiliary signs. This is certainly a greater impropriety than there can be in supposing an auxiliary and a participle to constitute a verb; for the mood and tense are the properties of the compound, and ought not to be ascribed to the principal term only. Not so with the preposition *to* before the infinitive, any more than with the conjunction *if* before the subjunctive. These may well be parsed as separate parts of speech; for these moods are sometimes formed, and are completely distinguished in each of their tenses, without the adding of these signs.

OBS. 7.—After a careful examination of what others have taught respecting this disputed point in grammar, I have given, in the preceding rule, that explanation which I consider to be the most correct and the most simple, and also as well authorized as any. Who first parsed the infinitive in this manner, I know not; probably those who first called the *to* a *preposition*; among whom were Lowth and the author of the old British Grammar. The doctrine did not originate with me, or with Comly, or with any American author. In Coar's English Grammar, published in London in 1796. the phrase *to trample* is parsed thus: "*To*—A preposition, serving for a sign of the infinitive mood to the verb *Trample*—A verb neuter, infinitive mood, present tense, *governed by the preposition* TO before it. RULE. The preposition *to* before a verb, is the sign of the infinitive mood." See the work, p. 263. This was written by a gentleman who speaks of his "long habit of teaching the Latin Tongue," and who was certainly partial enough to the principles of Latin grammar, since he adopts in English the whole detail of Latin cases.

OBS 8.—In Fisher's English Grammar, London, 1800, (of which there had been many earlier editions,) we find the following rule of syntax: "When two principal *Verbs* come together, the latter of them expresses an unlimited Sense, with the Preposition *to* before it; as *he loved to learn; I chose to dance*: and is called the *infinitive Verb*, which may also follow a Name or Quality; as, *a Time to sing; a Book delightful to read*." That this author supposed the infinitive to be *governed* by *to*, and not by the preceding verb, noun, or adjective, is plain from the following note, which he gives in his margin: "The Scholar will best understand this, by being told that *infinite* or *invariable Verbs*, having neither Number, Person, nor Nominative Word belonging to them, are known or *governed by the Preposition* TO coming before them. The Sign *to* is often understood; as, Bid Robert and his company (*to*) tarry."—*Fisher's New Gram.*, p. 95.

OBS. 9.—The forms of parsing, and also the rules, which are given in the early English grammars, are so very defective, that it is often impossible to say positively, what their authors did, or did not, intend to teach. Dr. Lowth's specimen of "grammatical resolution" contains four infinitives. In his explanation of the first, the preposition and the verb are parsed separately, as above; except that he says nothing about government. In his account of the other three, the two words are taken together, and called a "*verb*, in the infinitive *mode*." But as he elsewhere calls the particle *to* a preposition, and nowhere speaks of any thing else as governing the infinitive, it seems fair to infer, that he conceived the verb to be the regimen of this preposition.[404] If such was his idea, we have the learned Doctor's authority in opposition to that of his professed admirers and copyists. Of these, Lindley Murray is doubtless the most famous. But Murray's twelfth rule of syntax, while it expressly calls *to* before the infinitive a *preposition*, absurdly takes away from it this regimen, and leaves us a preposition that *governs nothing*, and has apparently nothing to do with the *relation* of the terms between which it occurs.

OBS. 10.—Many later grammarians, perceiving the absurdity of calling *to* before the infinitive a *preposition* without supposing it to govern the verb, have studiously avoided this name; and have either made the "*little word*" a supernumerary part of speech, or treated it as no part of speech at all. Among these, if I mistake not, are Allen, Lennie, Bullions, Alger, Guy, Churchill, Hiley, Nutting, Mulligan, Spencer, and Wells. Except Comly, the numerous modifiers of Murray's Grammar are none of them more consistent, on this point, than was Murray himself. Such of them as do not follow him literally, either deny, or forbear to affirm, that *to* before a verb is a *preposition*; and consequently either tell us not what it is, or tell us falsely; some calling it "*a part of the verb*," while they neither join it to the verb as a prefix, nor include it among the auxiliaries. Thus Kirkham: "*To* is not a preposition when *joined to* a verb in this mood; thus, *to* ride, *to* rule; but it should be parsed *with the verb*, and *as a part* of it."—*Gram. in Familiar Lect.*, p. 137. So R. C. Smith: "This little word *to* when *used before* verbs in this manner, is not a preposition, but forms a part of the verb, and, in parsing, should be so considered."—*Productive Gram.*, p. 65. How can that be "*a part* of the verb," which is *a word* used *before* it? or how is *to* "joined to the verb," or made a part of it, in the phrase, "*to* ride?" But Smith does not abide by his own doctrine; for, in an other part of his book, he adopts the phraseology of Murray, and makes *to* a preposition: saying, "The *preposition* TO, though generally used before the latter verb, is sometimes properly omitted; as, 'I heard him say it;' instead of '*to* say it.'"—*Productive Gram.*, p. 156. See *Murray's Rule* 12th.

OBS. 11.—Most English grammarians have considered the word *to* as a part of the infinitive, a part *of the verb*; and, like the teachers of Latin, have referred the government of this mood to a preceding verb. But the rule which they give, is partial, and often inapplicable; and their exceptions to it, or the heterogeneous parts into which some of them divide it, are both numerous and puzzling. They teach that at least half of the ten different parts of speech "*frequently* govern the infinitive:" if so, there should be a distinct rule for each; for why should the government of one part of speech be made an exception to that of an other? and, if this be done, with respect to the infinitive, why not also with respect to the objective case? In all instances to which their rule is applicable, the rule which I have given, amounts to the same thing; and it obviates the necessity for their numerous exceptions, and the embarrassment arising from other constructions of the infinitive not noticed in them. Why then is the simplest solution imaginable still so frequently rejected for so much complexity and inconsistency? Or how can the more common rule in question be suitable for a child, if its applicability depends on a relation between the two verbs, which the preposition *to* sometimes expresses, and sometimes does not?

OBS. 12.—All authors admit that in some instances, the sign *to* is "superfluous and improper," the construction and government appearing complete without it; and the "Rev. Peter Bullions, D. D., Professor of Languages in the Albany Academy," has recently published a grammar, in which he adopts the common rule, "One verb governs *another* in the infinitive mood; as, *I desire to learn*;" and then remarks, "The infinitive after a verb is governed by it *only when the attribute expressed by the infinitive is either the subject or* [the] *object of the other verb*. In such expressions as '*I read to learn*,' the infinitive is *not governed* by 'I read,' but depends on the phrase '*in order to*' understood."—*Bullions's Prin. of E. Gram.*, p. 110. But, "*I read 'in order to' to learn*," is not English; though it might be, if either *to* were any thing else than a preposition: as, "Now *set to to learn* your lesson." This broad exception, therefore, which embraces well-nigh half the infinitives in the language, though it contains some obvious truth, is both carelessly stated, and badly resolved. The single particle *to* is quite sufficient, both to govern the infinitive, and to connect it to any antecedent term which can make sense with such an adjunct. But, in fact, the reverend author must have meant to use the "*little word*" but once; and also to deny that it is a preposition; for he elsewhere says expressly, though, beyond question, erroneously, "A preposition should never be used before the infinitive."—*Ib.*, p. 92. And he also says, "The *Infinitive* mood expresses *a thing* in a general manner, without distinction of number, person, *or time*, and commonly has TO *before* it."—*Ib.*, Second Edition, p. 35. Now if TO is "*before*" the mood, it is certainly not *a part* of it. And again, if this mood had no distinction of "*time*," our author's two tenses of it, and his own two special rules for their application, would be as absurd as is his notion of its government. See his *Obs. 6 and 7, ib.*, p. 124.

OBS. 13.—Richard Hiley, too, a grammarian of perhaps more merit, is equally faulty in his explanation of the infinitive mood. In the first place, he absurdly says, "TO *before the infinitive mood*, is considered as forming *part of the verb*; but in *every other* situation it is a preposition."—*Hiley's Gram.*, Third Edition, p. 28. To teach that a "*part of the verb*" stands "*before the mood*," is an absurdity manifestly greater, than the very opposite notion of Dr. Ash, that what is *not a part of the verb*, may yet be included *in the mood*. There is no need of either of these false suppositions; or of the suggestion, doubly false, that *to* "in *every other* situation, is a preposition." What does *preposition* mean? Is *to* a preposition when it is placed *after* a verb, and *not* a preposition when it is placed *before* it? For example: "I rise *to shut to* the door."—See *Luke*, xiii, 25.

OBS. 14.—In his syntax, this author further says, "When two verbs come together, the latter *must be in the infinitive mood, when it denotes the object* of the former; as, 'Study *to improve*.'" This is his *Rule*. Now look at his *Notes*. "1. When the latter verb *does not express* the object, *but the end*, or something remote, the word *for*, or the words *in order to*, are understood; as, 'I read *to learn*;' that is, 'I read *for* to learn,' or, '*in order* [TO] *to* learn.' The word *for*, however, is never, in such instances, expressed in good language. 2. The infinitive is *frequently governed* by adjectives, substantives, and participles; but in *this instance* also, a preposition is understood, though *never expressed*; as, 'Eager *to learn*;' that is, 'eager *for* to learn;' or, '*for* learning;' 'A desire *to improve*;' that is, '*for to improve*.'"— *Hiley's Gram.*, p. 89. Here we see the origin of some of Bullions's blunders. *To* is so small a word, it slips through the fingers of these gentlemen. Words utterly needless, and worse than needless, they foist into our language, in instances beyond number, to explain infinitives that occur at almost every breath. Their students must see that, "*I read to learn*," and, "*I study to improve*," with countless other examples of either sort, are very *different constructions*, and not to be parsed by the same rule! And here the only government of the infinitive which Hiley affirms, is immediately contradicted by the supposition of a needless *for* "understood."

OBS. 15.—In all such examples as, "I *read* to *learn*,"—"I *strive* to *learn*"—"Some *eat* to *live*,"—"Some *live* to *eat*,"—"She *sings* to *cheer* him,"—"I *come* to *aid* you,"—"I *go* to *prepare* a place for you,"—*the action and its purpose* are connected by the word *to*; and if, in the countless instances of this kind, the former verbs *do not govern* the latter, it is not because the phraseology is elliptical, or ever was elliptical,[405] but because in no case is there any such government, except in the construction of those verbs which take the infinitive after them without the preposition *to*. Professor Bullions will have the infinitive to be governed by a finite verb, "when the *attribute expressed by the infinitive is the subject* of the other verb." An infinitive may be made *the subject* of a finite verb; but this grammarian has mistaken the established meaning of *subject*, as well as of *attribute,* and therefore written nonsense. Dr. Johnson defines his *adverb* TO, "A particle coming between two verbs, and noting the second as the *object* of the first." But of all the words which, according to my opponents and their oracles, govern the infinitive, probably not more than a quarter are such verbs as usually *have an object* after them. Where then is the propriety of their notion of infinitive government? And what advantage has it, even where it is least objectionable?

OBS. 16.—Take for an example of this contrast the terms, "Strive to enter in—many will seek to enter in."—*Luke,* xiii, 24. Why should it be thought more eligible to say, that the verb *strive* or *will seek* governs the infinitive verb *to enter*; than to say, that *to* is a preposition, showing the relation between *strive* and *enter,* or between *will seek* and *enter,* and governing the latter verb? (See the exact and only needful form for parsing any such term, in the *Twelfth Praxis* of this work.) None, I presume, will deny, that in the Greek or the Latin of these phrases, the finite verbs govern the infinitive; or that, in the French, the infinitive *entrer* is governed first by one preposition, and then by an other. "*Contendite intrare—multi quærent intrare.*"—*Montanus.* "Efforcez-vous _d'_entrer—plusieurs chercheront *à* y entrer."—*French Bible.* In my opinion, *to* before a verb is as fairly a preposition as the French *de* or *à*; and it is the main design of these observations, while they candidly show the reader what others teach, *to prove it so.* The only construction which makes it any thing else, is that which puts it after a verb or a participle, in the sense of an adverbial supplement; as, "The infernal idol is bowed down *to*."—*Herald of Freedom.* "Going *to* and *fro*."—*Bible.* "At length he came *to*."—"Tell him to heave *to*."—"He was ready to set *to*." With singular absurdness of opinion, some grammarians call *to* a preposition, when it thus *follows* a verb and governs nothing, who resolutely deny it that name, when it *precedes* the verb, and *requires it to be in the infinitive mood,* as in the last two examples. Now, if this is not *government,* what is? And if *to,* without government, is not an *adverb,* what is? See Obs. 2d on the List of Prepositions.

OBS. 17.—The infinitive thus admits a simpler solution in English, than in most other languages; because we less frequently use it without a preposition, and seldom, if ever, allow any variety in this connecting and governing particle. And yet in no other language has its construction given rise to a tenth part of that variety of absurd opinions, which the defender of its true syntax must refute in ours. In French, the infinitive, though frequently placed in immediate dependence on an other verb, may also be governed by several different prepositions, (as, *à, de, pour, sans, après,*) according to the sense.[406] In Spanish and Italian, the construction is similar. In Latin and Greek, the infinitive is, for the most part, immediately dependent on an other verb. But, according to the grammars, it may stand for a noun, in all the six cases; and many have called it an *indeclinable noun.* See the Port-Royal Latin and Greek grammars; in which several peculiar constructions of the infinitive are referred to the government of a *preposition*—constructions that occur frequently in Greek, and sometimes even in Latin.

OBS. 18.—It is from an improper extension of the principles of these "learned languages" to ours, that much of the false teaching which has so greatly and so long embarrassed this part of English grammar, has been, and continues to be, derived. A late author, who supposes every infinitive to be virtually *a noun,* and who thinks he finds in ours *all the cases* of an English noun, not excepting the possessive, gives the following account of its origin and nature: "This mood, with almost all its properties and uses, has been adopted into our language from the ancient Greek and Latin tongues. * * * The definite article [Greek: tò] [,] *the,* which they [the Greeks] used before the infinitive, to mark, in an especial manner, its nature of a substantive, *is evidently the same word* that we use before our infinitive; thus, '*to* write,' signifies *the* writing; that is, the action of writing;—and when a verb governs an infinitive, it only governs it *as in the objective case.*"—*Nixon's English Parser*, p. 83. But who will believe, that our old Saxon ancestors borrowed from Greek or Latin what is now our construction of the very *root* of the English verb, when, in all likelihood, they could not read a word in either of those languages, or scarcely knew the letters in their own, and while it is plain that they took not thence even the inflection of a *single branch* of any verb whatever?

OBS. 19.—The particle *to*, being a very common preposition in the Saxon tongue, has been generally used before the English infinitive, ever since the English language, or any thing like it, existed. And it has always *governed the verb*, not indeed "as in the *objective case*," for no verb is ever declined by cases, but simply as the *infinitive mood*. In the Anglo-Saxon version of the Gospels, which was made as early as the eleventh century, the infinitive mood is sometimes expressed in this manner, and sometimes by the termination *on* without the preposition. Dr. Johnson's History of the English Language, prefixed to his large Dictionary, contains, of this version, and of Wickliffe's, the whole of the first chapter of Luke; except that the latter omits the first four verses, so that the numbers for reference do not correspond. Putting, for convenience, English characters for the Saxon, I shall cite here three examples from each; and these, if he will, the reader may compare with the 19th, the 77th, and the 79th verse, in our common Bible. SAXON: "And ic eom asend with the *sprecan.* and the this bodian."—*Lucæ*, i, 19. WICKLIFFE: "And Y am sent to thee *to speke* and *to evangelise* to thee these thingis."—*Luk*, i, 15. SAXON: "*To syllene* his folce hæle gewit on hyra synna forgyfnesse."—*Lucæ*, i, 77. WICKLIFFE: "*To geve* science of heelth to his puple into remissioun of her synnes."— *Luk*, i, 73. SAXON: "*Onlyhtan* tham the on thystrum and on deathes sceade sittath. ure fet *to gereccenne* on sibbe weg."—*Lucæ*, i, 79. WICKLIFFE: "*To geve* light to them that sitten in derknessis, and in schadowe of deeth, *to dresse* oure feet into the weye of pees."—*Luk*, i, 75. "In Anglo-Saxon," says Dr. Latham, "the dative of the infinitive verb ended in *-nne*, and was preceded by the preposition *to*: as, To lufienne = *ad amandum* [= *to loving*, or *to love*]; To bærnenne = *ad urendum* [= *to burning*, or *to burn*]; To syllanne = *ad dandum* [= *to giving*, or *to give*]."—*Hand-Book*, p. 205.

OBS. 20.—Such, then, has ever been the usual construction of the *English* infinitive mood; and a wilder interpretation than that which supposes *to* an *article*, and says, "*to write* signifies *the writing*," cannot possibly be put upon it. On this supposition, "I am going *to write* a letter," is a pure Grecism; meaning, "I am going *the writing* a letter," which is utter nonsense. And further, the infinitive in Greek and Latin, as well as in Saxon and English, is always in fact governed as a *mood*, rather than as a *case*, notwithstanding that the Greek article in any of its four different cases may, in some instances, be put before it; for even with an article before it, the Greek infinitive usually retains its regimen as a verb, and is therefore not "a *substantive*," or noun. I am well aware that some learned critics, conceiving that the essence of the verb consists in predication, have plainly denied that the infinitive is a verb; and, because it may be made the subject of a finite verb, or may be governed by a verb or a preposition, have chosen to call it "a mere noun substantive." Among these is the erudite Richard Johnson, who, with so much ability and lost labour, exposed, in his Commentaries, the errors and defects of Lily's Grammar and others. This author adduces several reasons for his opinion; one of which is the following: "Thirdly, it is found to have a Preposition set before it, an other *sure sign of a Substantive*; as, '*Ille nihil præter loqui, et ipsum maledicè et malignè, didicit.*' Liv. l. 45, p. 888. [That is, "He learned nothing *but to speak*, and that slanderously and maliciously."] '*At si quis sibi beneficium dat, nihil interest inter dare et accipere.*' Seneca, de Ben. l. 5, c. 10." [That is, "If any one bestows a benefit on himself, there is no difference *between give and take*;" [407]—or, "*between bestowing* and *receiving*."]—See *Johnson's Gram. Com.*, p. 342.

But I deny that a preposition is a "sure sign of a substantive." (See Obs. 2d on the Prepositions, and also Obs. 1st on the List of Prepositions, in the tenth chapter of Etymology.) And if we appeal to philological authorities, to determine whether infinitives are nouns or verbs, there will certainly be found more for the latter name, than the former; that is, more in number, if not in weight; though it must be confessed, that many of the old Latin grammarians did, as Priscian tells us, consider the infinitive a noun, calling it *Nomen Verbi*, the Name of the Verb.[408] If we appeal to reasons, there are more also of these;—or at least as many, and most of them better: as, 1. That the infinitive is often transitive; 2. That it has tenses; 3. That it is qualified by adverbs, rather than by adjectives; 4. That it is never declined like a noun; 5. That the action or state expressed by it, is not commonly abstract, though it may be so sometimes; 6. That in some languages it is *the root* from which all other parts of the verb are derived, as it is in English.

OBS. 21.—So far as I know, it has not yet been denied, that *to* before a *participle* is a preposition, or that a preposition before a participle *governs* it; though there are not a few who erroneously suppose that participles, by virtue of such government, are necessarily converted into *nouns*. Against this latter idea, there are many sufficient reasons; but let them now pass, because they belong not here. I am only going to prove, in this place, that *to* before the infinitive is *just such a word* as it is before the participle; and this can be done, call either of them what you will. It is plain, that if the infinitive and the participle are ever *equivalent to each other*, the same word *to* before them both must needs be equivalent *to itself*. Now I imagine there are some examples of each equivalence; as, "When we are habituated *to doing* [or *to do*] any thing wrong, we become blinded by it."—*Young Christian*, p. 326. "The lyre, or harp, was best adapted *to accompanying* [or *to accompany*] their declamations."—*Music of Nature*, p. 336. "The new beginner should be accustomed *to giving* [or *to give*] all the reasons for each part of speech."—*Nutting's Gram.*, p. 88. "Which, from infecting our religion and morals, fell *to corrupt* [say, *to corrupting*] our language."—SWIFT: *Blair's Rhet.*, p. 108. Besides these instances of *sameness in the particle*, there are some cases of *constructional ambiguity*, the noun and the verb having the same form, and the *to* not determining which is meant: as, "He was inclined *to sleep*."—"It must be a bitter experience, to be more accustomed *to hate* than *to love*." Here are *double* doubts for the discriminators: their "*sign of the infinitive*" fails, or becomes uncertain; *because they do not know it from a preposition*. Cannot my opponents see in these examples an argument against the distinction which they attempt to draw between *to* and *to*? An other argument as good, is also afforded by the fact, that our ancestors often used the participle after *to*, in the very same texts in which we have since adopted the infinitive in its stead; as, "And if yee wolen resceyue, he is Elie that is *to comynge*."—*Matt.*, xi, 14. "Ihesu that delyueride us fro wraththe *to comynge*."—*1 Thes.*, i, 10. These, and seventeen other examples of the same kind, may be seen in *Tooke's Diversions of Purley*, Vol. ii. pp. 457 and 458.

OBS. 22.—Dr. James P. Wilson, speaking of the English infinitive, says: —"But if the appellation of *mode* be denied it, it is then a *verbal noun*. This is indeed *its truest character*, because *its idea ever represents* an *object of approach*. *To* supplies the defect of a termination characteristic of the infinitive, precedes it, and marks it either as *that, towards which* the preceding verb is directed;[409] or it signifies *act*, and shows the word to import an action. When the infinitive is the expression of an *immediate* action, which it must be, after the verbs, *bid, can, dare, do, feel, hear, let, make, may, must, need, see, shall*, and *will*, the *preposition* TO is omitted."—*Essay on Grammar*, p. 129. That the truest character of the infinitive is that of a verbal noun, is not to be conceded, in weak abandonment of all the reasons for a contrary opinion, until it can be shown that the action or being expressed by it, must needs assume a *substantive* character, in order to be "that *towards which* the preceding verb is directed."

But this character is manifestly not supposable of any of those infinitives which, according to the foregoing quotation, must follow other verbs without the intervention of the preposition *to*: as, "Bid him *come*;"—"He can *walk*." And I see no reason to suppose it, where the relation of the infinitive to an other word is *not "immediate"* but marked by the preposition, as above described. For example: "And he laboured till the going-down of the sun TO *deliver* him."—*Dan.*, vi, 14. Here *deliver* is governed by *to*, and connected by it to the finite verb *laboured*; but to tell us, it is to be understood *substantively* rather than *actively*, is an assumption as false, as it is needless.

OBS. 23.—To deny to the infinitive the appellation of *mood*, no more makes it a *verbal noun*, than does the Doctor's solecism about what "ITS IDEA *ever represents*." "The infinitive therefore," as Horne Tooke observes, "appears plainly to be what the Stoics called it, *the very verb itself*, pure and uncompounded."—*Diversions of Purley*, Vol. i, p. 286. Not indeed as including the particle *to*, or as it stands in the English perfect tense, but as it occurs in the *simple root*. But I cited Dr. Wilson, as above, not so much with a design of animadverting again on this point, as with reference to the *import* of the particle *to*; of which he furnishes a twofold explanation, leaving the reader to take which part he will of the contradiction. He at first conceives it to convey in general the idea of "*towards*," and to mark the infinitive as a term "*towards which*" something else "*is directed*." If this interpretation is the true one, it is plain that *to* before a verb is no other than the common preposition *to*; and this idea is confirmed by its ancient usage, and by all that is certainly known of its derivation. But if we take the second solution, and say, "it signifies *act*," we make it not a preposition, but either a noun or a verb; and then the question arises, *Which of these is it*? Besides, what sense can there be, in supposing *to go* to mean *act go*, or to be equivalent to *do go*.[410]

OBS. 24.—Though the infinitive is commonly made an adjunct to some finite verb, yet it may be connected to almost all the other parts of speech, or even to an other infinitive. The preposition *to* being its only and almost universal index, we seldom find any other preposition put before this; unless the word *about,* in such a situation, is a preposition, as I incline to think it is.[411] Anciently, the infinitive was sometimes preceded by *for* as well as *to*; as, "I went up to Jerusalem *for to* worship."—*Acts,* xxiv, 11. "What went ye out *for to* see?"—*Luke,* vii, 26. "And stood up *for to* read."—*Luke,* iv, 16. Here modern usage rejects the former preposition: the idiom is left to the uneducated. But it seems practicable to subjoin the infinitive to every one of the ten parts of speech, except the article: as,

1. To a noun; as, "If there is any *precept to obtain* felicity."—*Hawkesworth.* "It is high *time to awake* out of sleep."—*Rom.,* xiii, 11. "To flee from the *wrath to come.*"—*Matt.,* iii, 7.

2. To an adjective; as, "He seemed *desirous to speak,* yet *unwilling to offend.*"—*Hawkesworth.* "He who is the *slowest to promise,* is *the quickest to perform.*"—*Art of Thinking,* p. 35.

3. To a pronoun; as, "I discovered *him to be* a scholar."—*W. Allen's Gram.,* p. 166. "Is it lawful for *us to give* tribute to Cæsar?"—*Luke,* xx, 22. "Let me desire *you to reflect* impartially."—BLAIR: *Murray's Eng. Reader,* p. 77. "Whom hast thou then or *what t' accuse*?"—*Milton,* P. L., iv, 67.

4. To a finite verb; as, "Then Peter *began to rebuke* him."—*Matt.,* xvi, 22. "The Son of man *is come to seek and to save* that which was lost."—*Luke,* xix, 10.

5. To an other infinitive; as, "*To go to enter* into Egypt."—*Jer.,* xli, 17. "We are not often willing *to wait to consider.*"—*J. Abbott.* "For what had he *to do to chide* at me?"—*Shak.*

6. To a participle; as, "Still *threatening to devour* me."—*Milton.* "Or as a thief *bent to unhoard* the cash of some rich burgher."—*Id.*

7. To an adverb; as, "She is old *enough to go* to school."—"I know not *how to act.*"—*Nutting's Gram.*, p. 106. "Tell me *when to come*, and *where to meet* you."—"He hath not *where to lay* his head."

8. To a conjunction; as, "He knows better *than to trust* you."—"It was so hot *as to melt* these ornaments."—"Many who praise virtue, do no more *than praise* it."—*Dr. Johnson.*

9. To a preposition; as, "I was *about to write.*"—*Rev.*, x, 4. "Not *for to hide* it in a hedge."—*Burns's Poems*, p. 42. "Amatum iri, To be *about to be loved.*"—*Adam's Gram.*, p. 95.[412]

10. To an interjection; as, "*O to forget* her!"—*Young's Night Thoughts.*

OBS. 25.—The infinitive is the mere verb, without affirmation, without person or number, and therefore without the agreement peculiar to a finite verb. (See Obs. 8th on Rule 2d.) But, in most instances, it is not without *limitation* of the being, action, or passion, to some particular person or persons, thing or things, that are said, supposed, or denied, to be, to act, or to be acted upon. Whenever it is not thus limited, it is taken *abstractly*, and has some resemblance to a noun: because it then suggests the being, action, or passion alone: though, even then, the active infinitive may still govern the objective case; and it may also be easy to *imagine* to whom or to what the being, action, or passion, naturally pertains. The uses of the infinitive are so many and various, that it is no easy matter to classify them accurately. The following are unquestionably *the chief* of the things for which it may stand:

1. For the *supplement* to an other verb, to complete the sense; as, "Loose him, and *let* him *go*."—*John*, xi, 44. "They that *go to seek* mixed wine."—*Prov.*, xxiii, 30. "His hands *refuse* to *labour*."—*Ib.*, xxi, 25. "If you *choose to have* those terms."—*Tooke's D. P.*, ii, 374. "How our old translators first *struggled to express* this."—*Ib.*, ii, 456. "To any one who *will please to examine* our language."—*Ib.*, ii, 444. "They *are forced to give up* at last."—*Ib.*, ii, 375. "Which *ought to be done*."—*Ib.*, ii, 451. "Which *came to pass*."—*Acts*, xi, 28. "I *dare engage to make* it out."—*Swift*.

2. For the *purpose*, or *end*, of that to which it is added; as, "Each has employed his time and pains *to establish* a criterion."—*Tooke's D. P.*, ii, 374. "I shall not stop now, *to assist* in their elucidation."—*Ib.*, ii, 75. "Our purposes are not endowed with words *to make* them known."—*Ib.*, ii, 74. [A] "TOOL is some instrument taken up *to work* with."—*Ib.*, ii, 145. "Labour not *to be* rich."—*Prov.*, xxiii, 4. "I flee unto thee *to hide* me."—*Ps.*, cxliii, 9. "Evil shall hunt the violent man *to overthrow* him."—*Ib.*, cxl, 11.

3. For the *object* of an affection or passion; as, "He *loves to ride*."—"I *desire to hear* her *speak* again."—*Shale*. "If we *wish to avoid* important error."—*Tooke's D. P.*, ii, 3. "Who *rejoice to do* evil."—*Prov.*, ii, 14. "All agreeing in *earnestness to see* him."—*Shak.* "Our *curiosity* is raised *to know* what lies beyond."—*Kames, El. of Crit.*, ii, 335.

4. For the *cause* of an affection or passion; as, "I rejoice *to hear* it."—"By which I hope *to have laid* a foundation," &c.—*Blair's Rhet.*, p. 34. "For he made me mad, *to see* him *shine* so brisk, and *smell* so sweet."—*Beauties of Shak.*, p. 118. "Thou didst eat strange flesh, which some did die *to look* on."—*Ib.*, p. 182. "They grieved *to see* their best allies at variance."—*Rev. W. Allen's Gram.*, p. 165.

5. For the *subject* of a proposition, or the chief term in such subject; as, "*To steal* is sinful."—"*To do* justice and judgement, is more acceptable to the Lord than sacrifice."—*Prov.*, xxi, 3. "*To do* RIGHT, is, to do that which is ordered to be done."—*Tooke's D. P.*, ii, 7. "*To go* to law to plague a neighbour, has in it more of malice, than of love to justice."—*Seattle's Mor. Sci.*, i, 177.

6. For the *predicate* of a proposition, or the chief term in such predicate; as, "To enjoy is *to obey*."—*Pope.* "The property of rain is *to wet*, and fire, *to burn*."—*Beauties of Shak.*, p. 15. "To die is *to be banished* from myself."—*Ib.*, p. 82. "The best way is, *to slander* Valentine."—*Ib.*, p. 83. "The highway of the upright is *to depart* from evil."—*Prov.*, xvi, 17.

7. For a *coming event*, or what *will* be; as, "A mutilated structure soon *to fall*."—*Cowper.* "He being dead, and I speedily *to follow* him."—*Tooke's D. P.*, ii, 111. "She shall rejoice in time *to come*."—*Prov.*, xxxi, 25. "Things present, or things *to come*."—*1 Cor.*, iii, 22.

8. For a *necessary event*, or what *ought* to be; as, "It is *to be remembered*."—"It is never *to be forgotten*."—*Tooke's D. P.*, ii, 2. "An oversight much *to be deplored*."—*Ib.*, ii, 460. "The sign is not *to be used* by itself, or *to stand* alone; but is *to be joined* to some other term."—*Ib.*, ii, 372. "The Lord's name is *to be praised*."—*Ps.*, cxiii, 3.

9. For what is *previously suggested* by another word; as, "I have *faith to believe*."—"The glossarist *did well* here *not to yield* to his inclination."—*Tooke's D. P.*, ii, 329. "It is a good *thing to give* thanks unto the Lord."—*Ps.*, xcii, 1. "*It* is *as sport* to a fool *to do* mischief."—*Prov.*, x, 23. "They have the *gift to know* it."—*Shak.* "We have no remaining *occupation* but *to take* care of the public."—*Art of Thinking*, p. 52.

10. For a term of *comparison* or *measure*; as, "He was so much affected as *to weep*."—"Who could do no less than *furnish* him."—*Tooke's D. P.*, ii, 408. "I shall venture no farther than *to explain* the nature and convenience of these abbreviations."—*Ib.*, ii, 439. "I have already said enough *to show* what sort of operation that is."—*Ib.*, ii, 358.

OBS. 26.—After dismissing all the examples which may fairly be referred to one or other of the ten heads above enumerated, an observant reader may yet find *other uses* of the infinitive, and those so dissimilar that they can hardly be reduced to any one head or rule; except that all are governed by the preposition to, which points towards or to the verb; as, "A great altar *to see to*."—*Joshua*, xxii, 10. "[Greek: Bomon megan tou idein]."—*Septuagint*. That is, "An altar *great to behold*." "Altare infinitæ magnitudinis."—*Vulgate*. "Un fort grand autel."—*French Bible*. "Easy *to be entreated*."—*Jos.*, iii, 17. "There was none *to help*."—*Ps.*, cvii, 12. "He had rained down manna upon them *to eat*."—*Ps.*, lxxviii, 24. "Remember his commandments *to do* them."—*Ps.*, viii, 18. "Preserve thou those that are appointed *to die*."—*Ps.*, lxxix, 11. "As coals to burning coals, and as wood to fire; so is a contentious man *to kindle* strife."—*Prov.*, xxvi, 21. "These are far beyond the reach and power of any kings *to do* away."—*Tooke's D. P.*, ii, 126. "I know not indeed what *to do* with those words."—*Ib.*, ii, 441. "They will be as little able *to justify* their innovation."—*Ib.*, ii, 448. "I leave you *to compare* them."—*Ib.*, ii, 458. "There is no occasion *to attribute* it."—*Ib.*, ii, 375. "There is no day for me *to look* upon."—*Beauties of Shak.*, p. 82. "Having no external thing *to lose*."—*Ib.*, p. 100. "I'll never be a gosling *to obey* instinct."—*Ib.*, p. 200. "Whereto serves mercy, but *to confront* the visage of offence?"—*Ib.*, p. 233. "If things do not go *to suit* him."—*Liberator*, ix, 182. "And, *to be* plain, I think there is not half a kiss *to choose*, who loves an other best."—*Shak.*, p. 91. "But *to return* to R. Johnson's instance of *good man*."—*Tooke's D. P.*, ii, 370. Our common Bibles have this text: "And a certain woman cast a piece of a millstone upon

Abimelech's head, and *all to break* his skull."—*Judges,* ix, 53. Perhaps the interpretation of this may be, "and *so as completely to break* his skull." The octavo edition stereotyped by "the Bible Association of Friends in America," has it, "and *all-to brake* his skull." This, most probably, was supposed by the editors to mean, "and *completely broke* his skull;" but *all-to* is no proper compound word, and therefore the change is a perversion. The Septuagint, the Vulgate, and the common French version, all accord with the simple indicative construction, "and *broke* his skull."

OBS. 27.—According to Lindley Murray, "The infinitive mood is often *made absolute,* or used independently *on* [say *of*] the rest of the sentence, supplying the place of the conjunction *that* with the potential mood: as, '*To confess* the truth, I was in fault;' '*To begin* with the first;' '*To proceed;*' '*To conclude;*' that is, 'That I may confess,' &c."—*Murray's Gram.,* 8vo, p. 184; *Ingersoll's Gram.,* p. 244. Some other compilers have adopted the same doctrine. But on what ground the *substitution* of one mood for the other is imagined, I see not. The reader will observe that this potential mood is here just as much "*made absolute,*" as is the infinitive; for there is nothing expressed to which the conjunction *that* connects the one phrase, or the preposition *to* the other. But possibly, in either case, there may be an ellipsis of some antecedent term; and surely, if we imagine the construction to be complete without any such term, we make the conjunction the more anomalous word of the two. Confession of the truth, is here the aim of speaking, but not of what is spoken. The whole sentence may be, "*In order* to confess the truth, *I admit that* I was in fault." Or, "*In order* that I may confess the truth, *I admit that* I was in fault." I do not deny, that the infinitive, or a phrase of which the infinitive is a part, is sometimes put *absolute*; for, if it is not so in any of the foregoing examples, it appears to be so in the following: "For every object has several faces, *so to speak,* by which it may be presented to us."—*Blair's Rhet.,* p. 41. "*To declare* a thing shall be, long before it is in being, and then *to bring about* the accomplishment of that very thing, according to the same declaration; this, or nothing, is the work of God."—*Justin Martyr.*

"*To be*, or *not to be*;—that is the question."—*Shakspeare.*

"*To die;—to sleep;—To sleep*! perchance, *to dream*!"—*Id., Hamlet.*

OBS. 28.—The infinitive usually *follows* the word on which it depends, or to which the particle *to* connects it; but this order is sometimes reversed: as, "To beg I am ashamed."—*Luke*, xvi, 3. "To keep them no longer in suspense, [I say plainly,] Sir Roger de Coverly is dead."—*Addison.* "To suffer, as to do, Our strength is equal."—*Milton.*

"To catch your vivid scenes, too gross her hand."—*Thomson.*

OBS. 29.—Though, in respect to its syntax, the infinitive is oftener connected with a verb, a participle, or an adjective, than with a noun or a pronoun, it should never be so placed that the reader will be liable to mistake the *person* to whom, or the *thing* to which, the being, action, or passion, pertains. Examples of error: "This system will require a long time to be executed as it should be."—*Journal of N. Y. Lit. Convention*, 1830, p. 91. It is not the *time*, that is to be executed; therefore say, "This system, to be executed as it should be, will require a long time." "He spoke in a *manner distinct enough to be heard* by the whole assembly."—*Murray's Key*, 8vo, p. 192. This implies that the orator's *manner* was *heard*! But the grammarian interprets his own meaning, by the following alternative: "Or—*He spoke distinctly enough to be heard* by the whole assembly."—*Ibid.* This suggests that the man himself was heard. "When they hit upon a figure that pleases them, they are loth to part with it, and frequently continue it so long, as to become tedious and intricate."—*Murray's Gram.*, p. 341. Is it the *authors*, or their *figure*, that becomes tedious and intricate? If the latter, strike out, "*so long, as to become*," and say, "*till it becomes*." "Facts are always of the greatest consequence *to be remembered* during the course of the pleading."—*Blair's Rhet.*, p. 272. The rhetorician here meant: "The facts stated in an argument, are always those parts of it, which it is most important that the hearers should be made to remember."

OBS. 30.—According to some grammarians, "The Infinitive of the verb *to be*, is often *understood*; as, 'I considered it [*to be*] necessary to send the dispatches.'"—*W. Allen's Gram.*, p. 166. In this example, as in thousands more, of various forms, the verb *to be* may be inserted without affecting the sense; but I doubt the necessity of supposing an ellipsis in such sentences. The adjective or participle that follows, always relates to the preceding objective; and if a noun is used, it is but an other objective in apposition with the former: as, "I considered *it* an *imposition*." The verb *to be*, with the perfect participle, forms the passive infinitive; and the supposition of such an ellipsis, extensively affects one's mode of parsing. Thus, "He considered himself *insulted*," "I will suppose the work *accomplished*," and many similar sentences, might be supposed to contain passive infinitives. Allen says, "In the following construction, the words in *italics* are (elliptically) passive infinitives; I saw the bird *caught*, and the hare *killed*; we heard the letters *read*."—*W. Allen's Gram.*, p. 168. Dr. Priestley observes, "There is a remarkable ambiguity in the use of the participle *preterite*, as the same word may express a thing either doing, or done; as, I went to see the child *dressed*."—*Priestley's Gram.*, p. 125. If the Doctor's participle is ambiguous, I imagine that Allen's infinitives are just as much so. "The *participle* which we denominate *past*, often means an action *whilst performing*: thus, I saw the *battle fought*, and the *standard lowered*."—*Wilson's Essay*, p. 158. Sometimes, especially in familiar conversation, an infinitive verb is suppressed, and the sign of it retained; as, "They might have aided us; they ought *to*" [have aided us].—*Herald of Freedom*. "We have tried to like it, but it's hard *to*."—*Lynn News*.

OBS. 31.—After the verb *make*, some writers insert the verb *be*, and suppress the preposition *to*; as, "He *must make* every syllable, and even every letter, in the word which he pronounces, *be heard* distinctly."—*Blair's Rhet.*, p. 329; *Murray's E. Reader*, p. 9. "You *must make* yourself *be heard* with pleasure and attention."—*Duncan's Cicero*, p. 84. "To *make* himself *be heard* by all."—*Blair's Rhet.*, p. 328. "To *make* ourselves *be heard* by one."—*Ibid.* "Clear enough to *make* me *be* understood."—*Locke, on Ed.*, p. 198. In my opinion, it would be better, either to insert the *to*, or to use the participle only; as, "The information which he possessed, *made* his company *to be* courted."—*Dr. M'Rie.* "Which will both show the importance of this rule, and *make* the application of it *to be* understood."—*Blair's Rhet.*, p. 103. Or, as in these brief forms: "To *make* himself *heard* by all."—"Clear enough to *make* me *understood.*"

OBS. 32.—In those languages in which the infinitive is distinguished as such by its termination, this part of the verb may be used alone as the subject of a finite verb; but in English it is always necessary to retain the sign *to* before an abstract infinitive, because there is nothing else to distinguish the verb from a noun. Here we may see a difference between our language and the French, although it has been shown, that in their government of the infinitive they are in some degree analogous:—"HAÏR est un tourment; AIMER est un besoin de l'âme."—*M. de Ségur. "To hate* is a torment; *to love* is a requisite of the soul." If from this any will argue that *to* is not here a preposition, the same argument will be as good, to prove that *for* is not a preposition when it governs the objective case; because that also may be used without any antecedent term of relation: as, "They are by no means points of equal importance, *for me to be deprived* of your affections, and *for him to be defeated* in his prosecution."—*Anon., in W. Allen's Gram.*, p. 166. I said, the sign *to* must *always* be put before an abstract infinitive: but possibly a *repetition* of this sign may not always be necessary, when several such infinitives occur in the same construction: as,

"But, *to fill* a heart with joy, *restore* content to the afflicted, or *relieve* the necessitous, these fall not within the reach of their five senses."—*Art of Thinking*, p. 66. It may be too much to affirm, that this is positively ungrammatical; yet it would be as well or better, to express it thus: "But *to relieve* the necessitous, *to restore* content to the afflicted, *and to fill* a heart with joy, these full not within the reach of their five senses."

OBS. 33.—In the use of the English infinitive, as well as of the participle in *ing*, the distinction of *voice* is often disregarded; the active form being used in what, with respect to the noun before it, is a passive sense: as, "There's no time *to waste*."—*W. Allen's Gram.*, p. 82. "You are *to blame*."—*Ib*. "The humming-bird is delightful *to look* upon."—*Ib*. "What pain it was *to drown*."—*Shak*. "The thing's *to do*."—*Id*. "When deed of danger was *to do*."—*Scott*. "The evil I bring upon myself, is the hardest *to bear*."—*Home's Art of Thinking*, p. 27. "Pride is worse *to bear* than cruelty."—*Ib*., p. 37. These are in fact active verbs, and not passive. We may suggest agents for them, if we please; as, "There is no time *for us* to waste." That the simple participle in *ing* may be used passively, has been proved elsewhere. It seems sometimes to have no distinction of voice; as, "What is worth *doing*, is worth *doing well*."—*Com. Maxim*. This is certainly much more agreeable, than to say, "What is worth *being done*, is worth *being done well*." In respect to the voice of the infinitive, and of this participle, many of our grammarians are obviously hypercritical. For example: "The active voice should not be used for the passive; as, I have work *to do*: a house *to sell, to let*, instead of *to be done, to be sold, to be let*."—*Sanborn's Gram.*, p. 220. "Active verbs are often used improperly with a passive signification, as, 'the house is *building*, lodgings to *let*, he has a house to *sell*, nothing is *wanting*;' in stead of 'the house is *being built*, lodgings to *be lett*, he has a house to *be* sold, nothing is *wanted*.'"—*Blair's Gram.*, p. 64. In punctuation, orthography, and the use of capitals, here are more errors than it is worth while to particularize. With regard to such phraseology as, "The house *is being built,*" see, in Part II, sundry Observations on the Compound Form of Conjugation. To say, "I have work *to do,*"—"He has a house *to sell,*"—or, "We have lodgings *to let,*" is just as good English, as to say, "I have meat *to eat.*"—*John,* iv, 32. And who, but some sciolist in grammar, would, in all such instances, prefer the passive voice?

IMPROPRIETIES FOR CORRECTION. FALSE SYNTAX UNDER RULE XVIII.

INFINITIVES DEMANDING THE PARTICLE TO.

"William, please hand me that pencil."—*R. C. Smith's New Gram.,* p. 12.

[FORMULE—Not proper, because the infinitive verb *hand* is not preceded by the preposition *to.* But, according to Rule 18th, "The preposition *to* governs the infinitive mood, and commonly connects it to a finite verb." Therefore, *to* should be here inserted; thus, "William, please *to* hand me that pencil."]

"Please insert points so as to make sense."—*Davis's Gram.,* p. 123. "I have known Lords abbreviate almost the half of their words."—*Cobbett's English Gram.,* ¶ 153. "We shall find the practice perfectly accord with the theory."—*Knight, on the Greek Alphabet,* p. 23. "But it would tend to obscure, rather than elucidate the subject."—*L. Murray's Gram.,* p. 95. "Please divide it for them as it should be."—*Willett's Arith.,* p. 193. "So as neither to embarrass, nor weaken the sentence."—*Blair's Rhet.,* p. 116; *Murray's Gram.,* 322. "Carry her to his table, to view his poor fare,[413] and hear his heavenly discourse."—SHERLOCK: *Blair's Rhet.,* p. 157; *Murray's Gram.,* 347. "That we need not be surprised to find this hold in eloquence."—*Blair's Rhet.,* p. 174. "Where he has no occasion either to divide or explain."—*Ib.*, p. 305. "And they will find their pupils improve by hasty and pleasant steps."—*Russell's Gram.*, Pref., p. 4. "The teacher however will please observe," &c.—*Infant School Gram.*, p. 8. "Please attend to a few rules in what is called syntax."—*Ib.*, p. 128. "They may dispense with the laws to favor their friends, or secure their office."—*Webster's Essays*, p. 39. "To take back a gift, or break a contract, is a wanton abuse."—*Ib.*, p. 41. "The legislature has nothing to do, but let it bear its own price."—*Ib.*, p. 315. "He is not to form, but copy characters."—*Rambler*, No. 122. "I have known a woman make use of a shoeing-horn."—*Spect.*, No. 536. "Finding this experiment answer, in every respect, their wishes."—*Sandford and Merton*, p. 51. "In fine let him cause his argument conclude in the term of the question."—*Barclay's Works*, Vol. iii, p. 443.

"That he permitted not the winds of heaven
Visit her face too roughly."—*Shakspeare, Hamlet.*

RULE XIX.—INFINITIVES. The active verbs, *bid, dare, feel, hear, let, make, need, see,* and their participles, usually take the Infinitive after them without the preposition *to*: as, "If he *bade* thee *depart*, how *darest* thou *stay*?"—"I *dare* not *let* my mind *be* idle as I walk in the streets."—*Cotton Mather.*

"Thy Hector, wrapt in everlasting sleep,
Shall neither *hear* thee *sigh*, nor *see* thee *weep*."
—*Pope's Homer.*

OBSERVATIONS ON RULE XIX.

OBS. 1.—Respecting the syntax of the infinitive mood when the particle *to* is not expressed before it, our grammarians are almost as much at variance, as I have shown them to be, when they find the particle employed. Concerning *verbs governed by verbs*, Lindley Murray, and some others, are the most clear and positive, where their doctrine is the most obviously wrong; and, where they might have affirmed with truth, that the former verb *governs the latter*, they only tell us that "the preposition TO *is sometimes properly omitted*,"—or that such and such verbs "*have commonly other verbs following them* without the sign TO."—*Murray's Gram.*, p. 183; *Alger's*, 63; *W. Allen's*, 167, and others. If these authors meant, that the preposition *to* is omitted *by ellipsis*, they ought to have said so. Then the many admirers and remodellers of Murray's Grammar might at least have understood him alike. Then, too, any proper definition of *ellipsis* must have proved both them and him to be clearly wrong about this construction also. If the word *to* is really "understood," whenever it is omitted after *bid, dare, feel*, &c., as some authors, affirm, then is it here the governing word, if anywhere; and this nineteenth rule, however common, is useless to the parser.[414] Then, too, does no English verb ever govern the infinitive without governing also a *preposition*, "expressed or understood." Whatever is omitted by ellipsis, and truly "*understood*," really belongs to the grammatical construction; and therefore, if inserted, it cannot be actually *improper*, though it may be unnecessary. But all our grammarians admit, that *to* before the infinitive is sometimes "superfluous *and improper*."—*Murray's Gram.*, p. 183. I imagine, there cannot be any proper ellipsis of *to* before the infinitive, except in some forms of comparison; because, wherever else it is necessary, either to the sense or to the construction, it ought to be inserted. And wherever the *to* is rightly used, it is properly the governing word; but where it cannot be inserted without *impropriety*, it is absurd to say, that it is "*understood*." The infinitive that is put after such a verb or participle as excludes the preposition *to*, is governed by this verb or participle, if it is governed by any thing: as,

"To make them *do, undo, eat, drink, stand, move,*
Talk, think, and *feel,* exactly as he chose."—*Pollok,* p. 69.

OBS. 2.—Ingersoll, who converted Murray's Grammar into "*Conversations,*" says, "I will just remark to you that the verbs in the infinitive mood, that follow *make, need, see, bid, dare, feel, hear, let,* and their participles, are *always* GOVERNED by them."—*Conv. on Eng. Gram.,* p. 120. Kirkham, who pretended to turn the same book into "*Familiar Lectures,*" says, "*To,* the sign of the infinitive mood, is *often understood* before the verb; as, 'Let me proceed;' that is, Let me *to* proceed."—*Gram. in Fam. Lect.,* p. 137. The lecturer, however, does not suppose the infinitive to be here governed by the preposition *to,* or the verb *let,* but rather by the pronoun *me.* For, in an other place, he avers, that the infinitive may be governed by a noun or a pronoun; as, "Let *him do* it."—*Ib.,* p. 187. Now if the government of the infinitive is to be referred to the objective noun or pronoun that intervenes, none of those verbs that take the infinitive after them without the preposition, will usually be found to govern it, except *dare* and *need*; and if *need,* in such a case, is an *auxiliary,* no government pertains to that. R. C. Smith, an other modifier of Murray, having the same false notion of ellipsis, says, "*To,* the usual sign of this mood, is *sometimes understood*; as, 'Let me go,' instead of, 'Let me *to* go.'"—*Smith's New Gram.,* p. 65. According to Murray, whom these men profess to follow, *let,* in all these examples, is *an auxiliary,* and the verb that follows it, is not in the *infinitive* mood, but in the *imperative.* So they severally contradict their oracle, and all are wrong, both he and they! The disciples pretend to correct their master, by supposing "*Let me to go,*" and "*Let me to proceed,*" good English!

OBS. 3.—It is often impossible to say *by what* the infinitive is governed, according to the instructions of Murray, or according to any author who does not parse it as I do. Nutting says, "The infinitive *mode* sometimes follows the comparative conjunctions, *as, than,* and *how,* WITHOUT GOVERNMENT."—*Practical Gram.*, p. 106. Murray's uncertainty[415] may have led to some part of this notion, but the idea that *how* is a "comparative conjunction," is a blunder entirely new. Kirkham is so puzzled by "the language of that eminent philologist," that he bolts outright from the course of his guide, and runs he knows not whither; feigning that other able writers have well contended, "that this mood IS NOT GOVERNED by any particular word." Accordingly he leaves his pupils at liberty to "*reject the idea of government,* as applied to the verb in this mood;" and even frames a rule which refers it always "To some noun or pronoun, as its subject or actor."—*Kirkham's Gram.*, p. 188. Murray teaches that the object of the active verb sometimes governs the infinitive that follows it: as, "They have a *desire* to improve."—*Octavo Gram.*, p. 184. To what extent, in practice, he would carry this doctrine, nobody can tell; probably to every sentence in which this object is the antecedent term to the preposition *to,* and perhaps further: as, "I *have* a *house* to *sell*"—*Nutting's Gram.*, p. 106. "I *feel* a *desire* to *excel*." "I *felt* my *heart* within me *die*."—*Merrick.*

OBS. 4.—Nutting supposes that the objective case before the infinitive always governs it wherever it denotes the agent of the infinitive action; as, "He commands *me* to *write* a letter."—*Practical Gram.*, p. 96. Nixon, on the contrary, contends, that the finite verb, in such a sentence, can govern only one object, and that this object is the infinitive. "The objective case preceding it," he says, "is the subject or agent of that infinitive, and not governed by the preceding verb." His example is, "Let *them* go."—*English Parser*, p. 97. "In the examples, 'He is endeavouring *to persuade* them *to learn,*'—'It is pleasant *to see* the sun,'—the pronoun *them,* the adjective *pleasant,* and the participle *endeavouring,* I consider as *governing* the following verb in the infinitive mode."—*Cooper's Plain and Pract. Gram.,* p. 144. "Some erroneously say that pronouns govern the infinitive mode in such examples as this: 'I expected *him* to be present.' We will change the expression: 'He was expected to be present.' *All will admit* that *to be* is governed by *was expected.* The same verb that governs it in the passive voice, governs it in the active."—*Sanborn's Gram.,* p. 144. So do our *professed grammarians* differ about the government of the infinitive, even in *the most common* constructions of it! Often, however, it makes but little difference in regard to the sense, which of the two words is considered the governing or antecedent term; but where the preposition is excluded, the construction seems to imply some immediate influence of the finite verb upon the infinitive.

OBS. 5.—The *extent* of this influence, or of such government, has never yet been clearly determined. "This *irregularity,*" says *Murray,* "extends only to *active or neuter* verbs: ['active *and* neuter verbs,' says *Fisk*:] for all the verbs above mentioned, when made *passive,* require the preposition *to* before the following verb: as, 'He was seen *to* go;' 'He was heard *to* speak;' 'They were bidden *to* be upon their guard.'"—*Murray's Gram.,* p. 183. Fisk adds with no great accuracy "In the *past* and *future* tenses of the active voice also, these verbs generally require the sign *to,* to be prefixed to the following verbs; as, 'You *have dared to proceed* without authority;' 'They *will* not *dare to attack* you.'"—*Gram. Simplified,* p. 125. What these gentlemen here call "*neuter verbs,*" are only the two words *dare* and *need,* which are, in most cases, active, though not always transitive; unless the infinitive itself can make them so—an inconsistent doctrine of theirs which I have elsewhere refuted. (See Obs. 3rd on Rule 5th.) These two verbs take the infinitive after them without the preposition, only when they are intransitive; while all the rest seem to have this power, only when they are transitive. If there are any exceptions, they shall presently be considered. A more particular examination of the construction proper for the infinitive after each of these eight verbs, seems necessary for a right understanding of the rule.

OBS. 6.—Of the verb BID. This verb, in any of its tenses, when it commands an action, usually governs an object and also an infinitive, which come together; as, "Thou *bidst* the *world adore*."—*Thomson*. "If the prophet *had bid thee do* some great thing."—*2 Kings*, v, 13. But when it means, *to promise* or *offer*, the infinitive that follows, must be introduced by the preposition *to*; as, "He *bids* fair *to excel* them all"—"Perhaps no person under heaven *bids* more unlikely *to* be saved."—*Brown's Divinity*, p. vii. "And each *bade* high *to* win him."—GRANVILLE: *Joh. Dict.* After the compound *forbid*, the preposition is also necessary; as, "Where honeysuckles *forbid* the sun *to* enter."—*Beauties of Shak..* p. 57. In poetry, if the measure happens to require it, the word *to* is sometimes allowed after the simple verb *bid*, denoting a command; as,

"*Bid* me *to* strike my dearest brother dead, *To* bring my aged father's hoary head."—*Rowe's Lucan*, B. i, l. 677.

OBS. 7.—Of the verb DARE. This verb, when used intransitively, and its irregular preterit *durst*, which is never transitive, usually take the infinitive after them without *to*; as, "I *dare do* all that may become a man: Who *dares do* more, is none."—*Shakspeare*. "If he *durst steal* any thing adventurously."—*Id.* "Who *durst defy* th' Omnipotent to arms."—*Milton*. "Like one who *durst* his destiny *control*."—*Dryden*. In these examples, the former verbs have some resemblance to auxiliaries, and the insertion of the preposition *to* would be improper. But when we take away this resemblance, by giving *dare* or *dared*, an objective case, the preposition is requisite before the infinitive; as, "Time! I *dare thee to* discover Such a youth or such a lover."—*Dryden*. "He *dares me to* enter the lists."—*Fisk's Gram.*, p. 125. So when *dare* itself is in the infinitive mood, or is put after an auxiliary, the preposition is not improper; as, "And *let* a private man *dare to say* that it will."—*Brown's Estimate*, ii, 147. "*Would* its compiler *dare to affront* the Deity?"—*West's Letters*, p. 151. "What power so great, *to dare to disobey?*"—*Pope's Homer*. "Some *would* even *dare* to die."—*Bible*. "What *would dare to molest* him?"—*Dr. Johnson*. "*Do* you *dare to prosecute* such a creature as Vaughan?"—*Junius*, Let. xxxiii. Perhaps these examples might be considered good English, either with or without the *to*; but the last one would be still better thus: "*Dare* you *prosecute* such a creature as Vaughan?" Dr. Priestley thinks the following sentence would have been better with the preposition inserted: "Who *have dared defy* the worst."—HARRIS: *Priestley's Gram.*, p. 132. *To* is sometimes used after the simple verb, in the present tense; as, "Those whose words no one *dares to* repeat."—*Opie, on Lying*, p. 147.

"*Dare* I *to* leave of humble prose the shore?"
—*Young*, p. 377.

"Against heaven's endless mercies pour'd, how *dar'st* thou *to* rebel?"
—*Id.*, p. 380.

"The man who *dares to* be a wretch, deserves still greater pain."
—*Id.*, p. 381.

OBS. 8.—Of the verb FEEL. This verb, in any of its tenses, may govern the infinitive without the sign *to*; but it does this, only when it is used transitively, and that in regard to a bodily perception: as, "I *feel* it *move*."—"I *felt* something *sting* me." If we speak of feeling any mental affection, or if we use the verb intransitively, the infinitive that follows, requires the preposition; as, "I *feel* it *to* be my duty."—"I *felt* ashamed *to* ask."—"I *feel* afraid *to* go alone."—"I *felt* about, *to* find the door." One may say of what is painful to the body, "I *feel* it *to* be severe."

OBS. 9.—Of the verb HEAR. This verb is often intransitive, but it is usually followed by an objective case when it governs the infinitive; as. "To *hear* a *bird sing*."—*Webster*. "You have never *heard me say* so." For this reason, I am inclined to think that those sentences in which it appears to govern the infinitive alone, are elliptical; as, "I *have heard tell* of such things."—"And I *have heard say* of thee, that thou canst understand a dream to interpret it."—*Gen*, xli, 15. Such examples may be the same as. "I have heard *people* tell,"—"I have heard *men* say," &c.

OBS. 10.—Of the verb LET. By many grammarians this verb has been erroneously called an *auxiliary* of the optative mood; or, as Dr. Johnson terms it, "a *sign* of the *optative* mood:" though none deny, that it is sometimes also a principal verb. It is, in fact, always a principal verb; because, as we now apply it, it is always transitive. It commonly governs an objective noun or pronoun, and also an infinitive without the sign *to*; as, "Rise up, *let us go*."—*Mark*. "Thou *shalt let it rest*."—*Exodus*. But sometimes the infinitive coalesces with it more nearly than the objective, so that the latter is placed after both verbs; as, "The solution *lets go* the *mercury*."—*Newton*. "One *lets slip* out of his account a good *part* of that duration."—*Locke*. "Back! on *your* lives; *let* be, said he, my *prey*."—*Dryden*. The phrase, *let go*, is sometimes spoken for, *let go your hold*; and *let be*, for *let him be, let it be*, &c. In such instances, therefore, the verb *let* is not really intransitive. This verb, even in the passive form, may have the infinitive after it without the preposition to; as, "Nothing *is let slip*."—*Walker's English Particles*, p. 165. "They *were let go* in peace."—*Acts*, xv, 33. "The stage was never empty, nor the curtain *let fall*."—*Blair's Rhet.*, p. 459. "The pye's question was wisely *let fall* without a reply."—*L'Estrange*. With respect to other passives, Murray and Fisk appear to be right; and sometimes the preposition is used after this one: as, "There's a letter for you, sir, if your name be Horatio, as I *am let to know* it is."—*Shakspeare*. *Let*, when used intransitively, required the preposition *to* before the following infinitive; as, "He would not *let* [i. e. *forbear*] *to counsel* the king."—*Bacon*. But this use of *let* is now obsolete.

OBS. 11.—Of the verb MAKE. This verb, like most of the others, never immediately governs an infinitive, unless it also governs a noun or a pronoun which is the immediate *subject* of such infinitive; as, "You *make me blush*."—"This only *made* the *youngster laugh*"—*Webster's Spelling-Book*. "Which soon *made* the young *chap hasten* down."—*Ib*. But in very many instances it is quite proper to insert the preposition where this verb is transitive; as, "He *maketh* both the deaf *to* hear, and the dumb *to* speak."—*Mark*, vii, 37. "He *makes* the excellency of a sentence *to* consist in four things."—*Blair's Rhet.*, p. 122; *Jamieson's*, 124. "It is this that *makes* the observance of the dramatic unities *to* be of consequence."—*Blair's Rhet.*, p. 464. "In *making* some tenses of the English verb *to* consist of principal and auxiliary."—*Murray's Gram.*, p. 76. "When *make* is intransitive, it has some qualifying word after it, besides the sign of the infinitive; as,—I think he *will make out* to pay his debts." Formerly, the preposition *to* was almost always inserted to govern the infinitive after *make* or *made*; as, "Lest I *make* my brother *to* offend."—*1 Cor.*, viii, 13. "He *made* many *to* fall."—*Jer.*, xlvi, 16. Yet, in the following text, it is omitted, even where the verb is meant to be *passive*: "And it was lifted up from the earth, and *made stand* upon the feet as a man."—*Dan.*, vii, 4. This construction is improper, and not free from ambiguity; because *stand* may be a noun, and *made*, an active verb governing it. There may also be uncertainty in the meaning, where the insertion of the preposition leaves none in the construction; for *made* may signify either *created* or *compelled*, and the infinitive after it, may denote either the *purpose* of creation, or the *effect* of any temporary compulsion: as, "We are *made to be serviceable* to others."—*Murray's Key*, 8vo, p. 167. "Man *was made to mourn*."—*Burns*. "Taste *was never made to cater* for vanity."—*Blair*. The primitive word *make* seldom, if ever, produces a construction that is thus equivocal. The infinitive following it without *to*, always denotes the effect of the making, and not the purpose of the maker; as, "He *made* his son Skjöld *be received* there as king."—*North. Antiq.*, p. 81. But the same meaning may be conveyed when the *to* is used; as,

> "The fear of God is freedom, joy, and peace;
> And *makes* all ills that vex us here *to* cease."—*Waller*, p. 56.

OBS. 12.—Of the verb NEED. I incline to think, that the word *need*, whenever it is rightly followed by the infinitive without *to*, is, in reality an *auxiliary* of the potential mood; and that, like *may, can,* and *must*, it may properly be used, in both the present and the perfect tense, without personal inflection: as, "He *need* not *go*, He *need* not *have gone*;" where, if *need* is a principal verb, and governs the infinitive without *to*, the expressions must be, "He *needs* not *go*, He *needed* not *go*, or, He *has* not *needed go*." But none of these three forms is agreeable; and the last two are never used. Wherefore, in stead of placing in my code of false syntax the numerous examples of the former kind, with which the style of our grammarians and critics has furnished me, I have exhibited many of them, in contrast with others, in the eighth and ninth observations on the Conjugation of Verbs; in which observations, the reader may see what reasons there are for supposing the word *need* to be sometimes an auxiliary and sometimes a principal verb. Because no other author has yet intentionally recognized the propriety of this distinction, I have gone no farther than to show on what grounds, and with what authority from usage, it might be acknowledged. If we adopt this distinction, perhaps it will be found that the regular or principal verb *need* always requires, or, at least, always admits, the preposition *to* before the following infinitive; as, "They *need* not *to* be specially indicated."—*Adams's Rhet.*, i, 302. "We *need* only *to* remark."—*Ib.*, ii, 224. "A young man *needed* only *to* ask himself," &c.—*Ib.*, i, 117. "Nor is it conceivable to me, that the lightning of a Demosthenes *could need to* be sped upon the wings of a semiquaver."—*Ib.*, ii, 226. "But these people *need to* be informed."—*Campbell's Rhet.*, p. 220. "No man *needed* less *to* be informed."—*Ib.*, p. 175. "We *need* only *to* mention the difficulty that arises."—*Kames, El. of Crit.*, ii, 362. "*Can* there *need to* be argument to prove so plain a point?"—*Graham's Lect.* "Moral instruction *needs to* have a more prominent place."—*Dr. Weeks.* "Pride, ambition, and selfishness, *need to* be restrained."—*Id.* "Articles are sometimes omitted, where they *need to* be used."—*Sanborn's Gram.*, p. 197. "Whose power *needs* not *to* be dreaded."—*Wilson's Hebrew Gram.*, p. 93. "A workman that *needeth* not *to* be ashamed."—*2 Tim.*, ii, 15. "The small boys *may have needed to* be managed according to the school system."—*T. D. Woolsey.* "The difficulty of making variety consistent, *needs* not *to* disturb him."—*Rambler*, No. 122. "A more cogent proof *needs* not *to* be introduced."—*Wright's Gram.*, p. 66. "No person *needs to* be informed, that *you* is used in addressing a single person."—*Wilcox's Gram.*, p. 19. "I hope I *need* not *to* advise you further."—*Shak., All's Well.*

"Nor me, nor other god, thou *needst to* fear,
For thou to all the heavenly host art dear."—*Congreve.*

OBS. 13.—If *need* is ever an auxiliary, the essential difference between an auxiliary and a principal verb, will very well account for the otherwise puzzling fact, that good writers sometimes inflect this verb, and sometimes do not; and that they sometimes use *to* after it, and sometimes do not. Nor do I see in what other way a grammarian can treat it, without condemning as bad English a great number of very common phrases which he cannot change for the better. On this principle, such examples as, "He *need* not *proceed*," and "He *needs* not *to* proceed," may be perfectly right in either form; though Murray, Crombie,[416] Fisk, Ingersoll, Smith, C. Adams, and many others, pronounce both these forms to be wrong; and unanimously, (though contrary to what is perhaps the best usage,) prefer, "He *needs* not *proceed*."—*Murray's Key*, 8vo, p. 180.

OBS. 14.—On questions of grammar, the *practice of authors* ought to be of more weight, than the *dogmatism of grammarians*; but it is often difficult to decide well by either; because errors and contradictions abound in both. For example: Dr. Blair says, (in speaking of the persons represented by *I* and *thou*,) "Their sex *needs* not *be* marked."—*Rhet.*, p. 79. Jamieson abridges the work, and says, "*needs* not *to* be marked."—*Gram. of Rhet.*, p. 28. Dr. Lowth also says, "*needs* not *be* marked."—*Gram.*, p. 21. Churchill enlarges the work, and says, "*needs* not *to* be marked."—*New Gram.*, p. 72. Lindley Murray copies Lowth, and says, "*needs* not *be* marked."—*Gram.*, 12mo, 2d Ed., p. 39; 23d Ed., p. 51; and perhaps all other editions. He afterwards enlarges his own work, and says, "*needs* not *to* be marked."—*Octavo Gram.*, p. 51. But, according to Greenleaf they all express the idea ungrammatically; the only true form being, "Their sex *need* not *be marked.*" See *Gram. Simplified*, p. 48. In the two places in which the etymology and the syntax of this verb are examined, I have cited from proper sources more than twenty examples in which *to* is used after it, and more than twenty others in which the verb is not inflected in the third person singular. In the latter, *need* is treated as an auxiliary; in the former, it is a principal verb, of the regular construction. If the principal verb *need* can also govern the infinitive without *to*, as all our grammarians have supposed, then there is a third form which is unobjectionable, and my pupils may take their choice of the three. But still there is a fourth form which nobody approves, though the hands of some great men have furnished us with examples of it: as, "A figure of thought *need* not *to* detort the words from their literal sense."—*J. Q. Adams's Lectures*, Vol. ii, p. 254. "Which a man *need* only *to* appeal to his own feelings immediately to evince."—*Clarkson's Prize-Essay on Slavery*, p. 106.

OBS. 15.—Webster and Greenleaf seem inclined to justify the use of *dare*, as well as of *need*, for the third person singular. Their doctrine is this: "In *popular practice* it is used in the third person, without the personal termination. Thus, instead of saying, 'He *dares* not do it;' WE *generally* say, 'He *dare* not do it.' In like manner, *need*, when an active verb, is regular in its inflections; as, 'A man *needs* more prudence.' But *when intransitive*, it drops the personal terminations in the present tense, and is followed by a verb without the prefix *to*; as, 'A man *need* not *be* uneasy.'"—*Greenleaf s Grammar Simplified*, p. 38; *Webster's Philosophical Gram.*, p. 178; *Improved Gram.*, 127. Each part of this explanation appears to me erroneous. In *popular practice*, one shall oftener hear, "He *dares n't* do it," or even, "*You dares n't* do it," than, "*He dare not* do it." But it is only in the trained practice of the schools, that he shall ever hear, "He *needs n't* do it," or, "He *needs not* do it." If *need* is sometimes used without inflection, this peculiarity, or the disuse of *to* before the subsequent infinitive, is not a necessary result of its "*intransitive*" character. And as to their latent *nominative*, "whereof there *is* no *account*," or, "whereof there *needs* no *account*;" their *fact*, of which "there *is* no *evidence*," or of which "there *needs* no *evidence*;" I judge it a remarkable phenomenon, that authors of so high pretensions, could find, in these *transpositions*, a nominative to "*is*," but none to "*needs*!" See a marginal note under Rule 14th, at p. 570.

OBS. 16.—Of the verb SEE. This verb, whenever it governs the infinitive without *to*, governs also an objective noun or pronoun; as, "*See me do* it."—"I *saw him do* it."—*Murray*. Whenever it is intransitive, the following infinitive must be governed by *to*; as, "I *will see to have* it done."—*Comly's Gram.*, p. 98; *Greenleaf's*, 38. "How *could* he *see to do* them?"—*Beauties of Shak.*, p. 43. In the following text, *see* is transitive, and governs the infinitive; but the two verbs are put so far apart, that it requires some skill in the reader to make their relation apparent: "When ye therefore *shall see* the abomination of desolation, spoken of by Daniel the prophet, *stand* in the holy place," &c.—*Matt.*, xxiv, 15. An other scripturist uses the *participle*, and says—"*standing* where it ought not," &c.—*Mark*, xiii, 14. The Greek word is the same in both; it is a participle, agreeing with the noun for *abomination.* Sometimes the preposition *to* seems to be admitted on purpose to protract the expression: as,

"Tranio, I *saw* her coral lips *to move,*
And with her breath she did perfume the air."—*Shak.*

OBS 17.—A few other verbs, besides the eight which are mentioned in the foregoing rule and remarks, sometimes have the infinitive after them without *to.* W. Allen teaches, that, "The sign *to* is *generally* omitted," not only after these eight, but also after eight others; namely, "*find, have, help, mark, observe, perceive, watch,* and the old preterit *gan,* for *began*; and *sometimes* after *behold* and *know.*"—*Elements of Gram.,* p. 167. Perhaps he may have found *some instances* of the omission of the preposition after all these, but in my opinion his rule gives a very unwarrantable extension to this "irregularity," as Murray calls it. The usage belongs only to particular verbs, and to them not in all their applications. Other verbs of the same import do not in general admit the same idiom. But, by a license for the most part peculiar to the poets, the preposition *to* is occasionally omitted, especially after verbs equivalent to those which exclude it; as, "And *force* them *sit.*"—*Cowper's Task,* p. 46. That is, "And *make* them *sit.*" According to Churchill, "To use *ought* or *cause* in this manner, is a Scotticism: [as,] 'Won't you *cause* them *remove* the hares?'—'You *ought* not *walk.*' SHAK."—*New Gram.,* p. 317. The verbs, *behold, view, observe, mark, watch,* and *spy,* are only other words for *see*; as, "There might you *behold* one joy *crown* an other."—*Shak.* "There I sat, *viewing* the silver stream *glide* silently towards the tempestuous sea."—*Walton.* "I *beheld* Satan as lightning *fall* from heaven."—*Luke,* x, 18.

"Thy drowsy nurse hath sworn she did them *spy*
Come tripping to the room where thou didst lie."—*Milton.*

————"Nor with less dread the loud

Ethereal trumpet from on high '*gan blow*."—*Id., P. L.*, vi, 60.

OBS. 18.—After *have, help,* and *find,* the infinitive sometimes occurs without the preposition *to,* but much oftener with it; as, "When enumerating objects which we wish to *have appear* distinct."—*Kirkham's Gram.*, p. 222. "Certainly, it is heaven upon earth, to *have* a man's mind *move* in charity, *rest* in Providence, and *turn* upon the poles of truth."—*Ld. Bacon.* "What wilt thou *have* me *to* do?"—*Acts*, ix, 6. "He will *have* us *to* acknowledge him."—*Scougal*, p. 102. "I *had to walk* all the way."—*Lennie's Gram.*, p. 85. "Would you *have* them *let go* then? No."—*Walker's Particles*, p. 248. According to Allen's rule, this question is ambiguous; but the learned author explains it in Latin thus: "Placet igitur eos *dimitti*? Minimé." That is, "Would you have them *dismissed* then? No." Had he meant, "Would you have them *to* let go then?" he would doubtless have said so. Kirkham, by adding *help* to Murray's list, enumerates nine verbs which he will have to exclude the sign of the infinitive; as, "*Help* me *do* it."—*Gram.*, p. 188. But good writers sometimes use the particle *to* after this verb; as, "And Danby's matchless impudence *helped to* support the knave."—DRYDEN: *Joh. Dict., w. Help.* Dr. Priestley says, "It must, I suppose, be according to the *Scotch* idiom that Mrs. Macaulay omits it after the verb *help*: 'To *help carry* on the new measures of the court.' *History*, Vol. iv, p. 150."—*Priestley's Gram.*, p. 133. "You will *find* the difficulty *disappear* in a short time."—*Cobbett's English Gram.*, ¶ 16. "We shall always *find* this distinction *obtain*."—*Blair's Rhet.*, p. 245. Here the preposition *to* might have been inserted with propriety. Without it, a plural noun will render the construction equivocal. The sentence, "You will find the *difficulties disappear* in a short time," will probably be understood to mean, "You will find *that* the difficulties disappear in a short time." "I do not *find* him *reject* his authority."—*Johnson's Gram. Com.*, p. 167. Here too the preposition might as well have been inserted. But, as this use of the infinitive is a sort of Latinism, some critics would choose to say, "I do not find *that he rejects* his authority." "Cyrus was extremely glad to find *them have* such sentiments of religion."—*Rollin*, ii, 117. Here the infinitive may be varied either by the participle or by the indicative; as, "to find *them having*," or, "to find *they had*." Of the three expressions, the last, I think, is rather the best.

OBS. 19.—When two or more infinitives are connected in the same construction, one preposition sometimes governs them both or all; a repetition of the particle not being always necessary, unless we mean to make the terms severally emphatical. This fact is one evidence that *to* is not a necessary part of each infinitive verb, as some will have it to be. Examples: "Lord, suffer me first TO *go* and *bury* my father."—*Matt.*, viii, 21. "To *shut* the door, means, TO *throw* or *cast* the door to."—*Tooke's D. P.*, ii, 105. "Most authors expect the printer TO *spell, point*, and *digest* their copy, that it may be intelligible to the reader."—*Printer's Grammar*.

"I'll not be made a soft and dull-eyed fool,
To *shake* the head, *relent*, and *sigh*, and *yield*."—*Shak.*

OBS. 20.—An infinitive that explains an other, may sometimes be introduced without the preposition *to*; because, the former having it, the construction of the latter is made the same by this kind of apposition: as, "The most accomplished way of using books at present is, TO *serve* them as some do lords; *learn* their *titles*, and, then *brag* of their acquaintance."—SWIFT: *Kames, El. of Crit.*, ii, 166.

OBS. 21.—After *than* or *as*, the sign of the infinitive is sometimes required, and sometimes excluded; and in some instances we can either insert it or not, as we please. The latter term of a comparison is almost always more or less elliptical; and as the nature of its ellipsis depends on the structure of the former term, so does the necessity of inserting or of omitting the sign of the infinitive. Examples: "No desire is more universal than [*is the desire*] to be exalted and honoured."—*Kames, El. of Crit.*, i, 197. "The difficulty is not so great to die for a friend, as [*is the difficulty*] to find a friend worth dying for."—*Id., Art of Thinking*, p. 42. "It is no more in one's power to love or not to love, than [*it is in one's power*] to be in health or out of order."—*Ib.*, p. 45. "Men are more likely to be praised into virtue, than [*they are likely*] to be railed out of vice."—*Ib.*, p. 48. "It is more tolerable to be always alone, than [*it is tolerable*] never to be so."—*Ib.*, p. 26. "Nothing [*is*] more easy than to do mischief [*is easy*]: nothing [is] more difficult than to suffer without complaining" [*is difficult*].—*Ib.*, p. 46. Or: "than [*it is easy*] to do mischief:" &c., "than [*it is difficult*] to suffer," &c. "It is more agreeable to the nature of most men to follow than [*it is agreeable to their nature*] to lead."—*Ib.*, p. 55. In all these examples, the preposition *to* is very properly inserted; but what excludes it from the former term of a comparison, will exclude it from the latter, if such governing verb be understood there: as, "You no more heard me *say* those words, than [*you heard me*] *talk* Greek." It may be equally proper to say, "We choose rather to lead than *follow*," or, "We choose rather to lead than *to* follow."—*Art of Thinking*, p. 37. The meaning in either case is, "We choose to lead rather than *we choose to* follow." In the following example, there is perhaps an ellipsis of *to* before *cite*: "I need do nothing more than *simply cite* the explicit declarations," &c.—*Gurney's Peculiarities*, p. 4. So in these: "Nature did no more than *furnish* the power and means."—*Sheridan's Elocution*, p. 147.

"To beg, than *work*, he better understands;
  Or we perhaps might take him off thy hands."
    —*Pope's Odyssey*, xvii, 260.

OBS. 22.—It has been stated, in Obs. 16th on Rule 17th, that good writers are apt to shun a repetition of any part common to two or more verbs in the same sentence; and among the examples there cited is this:

"They mean *to,* and will, hear patiently."—*Salem Register.* So one might say, "Can a man arrive at excellence, who has no desire *to*?"—"I do not wish to go, nor expect *to.*"—"Open the door, if you are going *to.*" Answer: "We want *to,* and try *to,* but can't." Such ellipses of the infinitive after *to,* are by no means uncommon, especially in conversation; nor do they appear to me to be always reprehensible, since they prevent repetition, and may contribute to brevity without obscurity. But Dr. Bullions has lately thought proper to *condemn* them; for such is presumed to have been the design of the following note: "*To,* the sign of the infinitive, should never be used for the infinitive itself. Thus, 'I have not written, and I do not intend *to,*' is a colloquial vulgarism for, 'I have not written, and I do not intend *to write.*'"—*Bullions's Analyt. and Pract. Gram.,* p. 179. His "Exercises to be corrected," here, are these: "Be sure to write yourself and tell him to. And live as God designed me to."—*Ib.,* 1st Ed., p. 180. It being manifest, that *to* cannot "be used *for*"—(that is, *in place of*—)what is implied *after* it, this is certainly a very awkward way of hinting "there should never be an ellipsis of the infinitive after *to.*" But, from the false syntax furnished, this appears to have been the meaning intended. The examples are severally faulty, but not for the reason suggested—not because "*to*" is used for "*write*" or "*live*"—not, indeed, for any one reason common to the three—but because, in the first, "*to write*" and "*have not written,*" have nothing in common which we can omit; in the second, the mood of "*tell*" is doubtful, and, without a comma after "yourself," we cannot precisely know the meaning; in the third, the mood, the person, and the number of "*live,*" are all unknown. See Note 9th to Rule 17th, above; and Note 2d to the General Rule, below.

OBS. 23.—Of some infinitives, it is hard to say whether they are transitive or intransitive; as, "Well, then, let us proceed; we have other forced marches to *make*; other enemies to *subdue*; more laurels to *acquire*;

and more injuries to *avenge.*"—BONAPARTE: *Columbian Orator*, p. 136. These, without ellipsis, are intransitive; but relatives may be inserted.

IMPROPRIETIES FOR CORRECTION.

FALSE SYNTAX UNDER RULE XIX.

INFINITIVES AFTER BID, DARE, FEEL, HEAR, LET, &c.

"I dare not to proceed so hastily, lest I should give offence."—*Murray's Exercises*, p. 63.

[FORMULE.—Not proper, because the preposition *to* is inserted before *proceed*, which follows the active verb *dare.* But, according to Rule 19th, "The active verbs, *bid, dare, feel, hear, let, make, need, see,* and their participles, usually take the infinitive after them without the preposition *to*;" and this is an instance in which the finite verb should immediately govern the infinitive. Therefore, the *to* should be omitted; thus, "I *dare* not *proceed* so hastily," &c.]

"Their character is formed, and made appear."—*Butler's Analogy*, p. 115.

[FORMULE.—Not proper, because the preposition *to* is not inserted between *made* and *appear*, the verb *is made* being passive. But, according to Obs. 5th and 10th on Rule 19th, those verbs which in the active form govern the infinitive without *to*, do not so govern it when they are made passive, except the verb *let.* Therefore, *to* should be here inserted; thus, "Their character is formed, and made *to* appear."]

"Let there be but matter and opportunity offered, and you shall see them quickly to revive again."—*Wisdom of the Ancients*, p. 53. "It has been made appear, that there is no presumption against a revelation."—*Butler's*

Analogy, p. 252. "MANIFEST, *v. t.* To reveal; to make to appear; to show plainly."—*Webster's American Dict.* "Let him to reign like unto good Aurelius, or let him to bleed like unto Socrates."—*Kirkham's Gram.*, p. 169. "To sing I could not; to complain I durst not."—*S. Fothergill.* "If T. M. be not so frequently heard pray by them."—*Barclay's Works*, iii, 132. "How many of your own church members were never heard pray?"—*Ib.*, iii, 133. "Yea, we are bidden pray one for another."—*Ib.*, iii, 145. "He was made believe that neither the king's death, nor imprisonment would help him."—*Sheffield's Works*, ii, 281. "I felt a chilling sensation to creep over me."—*Inst.*, p. 188. "I dare to say he has not got home yet."—*Ib.* "We sometimes see bad men to be honoured."—*Ib.* "I saw him to move."—*Felch's Comprehensive Gram.*, p. 62. "For see thou, ah! see thou a hostile world to raise its terrours."—*Kirkham's Gram.*, p. 167. "But that he make him to rehearse so."—*Lily's Gram.*, p. xv. "Let us to rise."—*Fowle's True Eng. Gram.*, p. 41.

"Scripture, you know, exhorts us to it;
Bids us to 'seek peace, and ensue it.'"—*Swift's Poems*, p. 336.

"Who bade the mud from Dives' wheel
To spurn the rags of Lazarus?
Come, brother, in that dust we'll kneel,
Confessing Heaven that ruled it thus."—*Christmas Book.*